THE LONE RANGER®

★ MATTHEWS ★ CARIELLO ★ POPE ★ CASSADAY ★

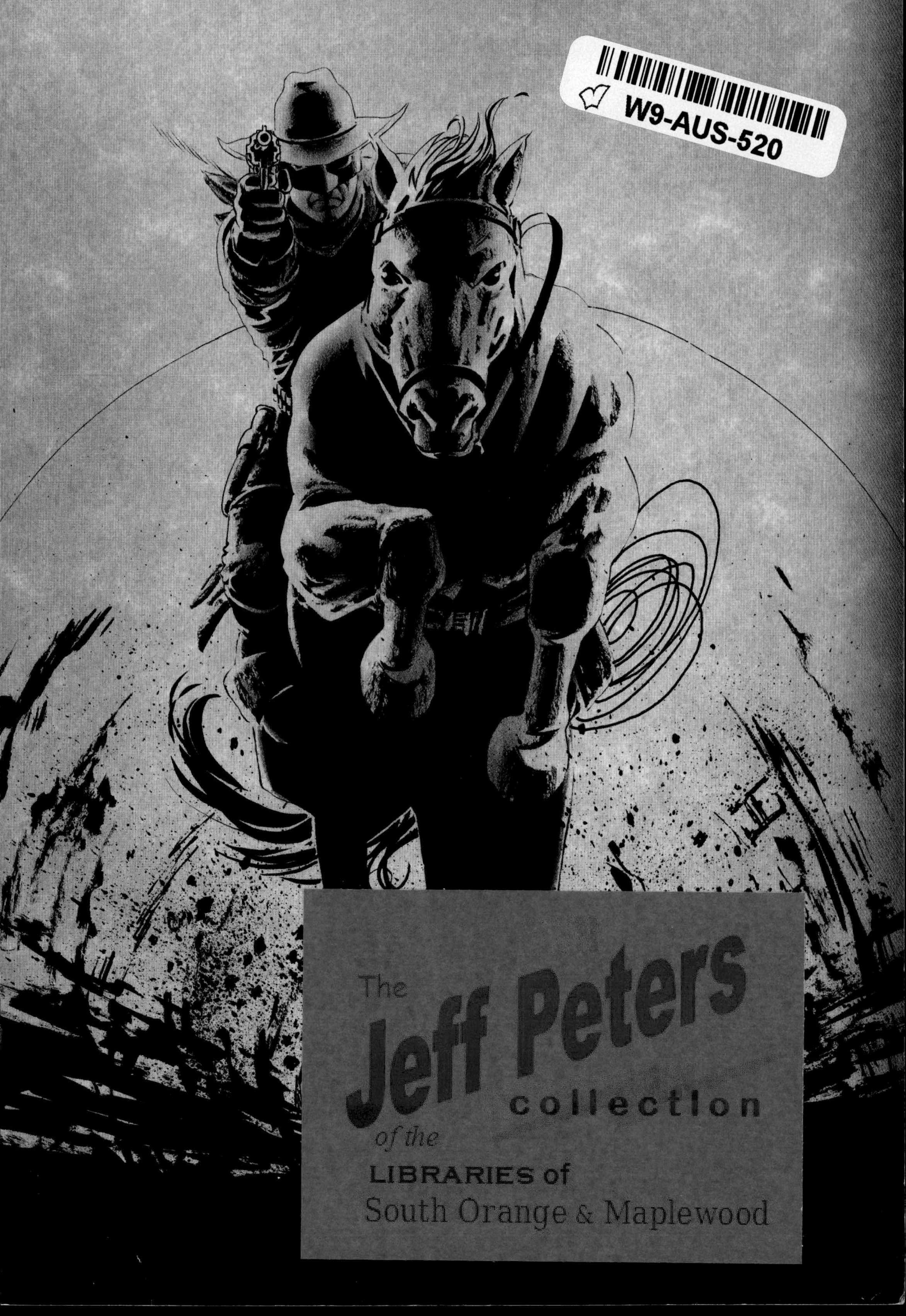

YA-G
MAT

LONE
★ VOLUME II:

DYNAMITE
ENTERTAINMENT

WWW.DYNAMITEENTERTAINMENT.COM

NICK BARRUCCI • PRESIDENT
JUAN COLLADO • CHIEF OPERATING OFFICER
JOSEPH RYBANDT • DIRECTOR OF MARKETING
JOSH JOHNSON • CREATIVE DIRECTOR
JASON ULLMEYER • GRAPHIC DESIGNER

To find a comic shop in your area,
call the comic shop locator service
toll-free **1-888-266-4226** or visit
comicshoplocator.com

THE LONE RANGER ® VOLUME 2: LINES NOT CROSSED. First printing. Contains materials originally published in THE LONE RANGER #7-11. Published by Dynamite Entertainment. 155 Ninth Ave. Suite B, Runnemede, NJ 08078. Lone Ranger: © 2008 Classic Media, Inc. THE LONE RANGER and associated character names, images and other indicia are trademarks of and copyrighted by Classic Media, Inc., an Entertainment Rights group company. All rights reserved. "DYNAMITE," "DYNAMITE ENTERTAINMENT" and its logo ® & © 2008 DFI. All names, characters, events, and locales in this publication are entirely fictional. Any resemblance to actual persons (living or dead), events or places, without satiric intent, is coincidental. No portion of this book may be reproduced by any means (digital or print) without the written permission of Dynamite Entertainment except for review purposes. The scanning, uploading and distribution of this book via the Internet or via any other means without the permission of the publisher is illegal and punishable by law. Please purchase only authorized electronic editions, and do not participate in or encourage electronic piracy of copyrighted materials.

For information regarding media rights, foreign rights, promotions, licensing, and advertising:
marketing@dynamiteentertainment.com

Printed in China

First Printing
HARDCOVER ISBN-10: 1-933305-66-5   ISBN-13: 9-781933-305660
SOFTCOVER ISBN-10: 1-933305-70-3   ISBN-13: 9-781933-305707
10 9 8 7 6 5 4 3 2 1

THE RANGER®
LINES NOT CROSSED★

Brett Matthews
WRITER

Sergio Cariello
ARTIST

Paul Pope
ARTIST (WOLF SEQUENCE)

Marcelo Pinto
COLORIST

Simon Bowland
LETTERER

John Cassaday
COVER ARTIST AND ART DIRECTOR

SPECIAL THANKS TO:
Lynn kim, Kim Anthony Jones, Tony Knight,
Evan Baily, Mike Weiss and John Fraser

This volume collects issues 7-11 of the Dynamite Entertainment series.

collection design by Jason Ullmeyer

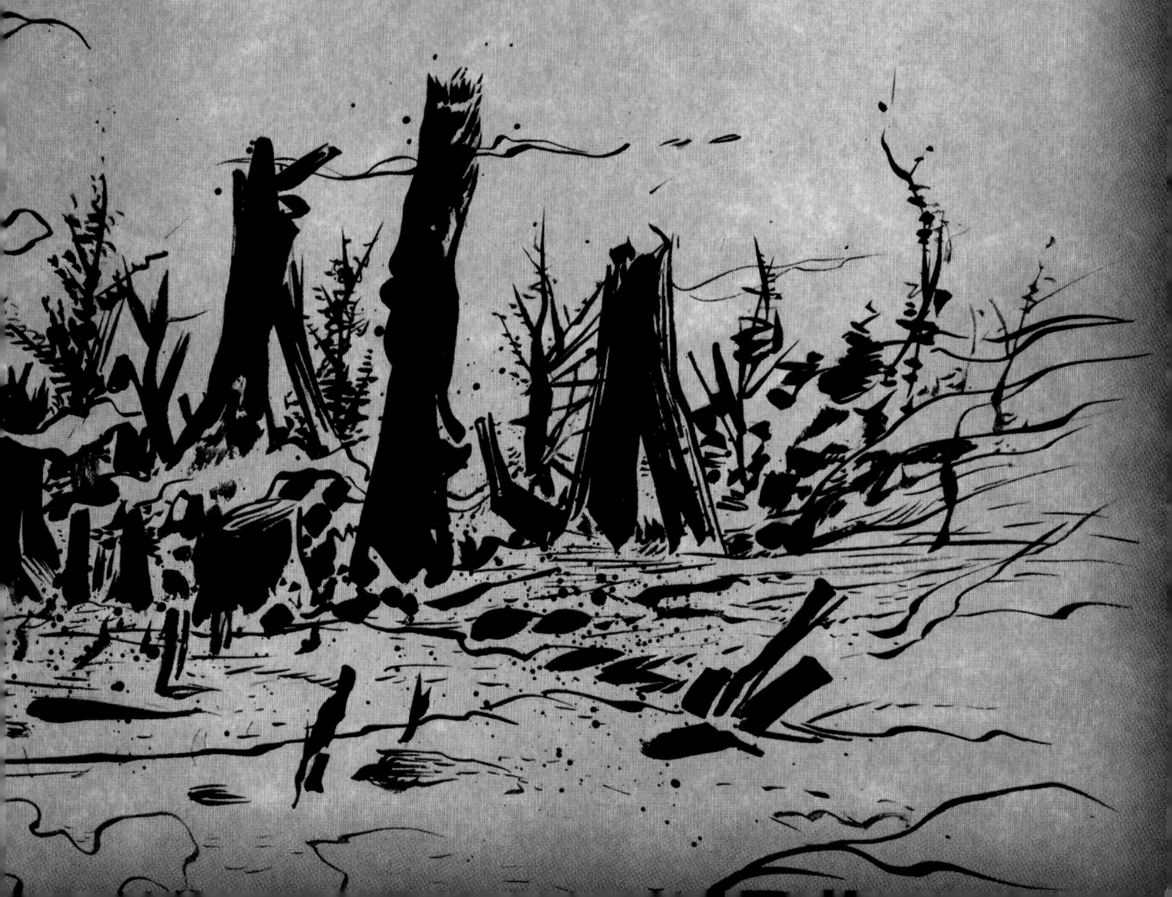

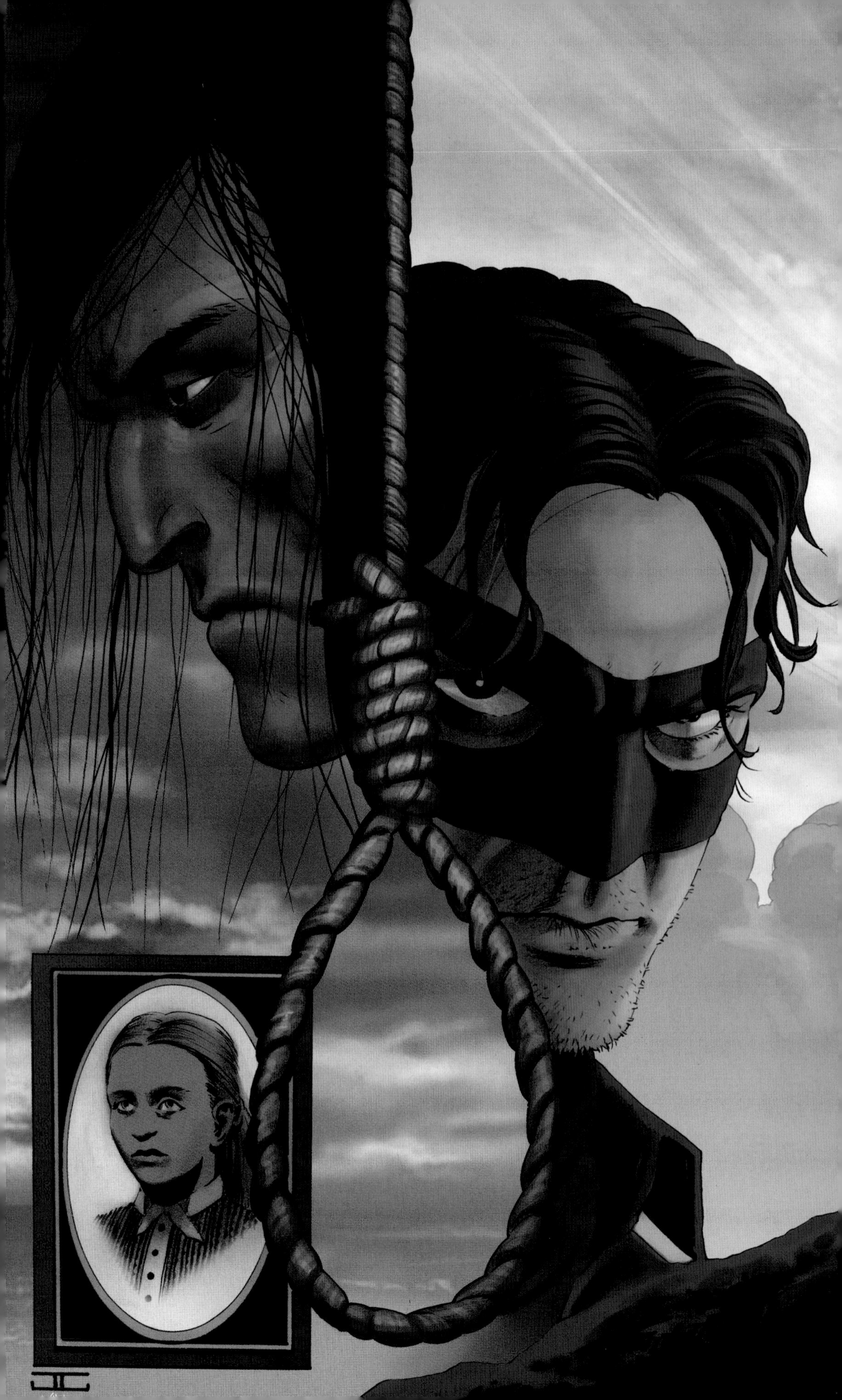

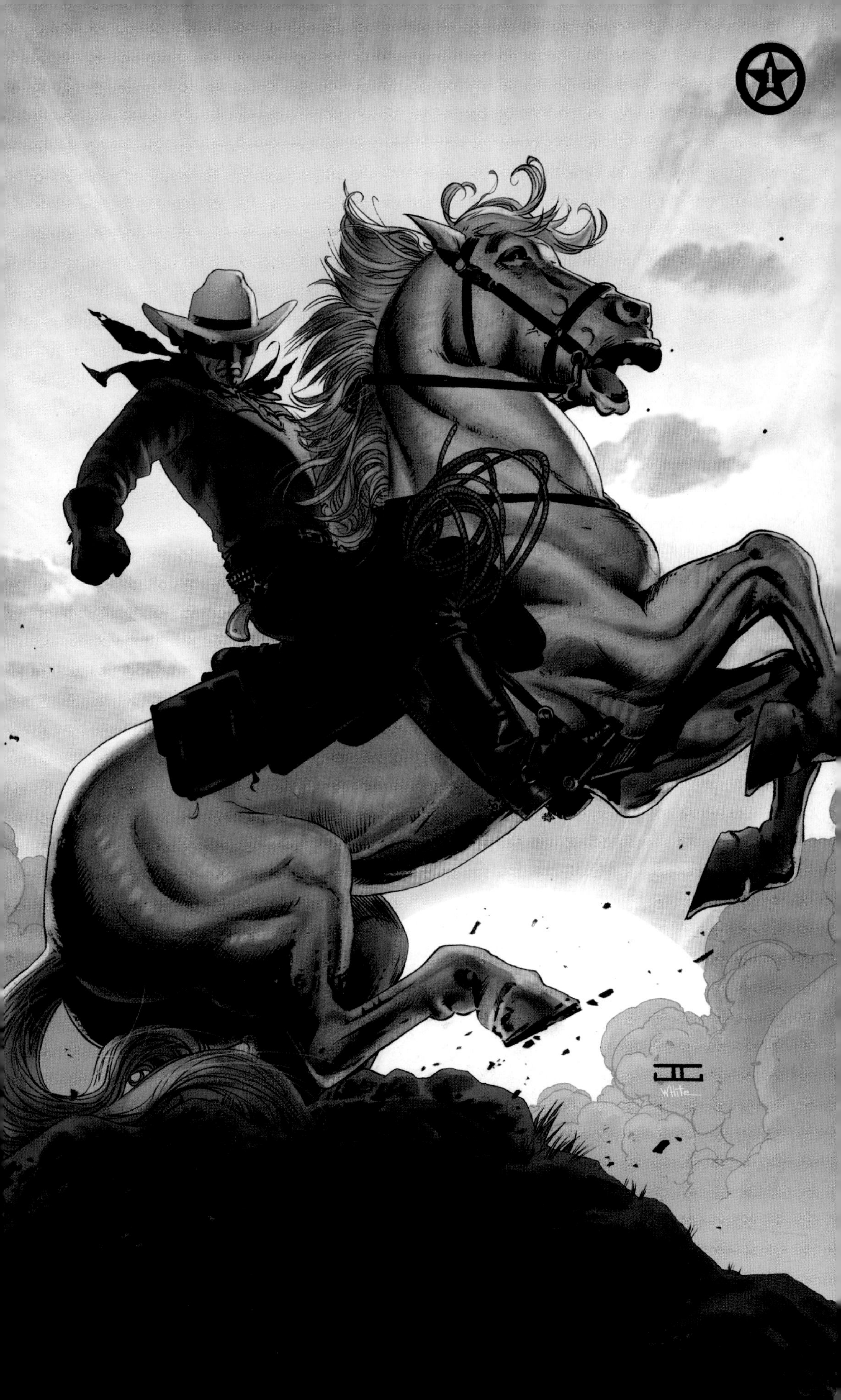
1
White

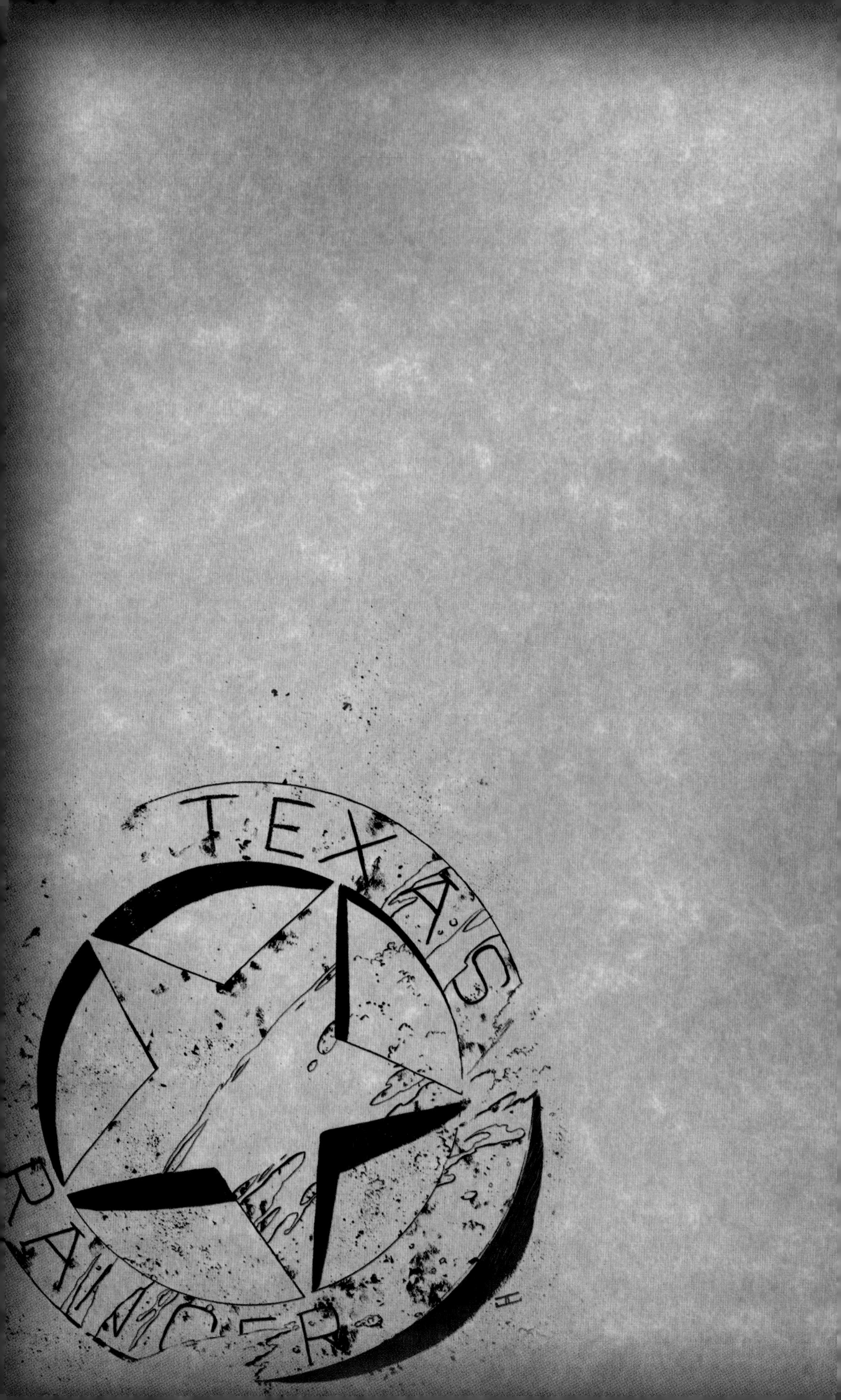
TEXAS
RANGER

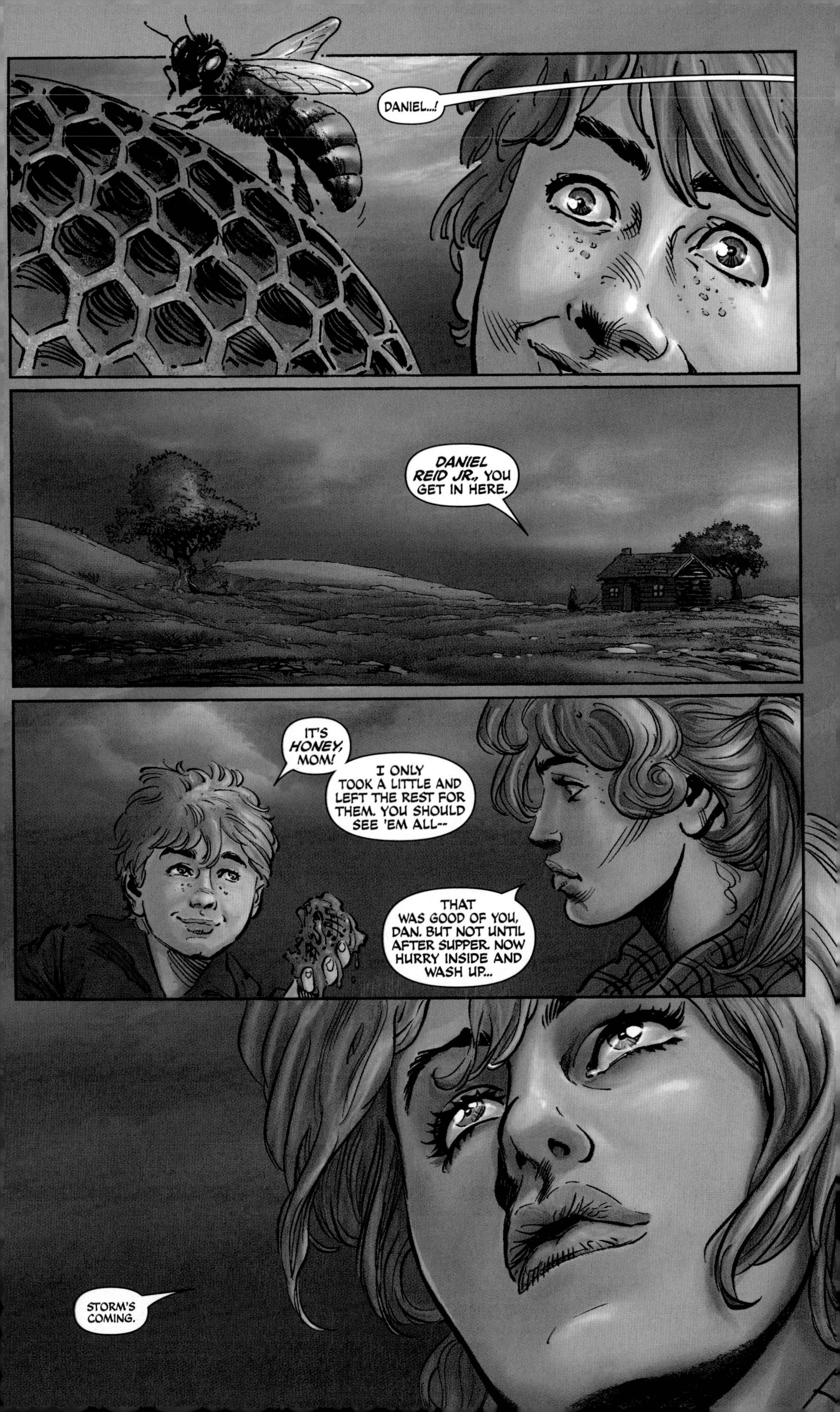
DANIEL...!
DANIEL REID JR., YOU GET IN HERE.
IT'S HONEY, MOM!
I ONLY TOOK A LITTLE AND LEFT THE REST FOR THEM. YOU SHOULD SEE 'EM ALL--
THAT WAS GOOD OF YOU, DAN. BUT NOT UNTIL AFTER SUPPER. NOW HURRY INSIDE AND WASH UP...
STORM'S COMING.

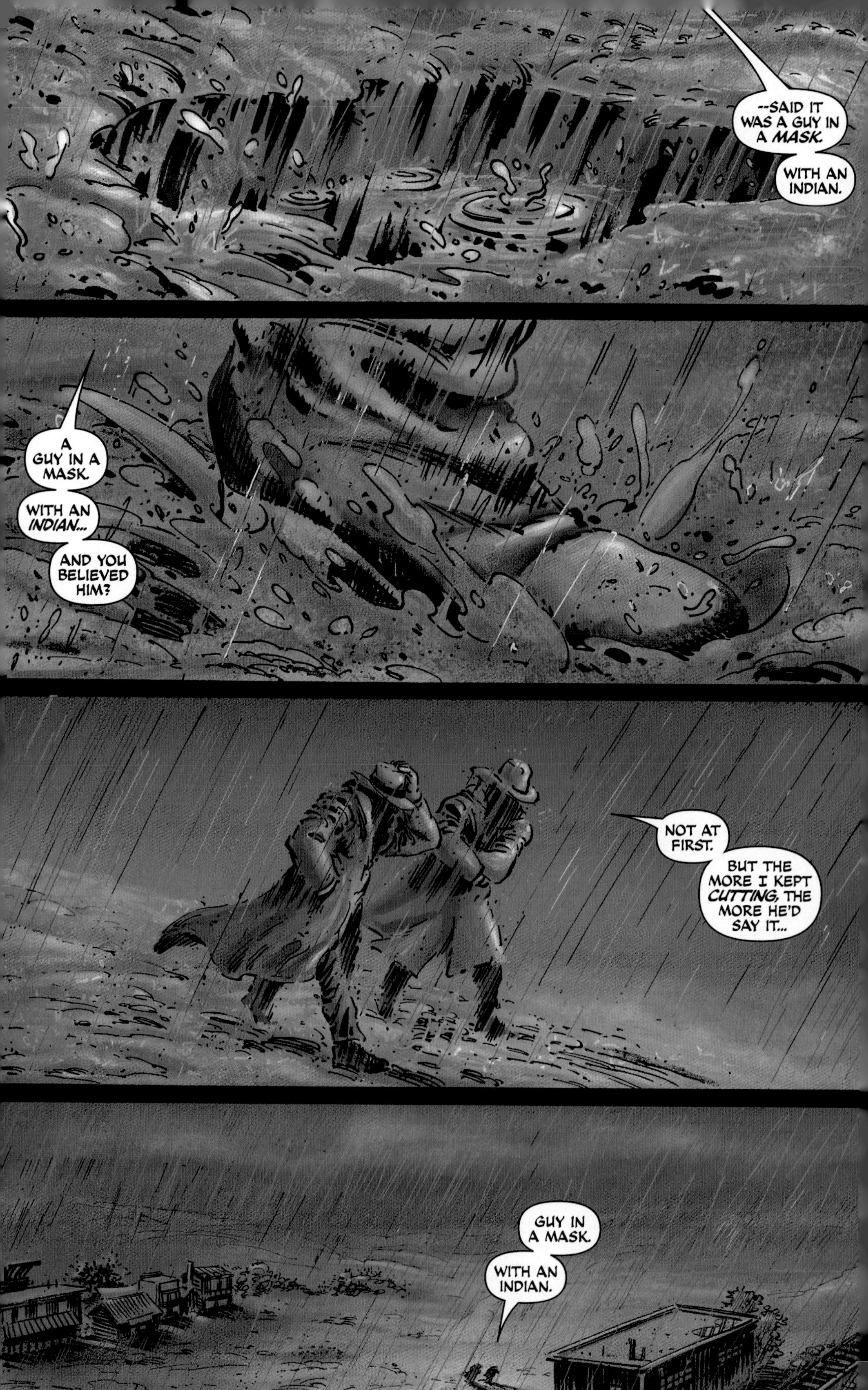
--SAID IT WAS A GUY IN A *MASK.*
WITH AN INDIAN.
A GUY IN A MASK.
WITH AN *INDIAN...*
AND YOU BELIEVED HIM?
NOT AT FIRST.
BUT THE MORE I KEPT *CUTTING,* THE MORE HE'D SAY IT...
GUY IN A MASK.
WITH AN INDIAN.

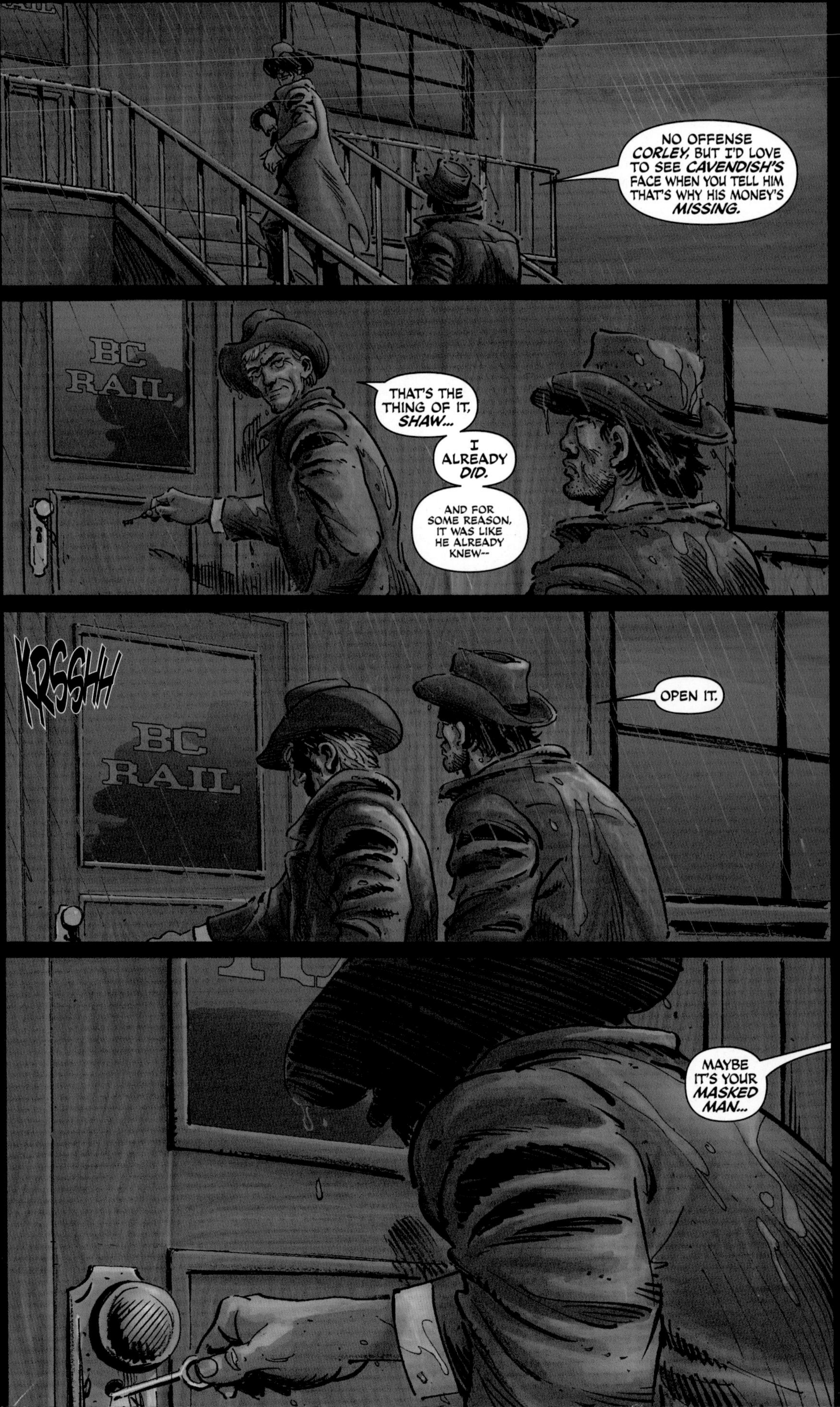
NO OFFENSE CORLEY, BUT I'D LOVE TO SEE CAVENDISH'S FACE WHEN YOU TELL HIM THAT'S WHY HIS MONEY'S MISSING.
BC RAIL
THAT'S THE THING OF IT, SHAW...
I ALREADY DID.
AND FOR SOME REASON, IT WAS LIKE HE ALREADY KNEW--
KRSSHH
BC RAIL
OPEN IT.
MAYBE IT'S YOUR MASKED MAN...

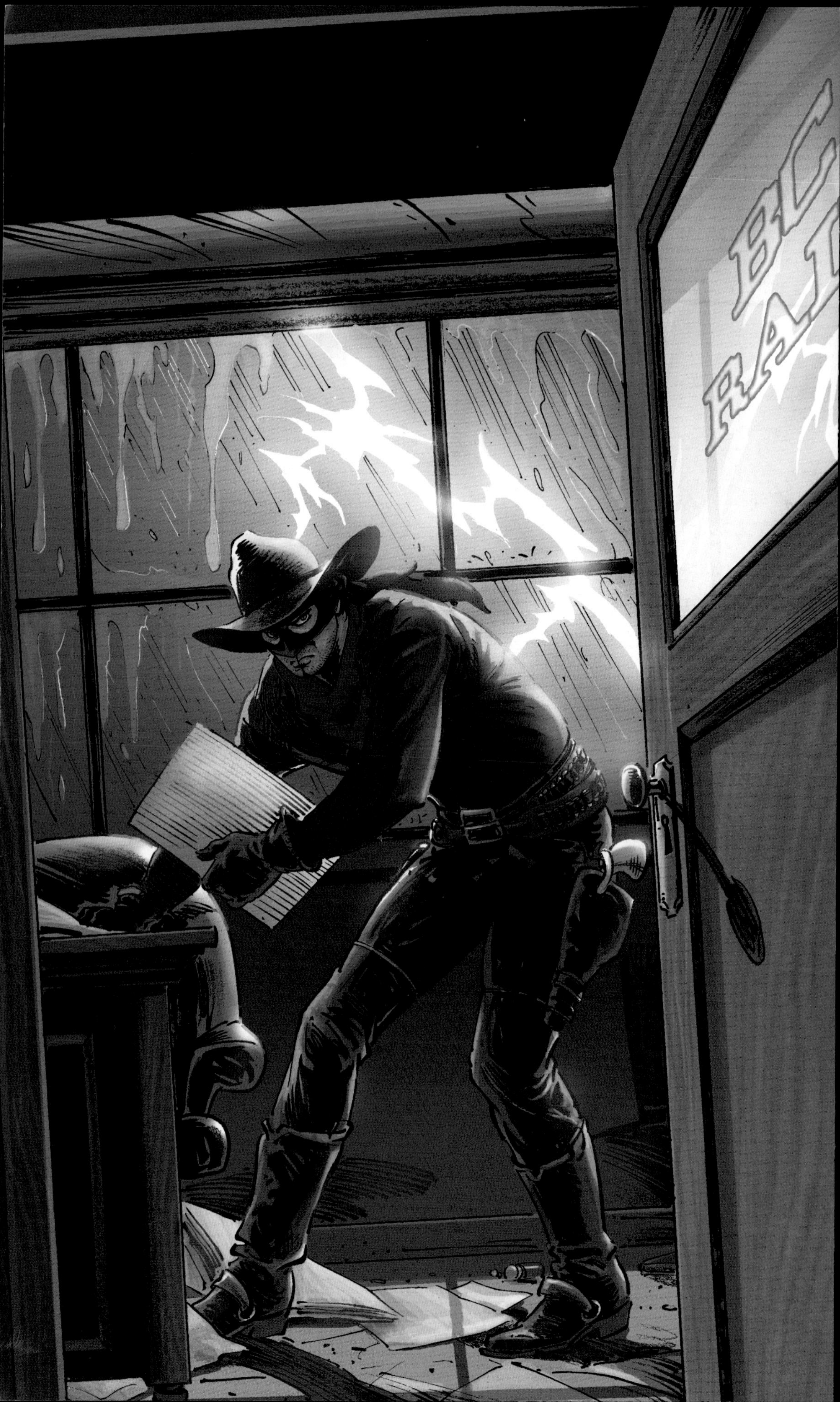

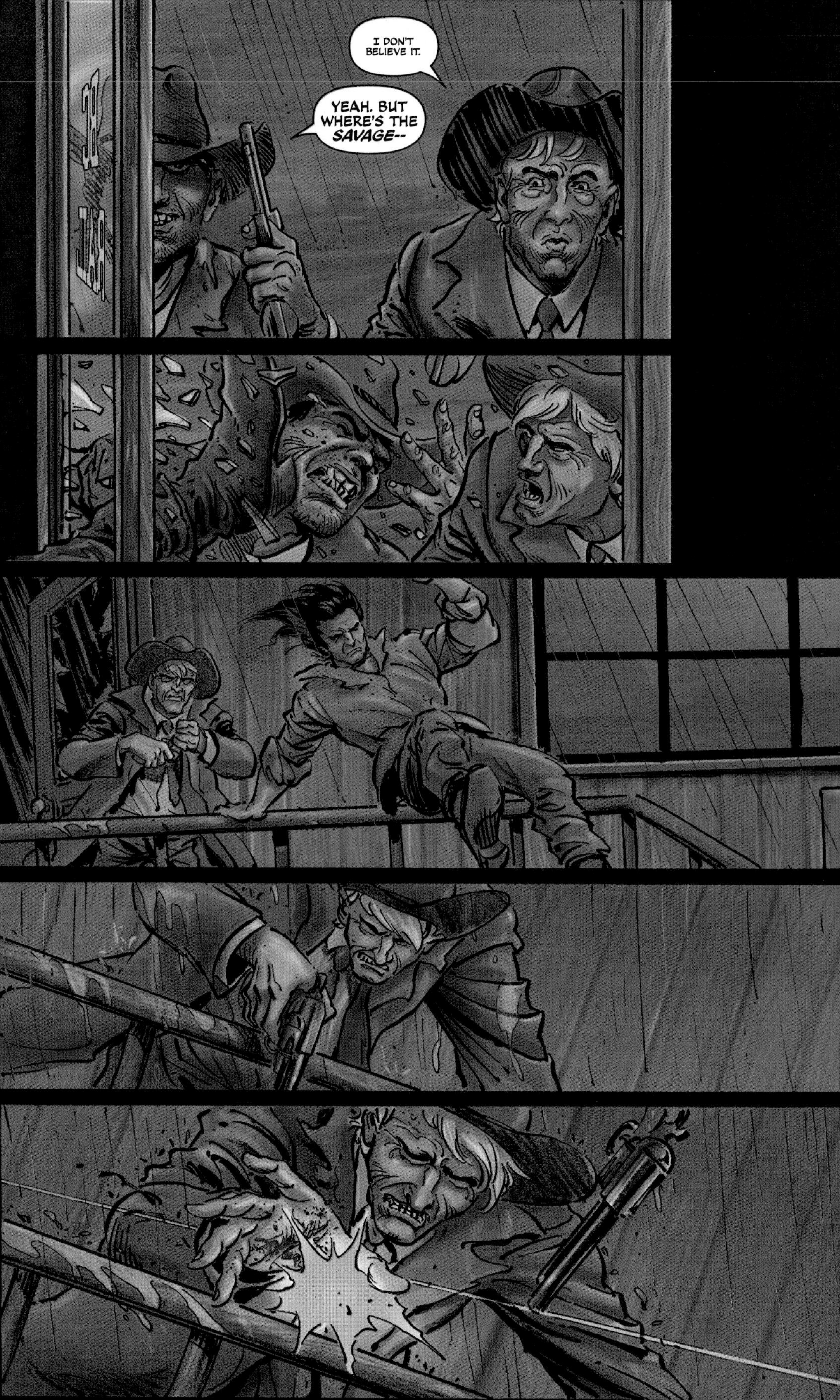
I DON'T BELIEVE IT.
YEAH. BUT WHERE'S THE *SAVAGE--*

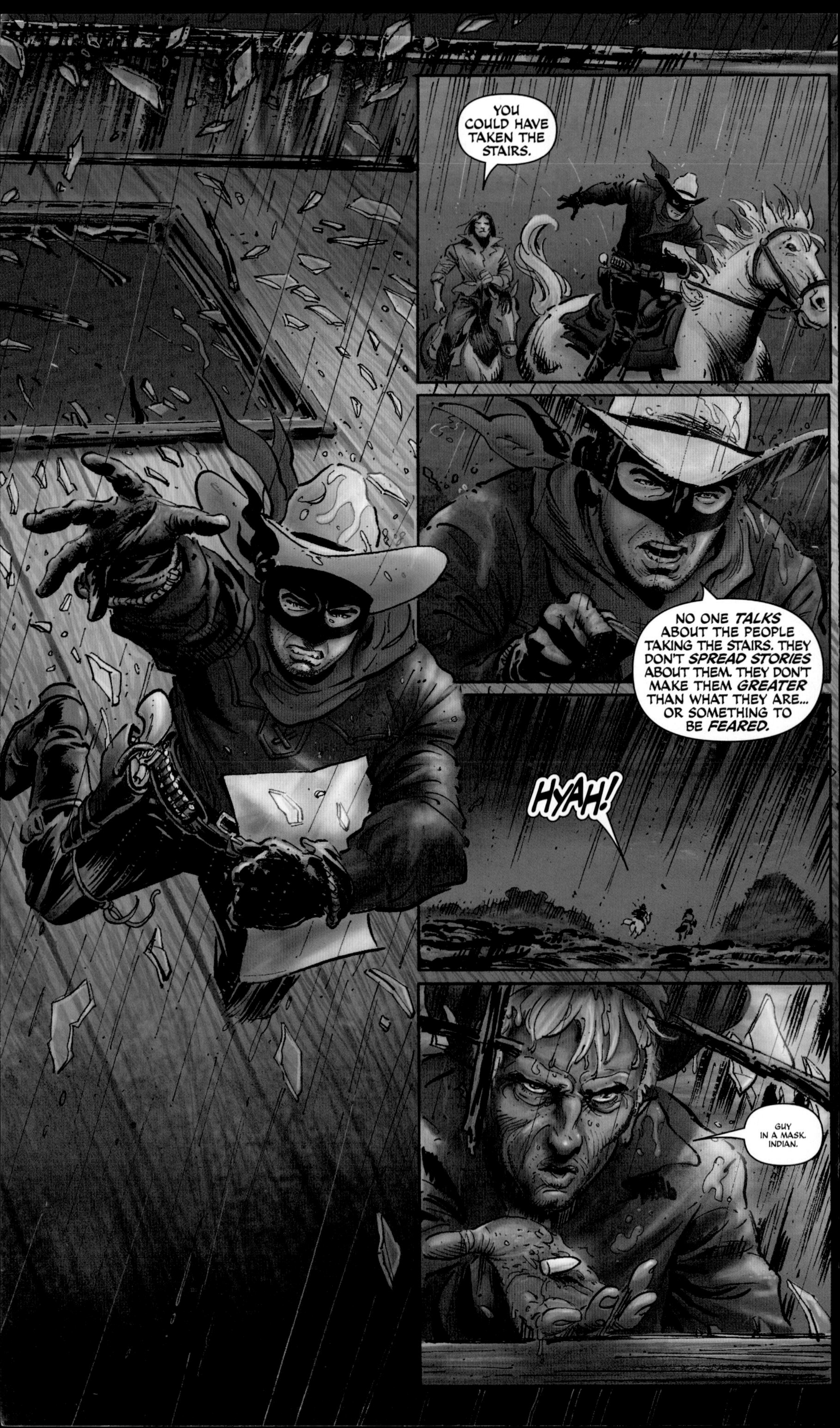
YOU COULD HAVE TAKEN THE STAIRS.
NO ONE *TALKS* ABOUT THE PEOPLE TAKING THE STAIRS. THEY DON'T *SPREAD STORIES* ABOUT THEM. THEY DON'T MAKE THEM *GREATER* THAN WHAT THEY ARE... OR SOMETHING TO BE *FEARED.*
HYAH!
GUY IN A MASK. INDIAN.

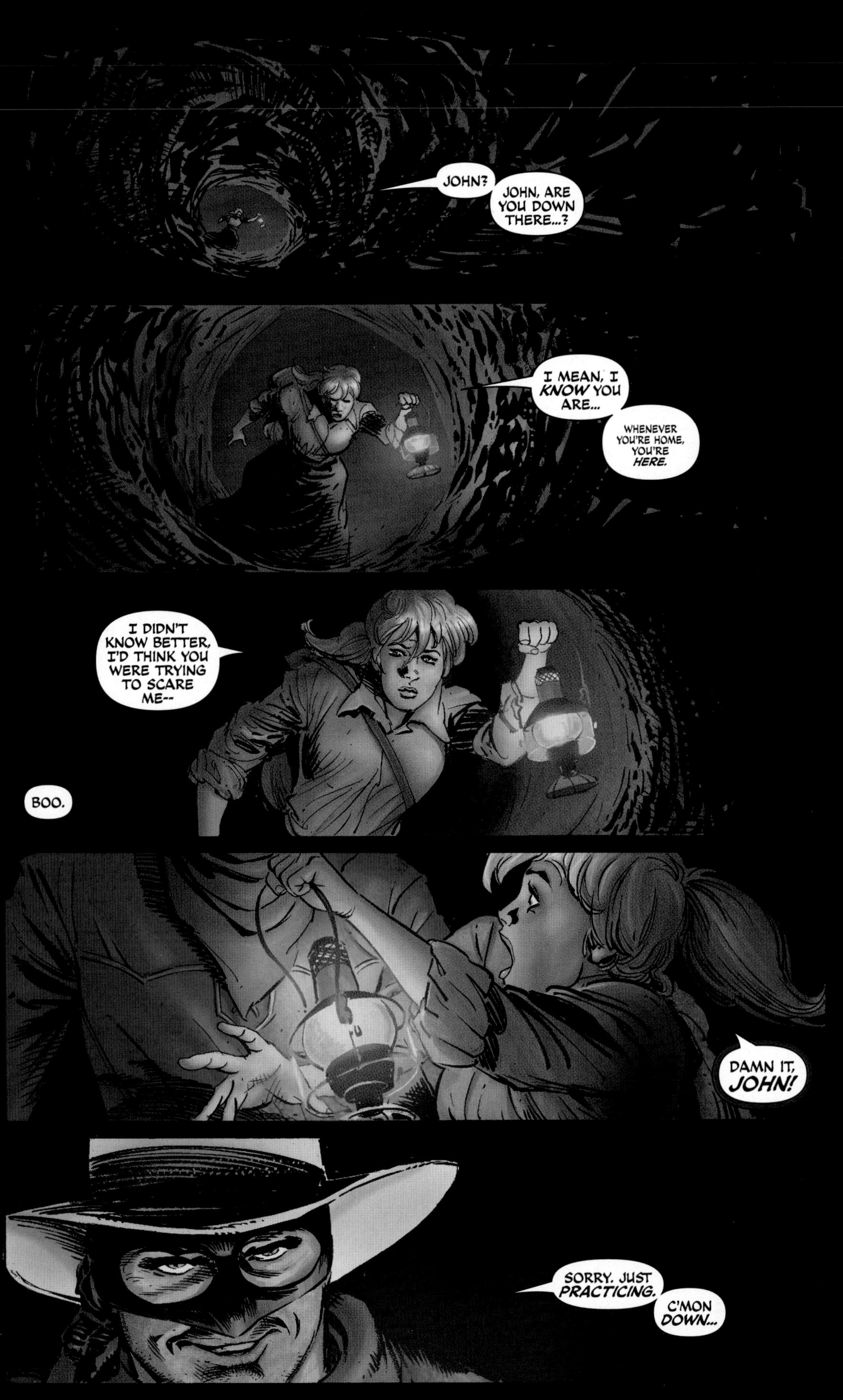
JOHN?
JOHN, ARE YOU DOWN THERE...?
I MEAN, I KNOW YOU ARE...
WHENEVER YOU'RE HOME, YOU'RE HERE.
I DIDN'T KNOW BETTER, I'D THINK YOU WERE TRYING TO SCARE ME--
BOO.
DAMN IT, JOHN!
SORRY. JUST PRACTICING.
C'MON DOWN...

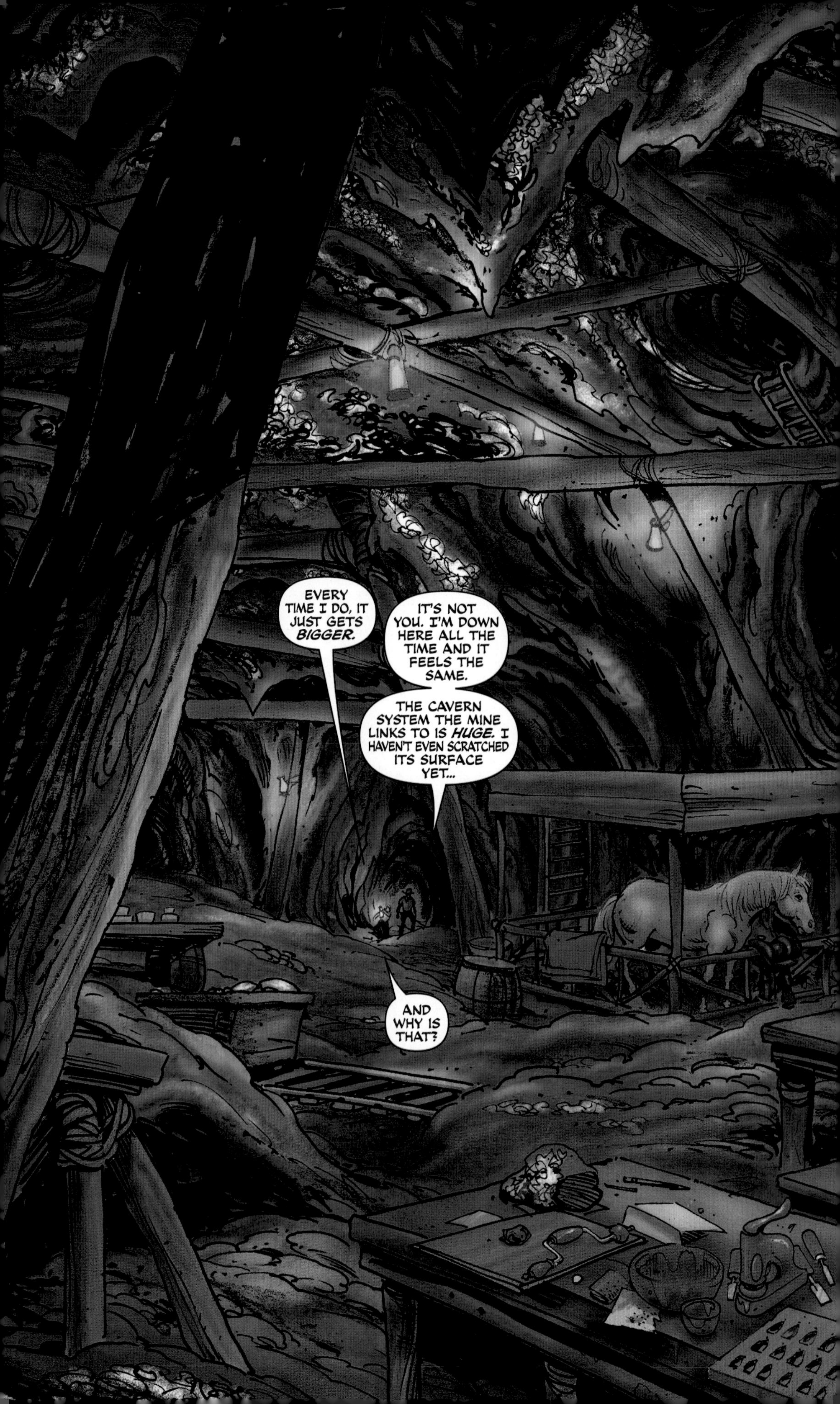
EVERY TIME I DO, IT JUST GETS *BIGGER.*
IT'S NOT YOU. I'M DOWN HERE ALL THE TIME AND IT FEELS THE SAME.
THE CAVERN SYSTEM THE MINE LINKS TO IS *HUGE.* I HAVEN'T EVEN SCRATCHED ITS SURFACE YET...
AND WHY IS THAT?

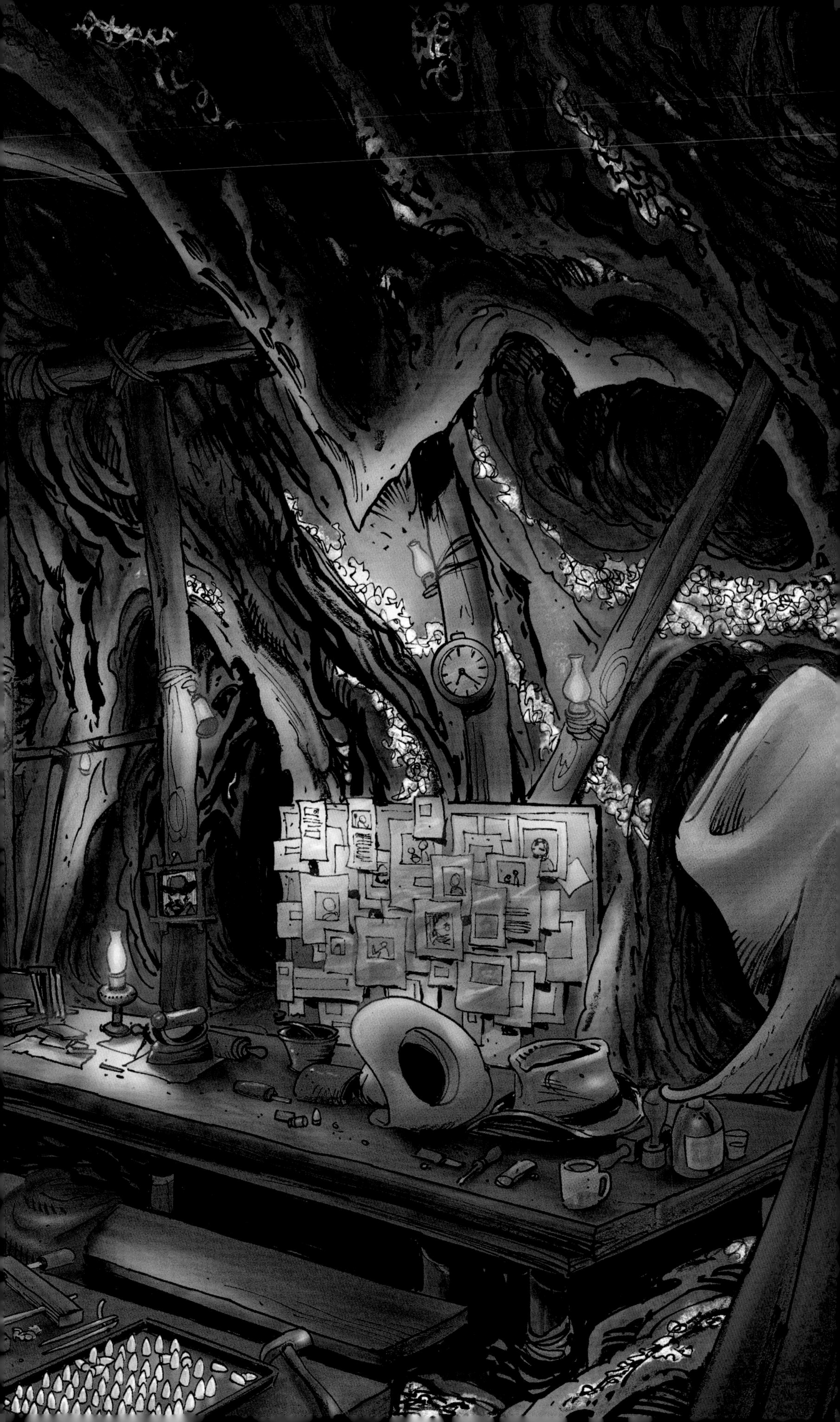

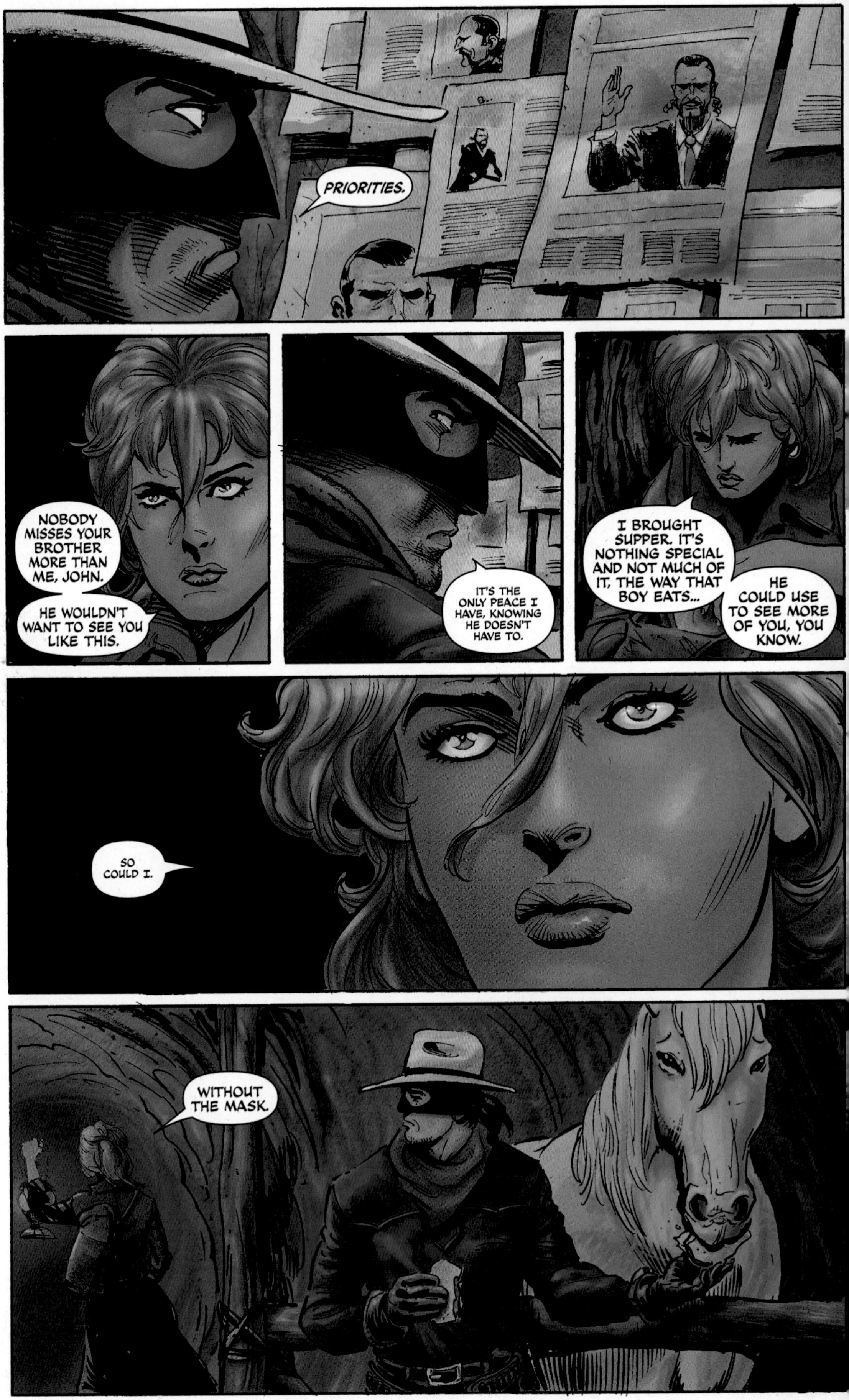
PRIORITIES.
NOBODY MISSES YOUR BROTHER MORE THAN ME, JOHN.
HE WOULDN'T WANT TO SEE YOU LIKE THIS.
IT'S THE ONLY PEACE I HAVE, KNOWING HE DOESN'T HAVE TO.
I BROUGHT SUPPER. IT'S NOTHING SPECIAL AND NOT MUCH OF IT, THE WAY THAT BOY EATS...
HE COULD USE TO SEE MORE OF YOU, YOU KNOW.
SO COULD I.
WITHOUT THE MASK.

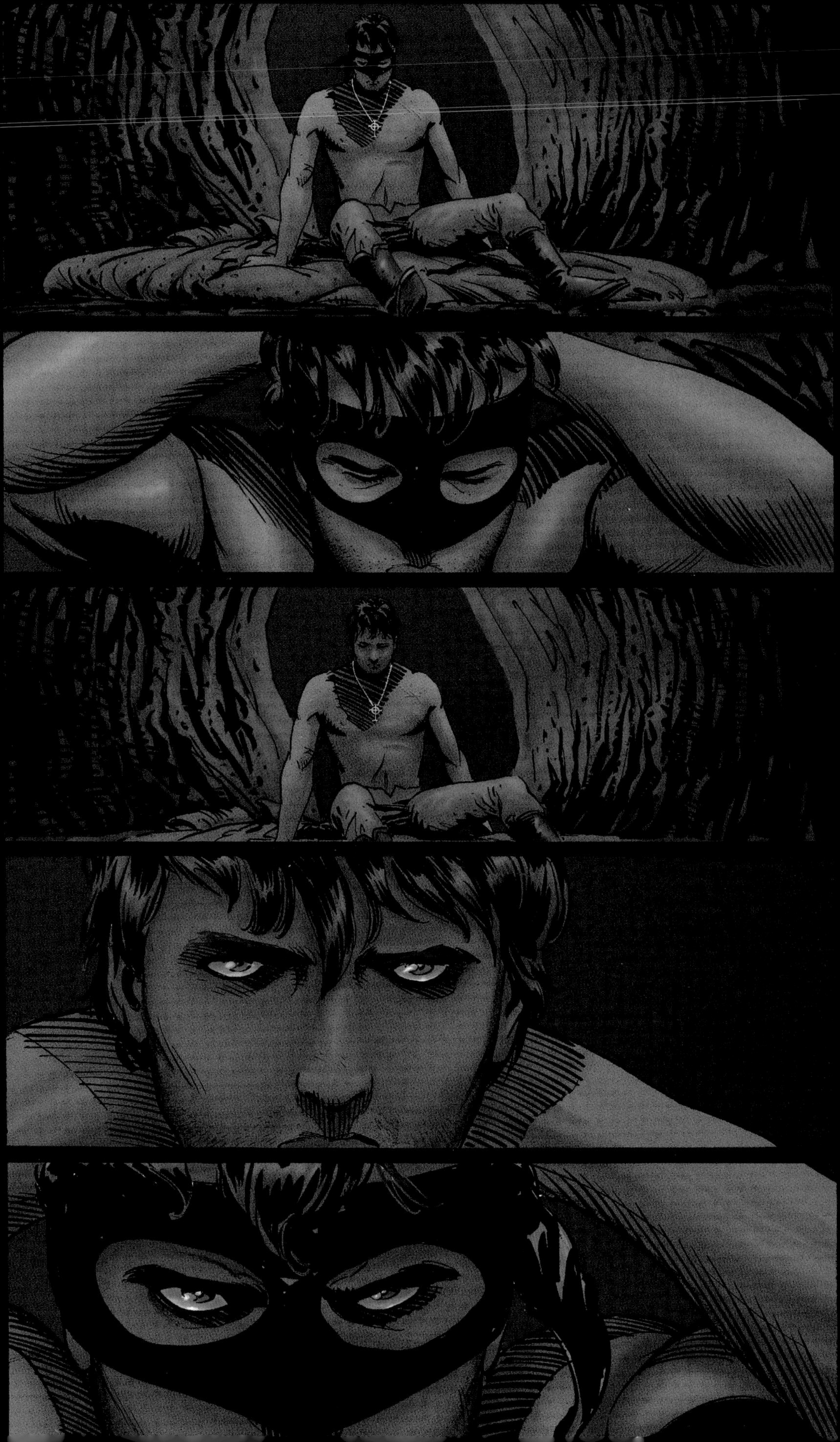

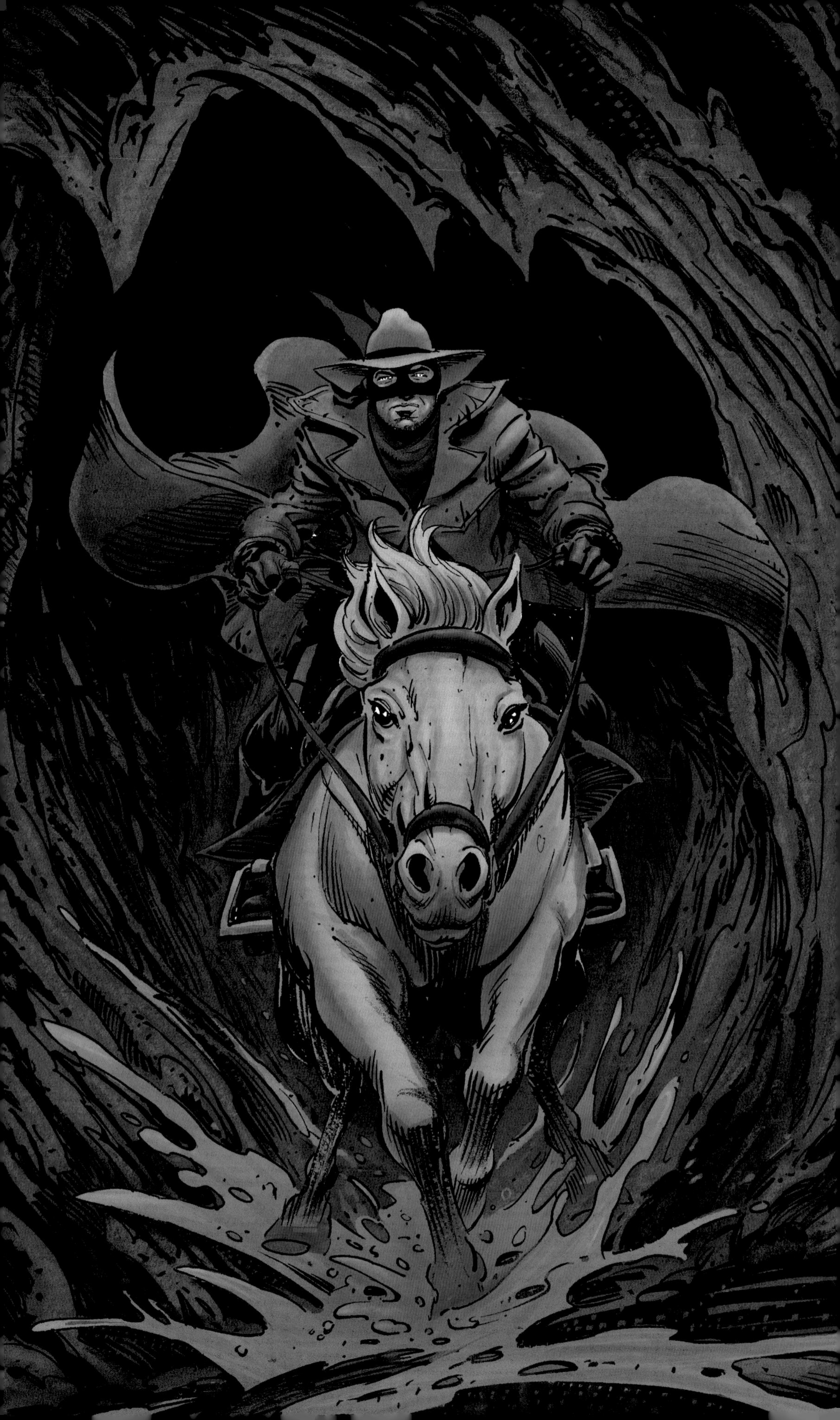

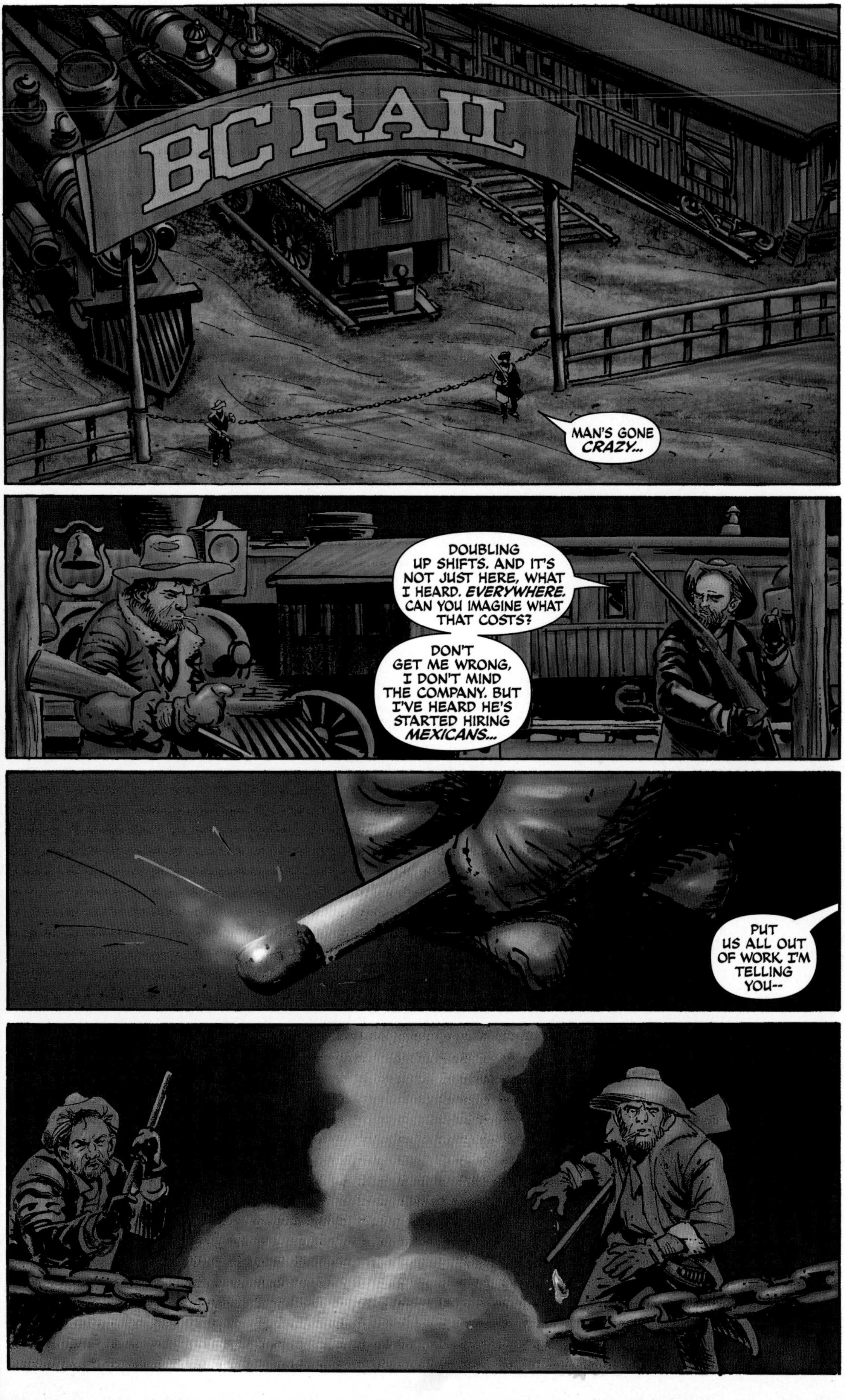
BC RAIL
MAN'S GONE CRAZY...
DOUBLING UP SHIFTS. AND IT'S NOT JUST HERE, WHAT I HEARD. EVERYWHERE. CAN YOU IMAGINE WHAT THAT COSTS?
DON'T GET ME WRONG, I DON'T MIND THE COMPANY. BUT I'VE HEARD HE'S STARTED HIRING MEXICANS...
PUT US ALL OUT OF WORK, I'M TELLING YOU--

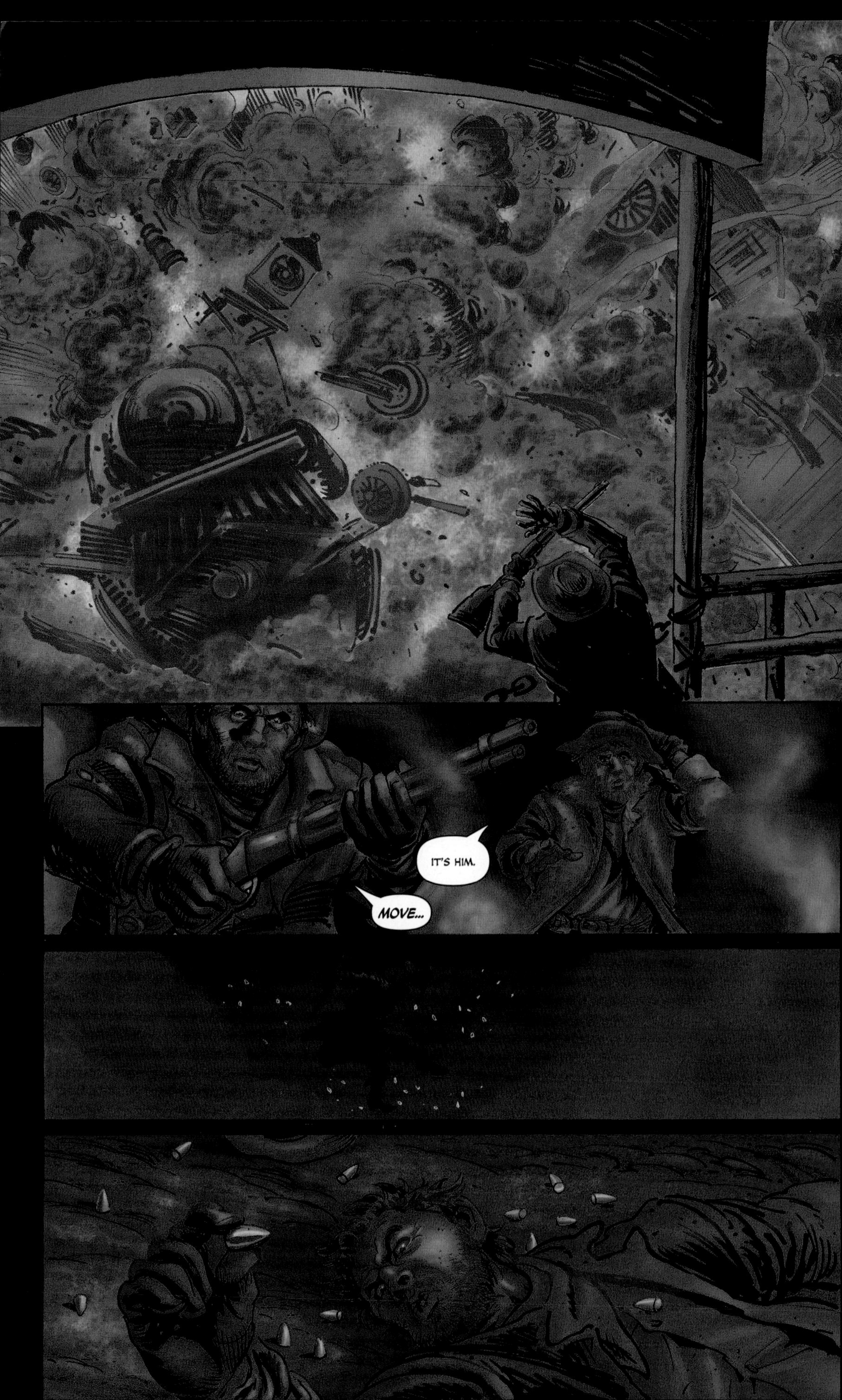
IT'S HIM.
MOVE...

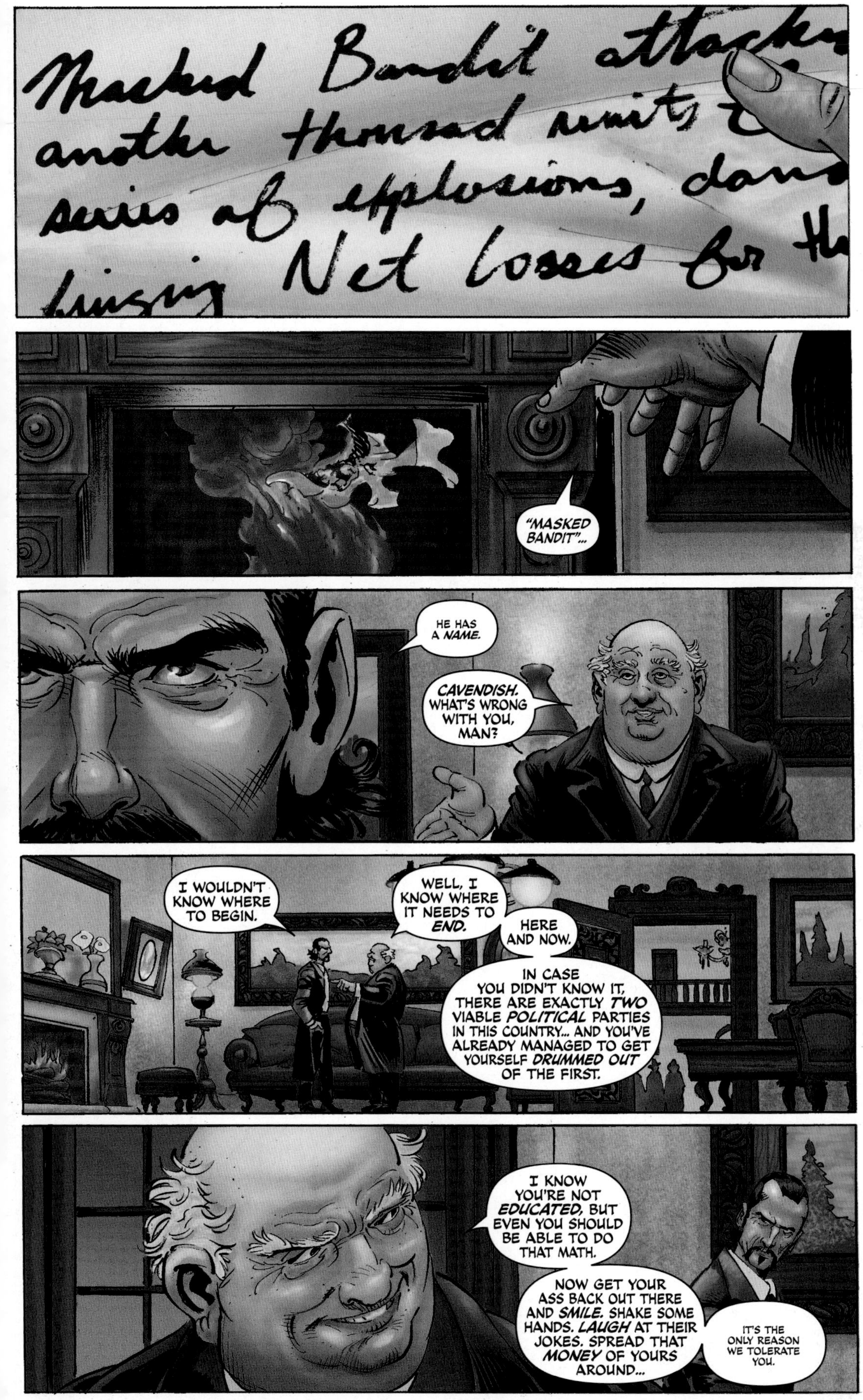
Masked Bandit
another thousand units,
series of explosions,
Net losses for
"MASKED BANDIT"...
HE HAS A NAME.
CAVENDISH. WHAT'S WRONG WITH YOU, MAN?
I WOULDN'T KNOW WHERE TO BEGIN.
WELL, I KNOW WHERE IT NEEDS TO END.
HERE AND NOW.
IN CASE YOU DIDN'T KNOW IT, THERE ARE EXACTLY TWO VIABLE POLITICAL PARTIES IN THIS COUNTRY... AND YOU'VE ALREADY MANAGED TO GET YOURSELF DRUMMED OUT OF THE FIRST.
I KNOW YOU'RE NOT EDUCATED, BUT EVEN YOU SHOULD BE ABLE TO DO THAT MATH.
NOW GET YOUR ASS BACK OUT THERE AND SMILE. SHAKE SOME HANDS. LAUGH AT THEIR JOKES. SPREAD THAT MONEY OF YOURS AROUND...
IT'S THE ONLY REASON WE TOLERATE YOU.

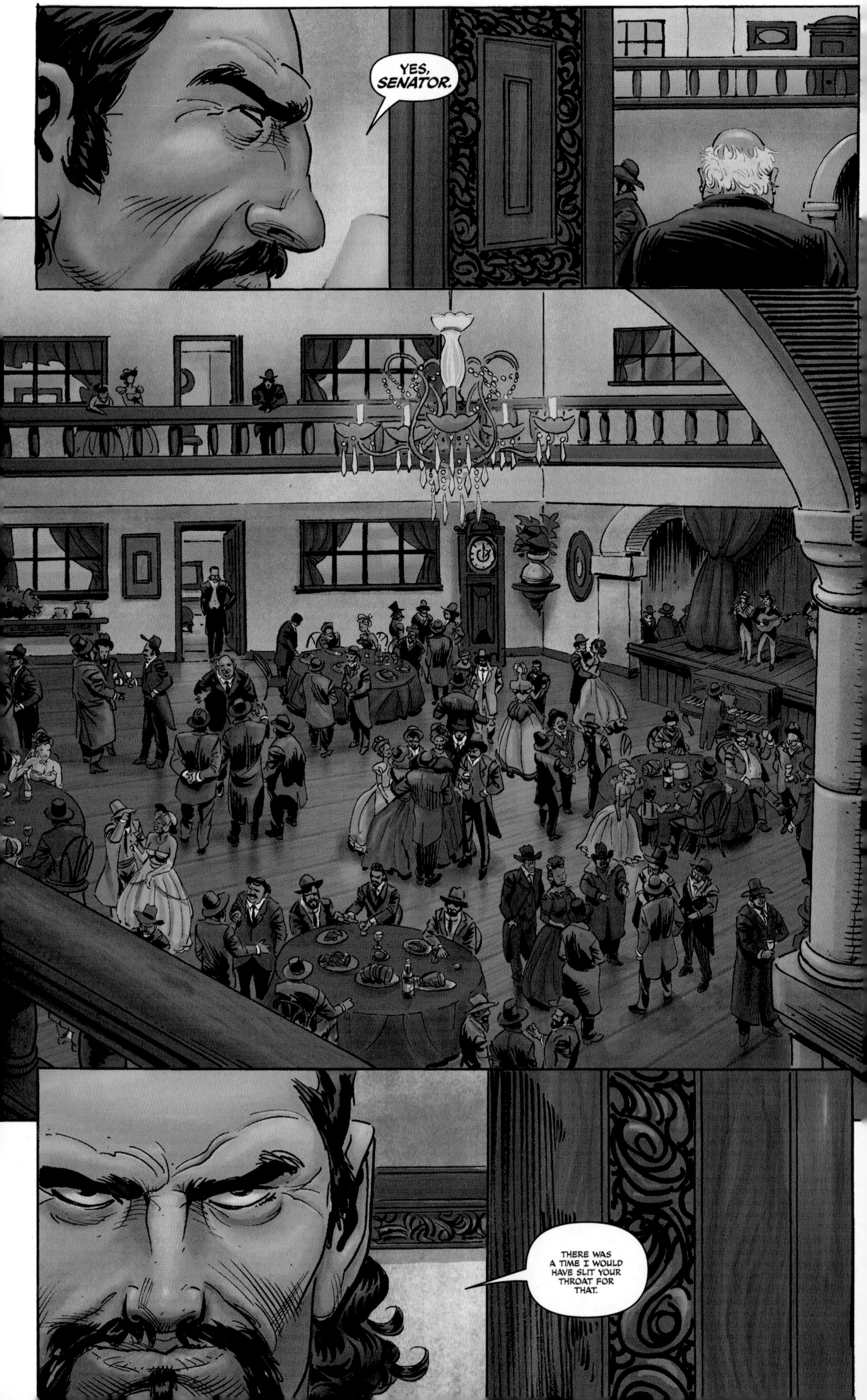
YES, SENATOR.
THERE WAS A TIME I WOULD HAVE SLIT YOUR THROAT FOR THAT.

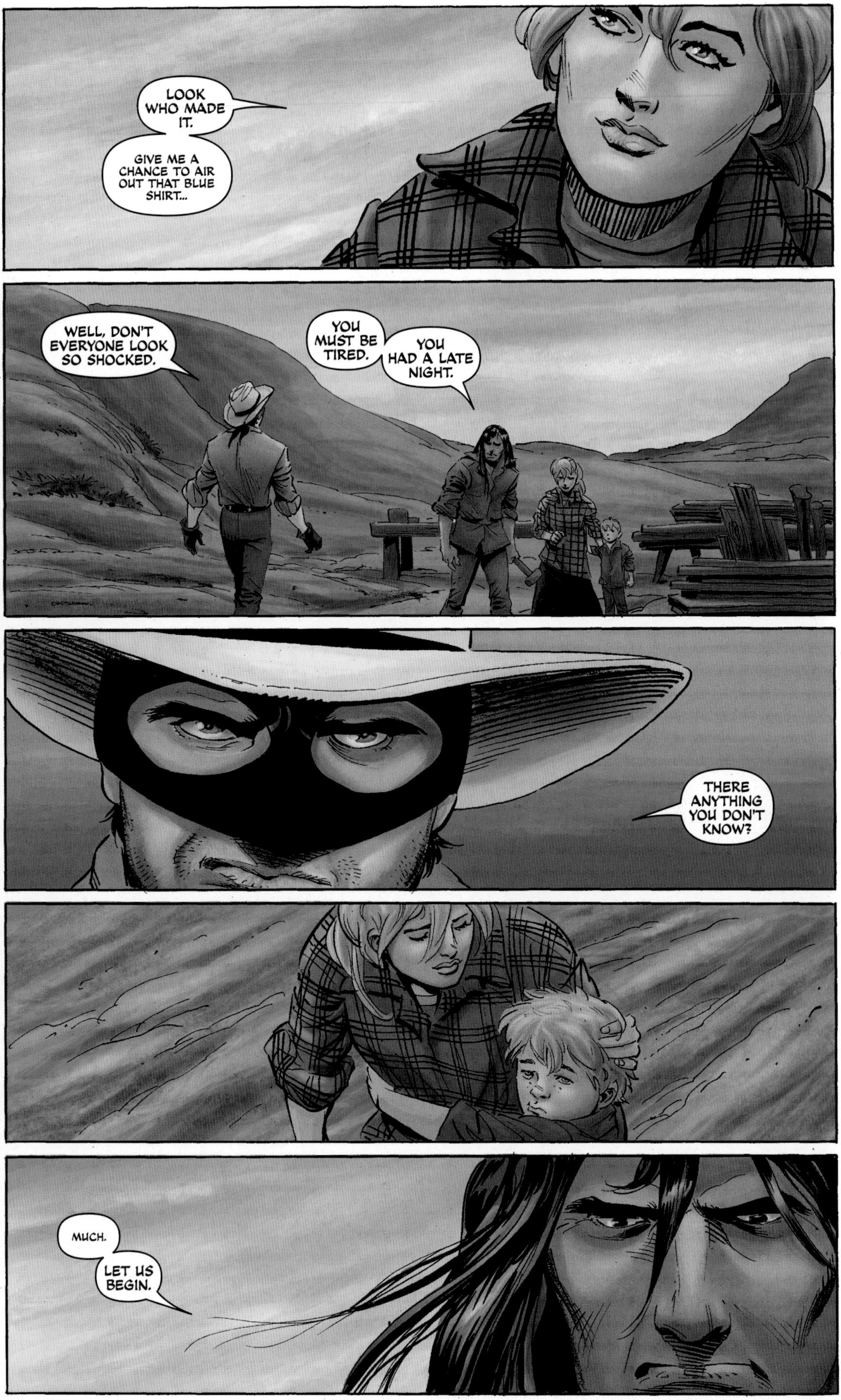
LOOK WHO MADE IT.
GIVE ME A CHANCE TO AIR OUT THAT BLUE SHIRT...
WELL, DON'T EVERYONE LOOK SO SHOCKED.
YOU MUST BE TIRED.
YOU HAD A LATE NIGHT.
THERE ANYTHING YOU DON'T KNOW?
MUCH.
LET US BEGIN.

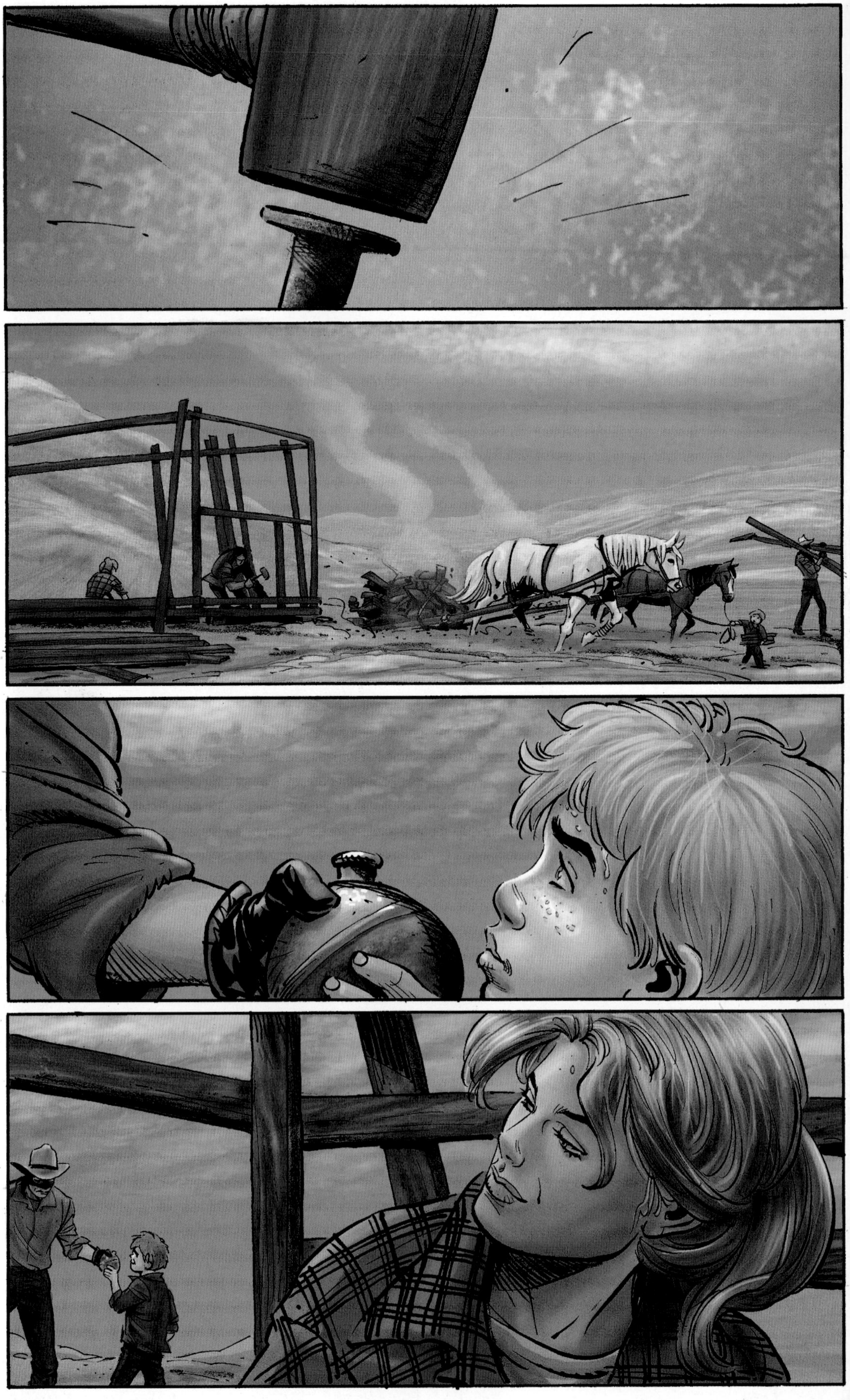

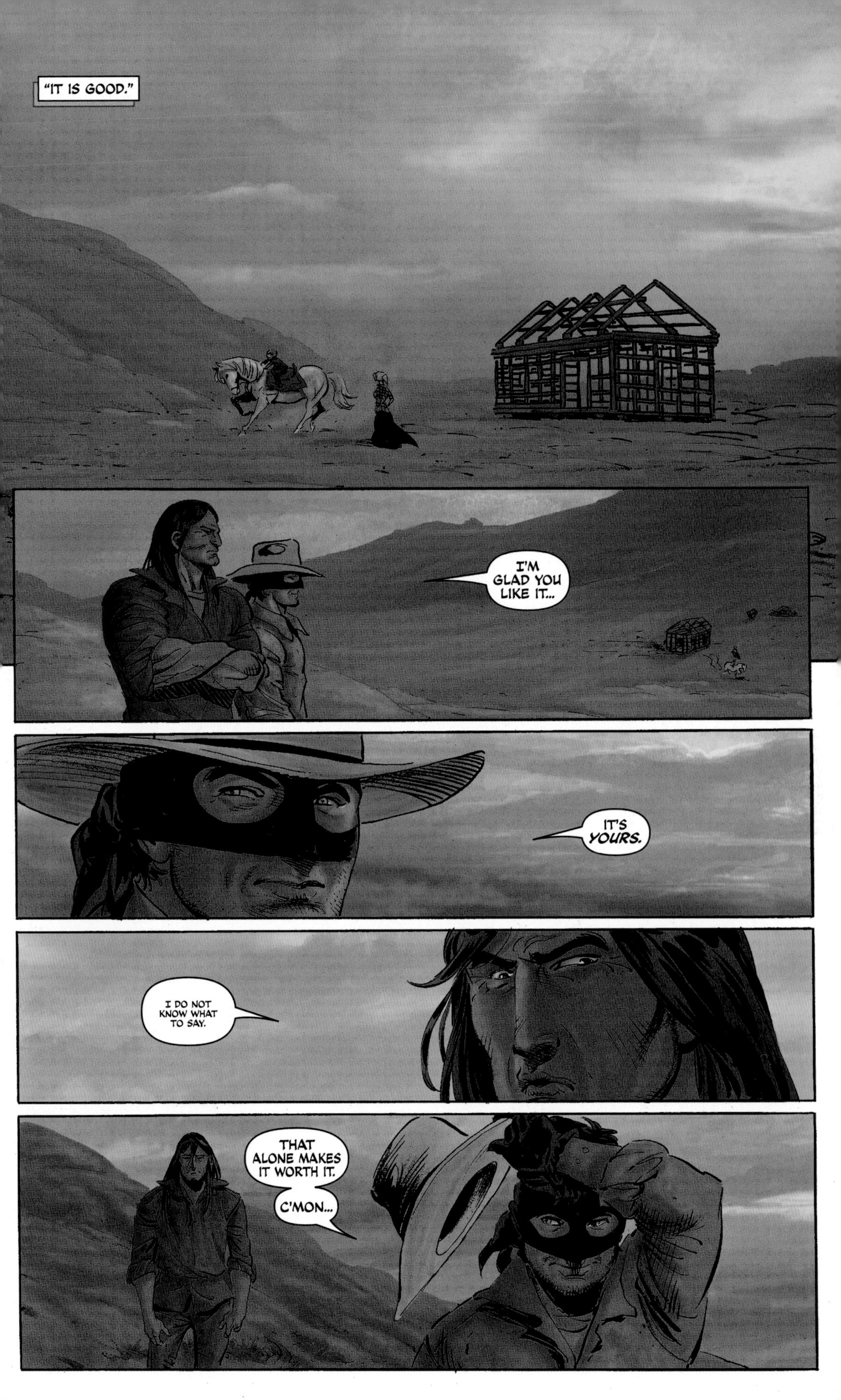
"IT IS GOOD."
I'M GLAD YOU LIKE IT...
IT'S *YOURS.*
I DO NOT KNOW WHAT TO SAY.
THAT ALONE MAKES IT WORTH IT.
C'MON...

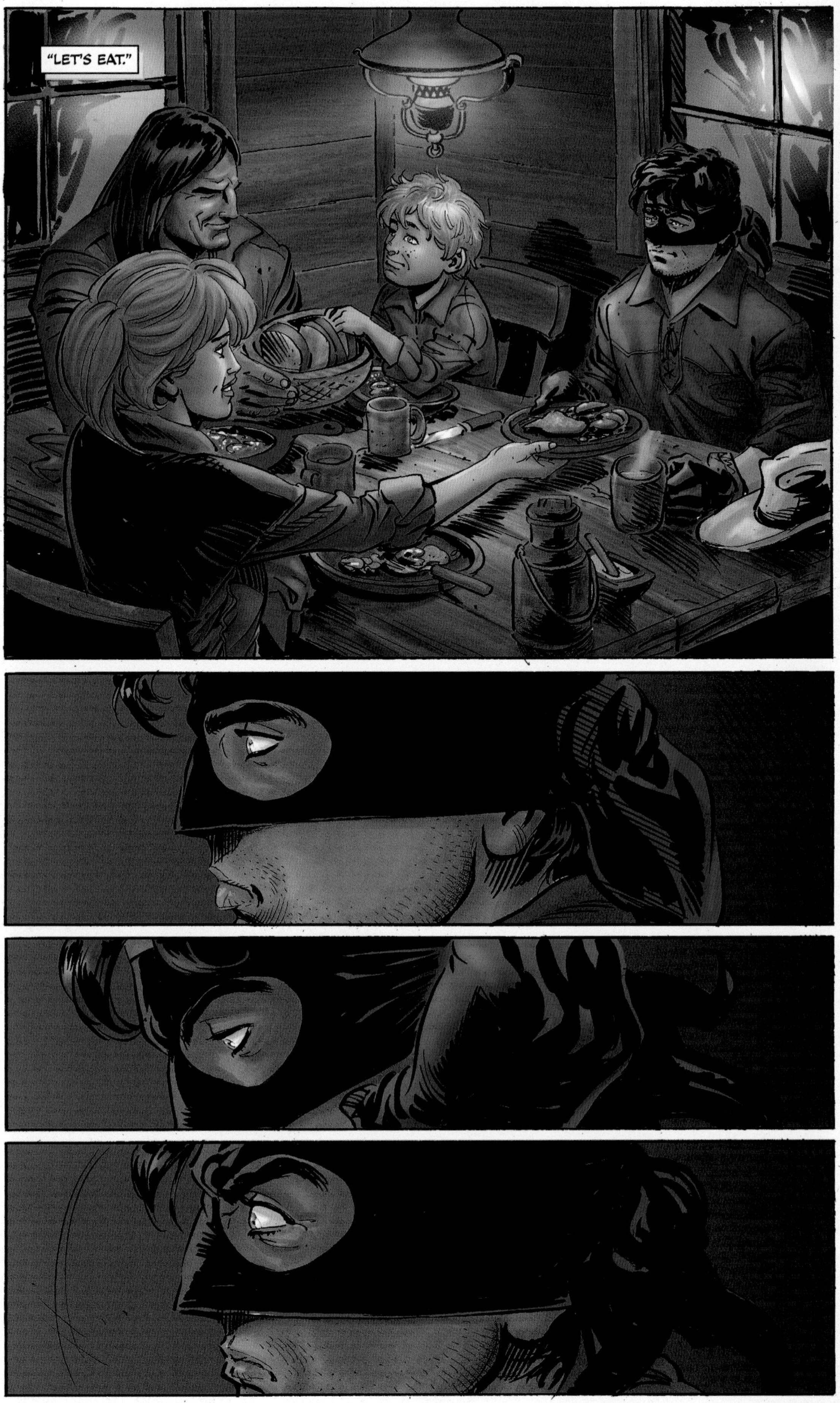
"LET'S EAT."

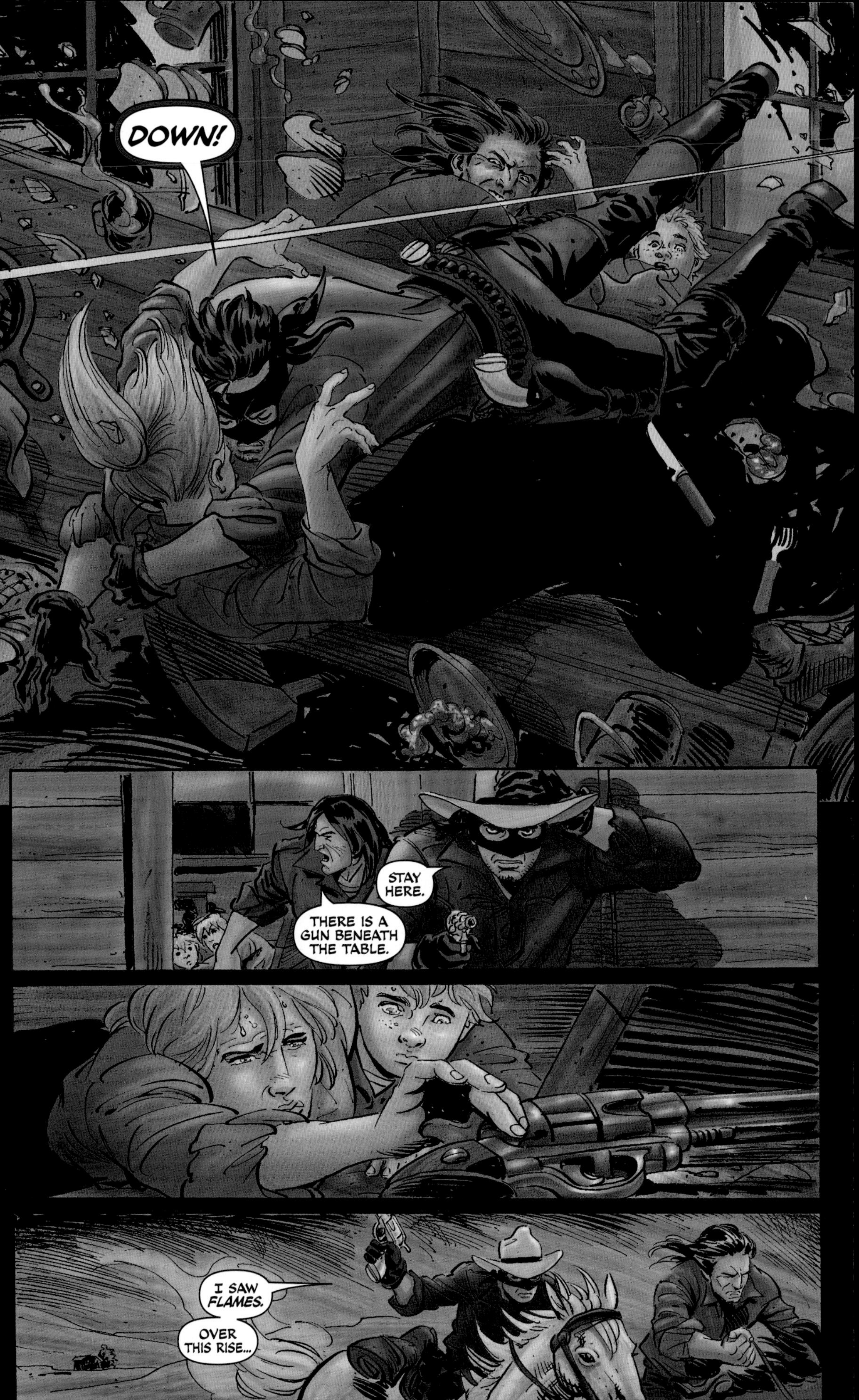
DOWN!
STAY HERE.
THERE IS A GUN BENEATH THE TABLE.
I SAW *FLAMES.*
OVER THIS RISE...

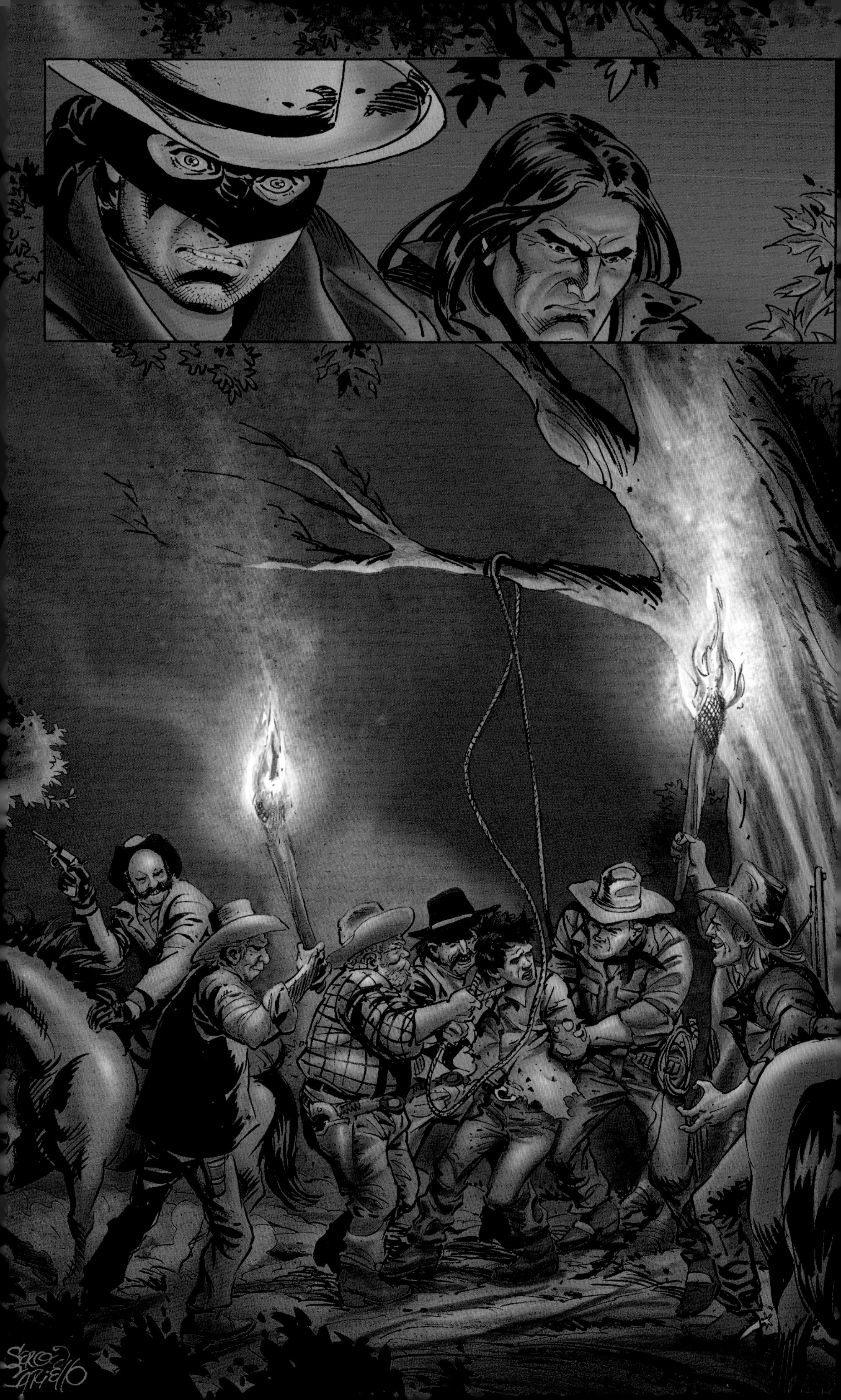

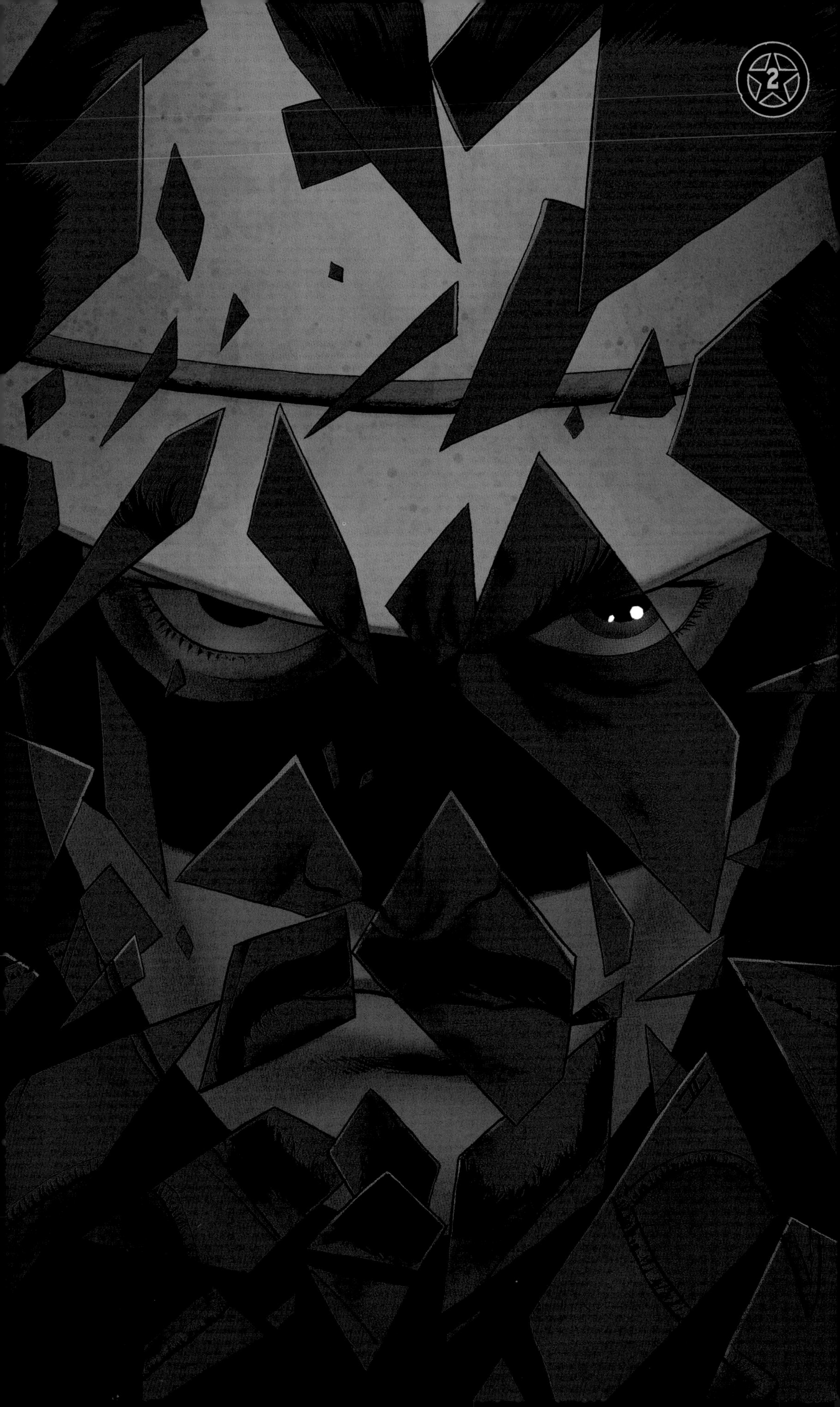
2

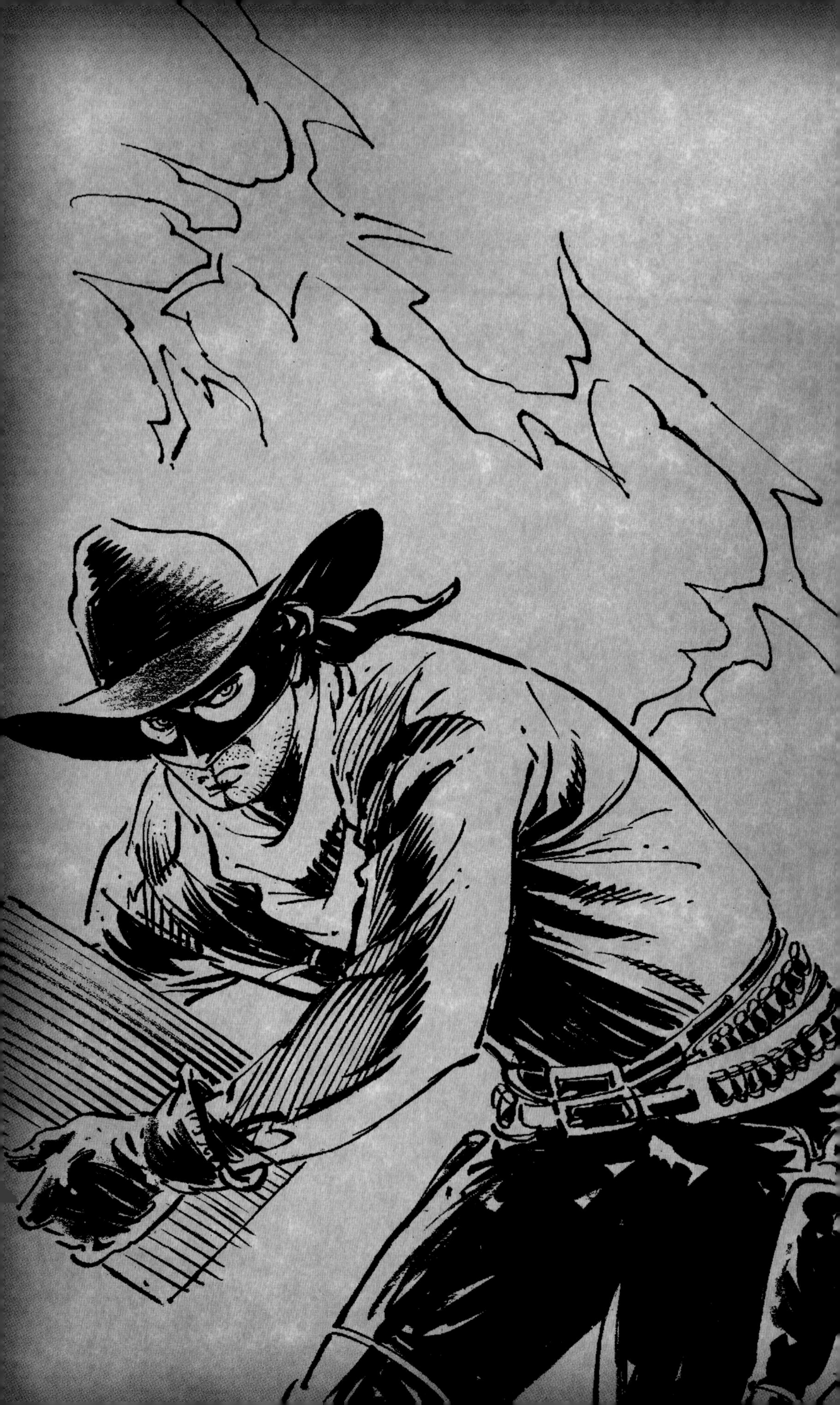

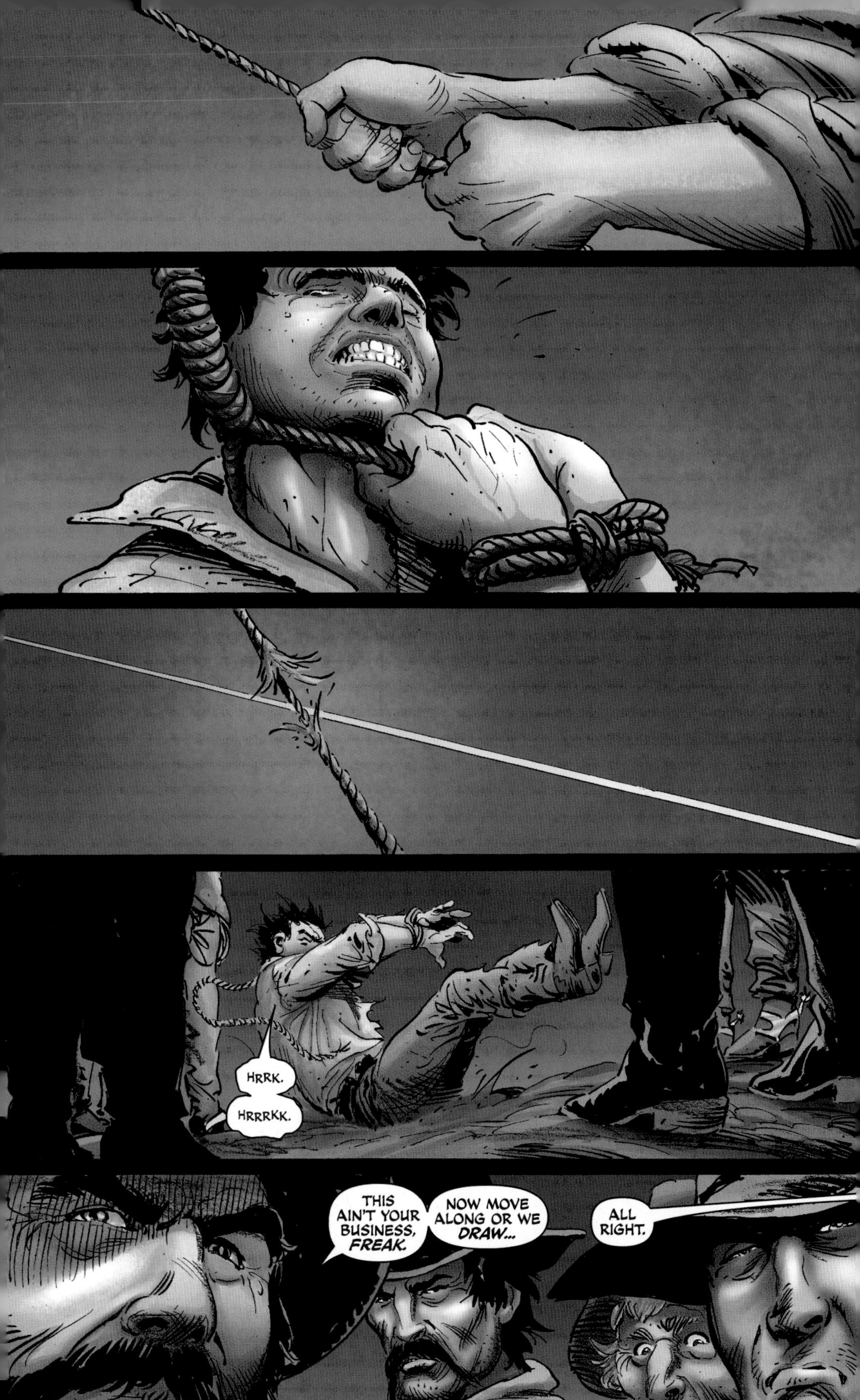
HRRK.
HRRRKK.
THIS AIN'T YOUR BUSINESS, FREAK.
NOW MOVE ALONG OR WE DRAW...
ALL RIGHT.

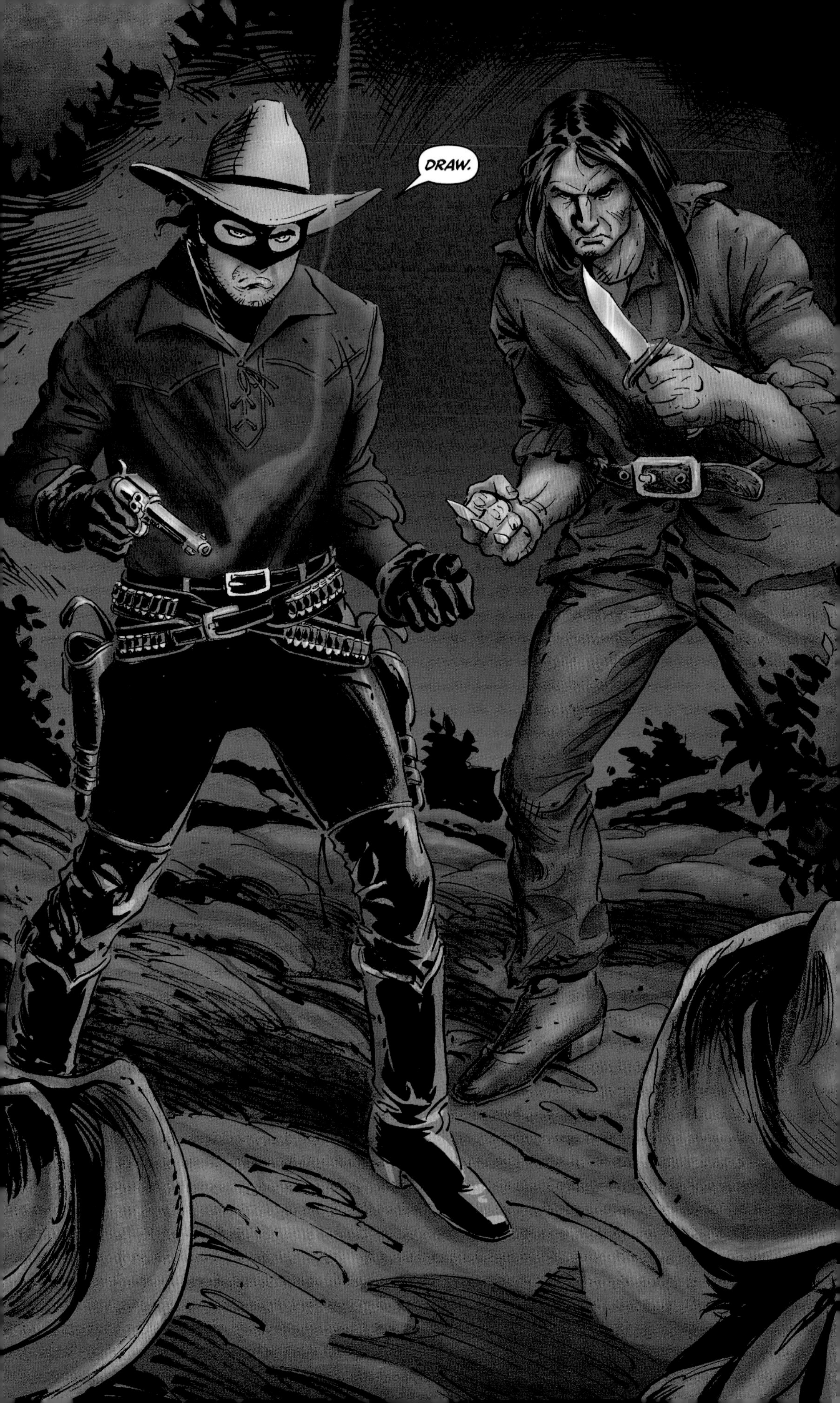
DRAW.

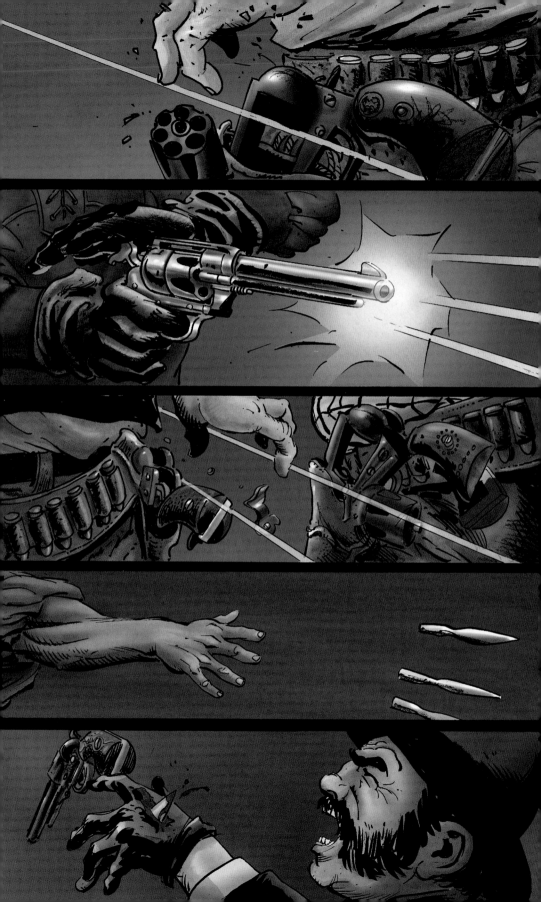

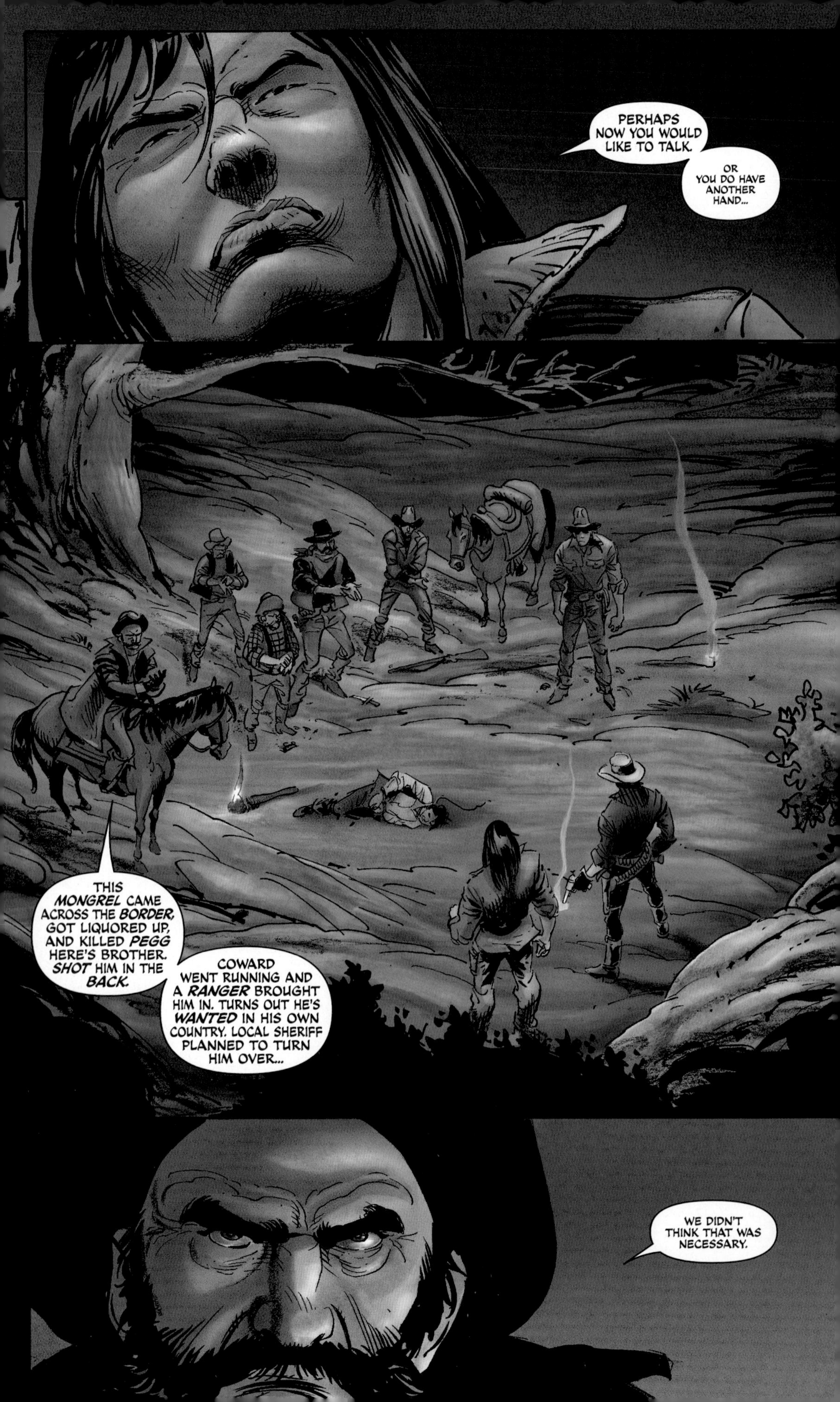
PERHAPS NOW YOU WOULD LIKE TO TALK.
OR YOU DO HAVE ANOTHER HAND...
THIS *MONGREL* CAME ACROSS THE *BORDER,* GOT LIQUORED UP, AND KILLED *PEGG* HERE'S BROTHER. *SHOT* HIM IN THE *BACK.*
COWARD WENT RUNNING AND A *RANGER* BROUGHT HIM IN. TURNS OUT HE'S *WANTED* IN HIS OWN COUNTRY. LOCAL SHERIFF PLANNED TO TURN HIM OVER...
WE DIDN'T THINK THAT WAS NECESSARY.

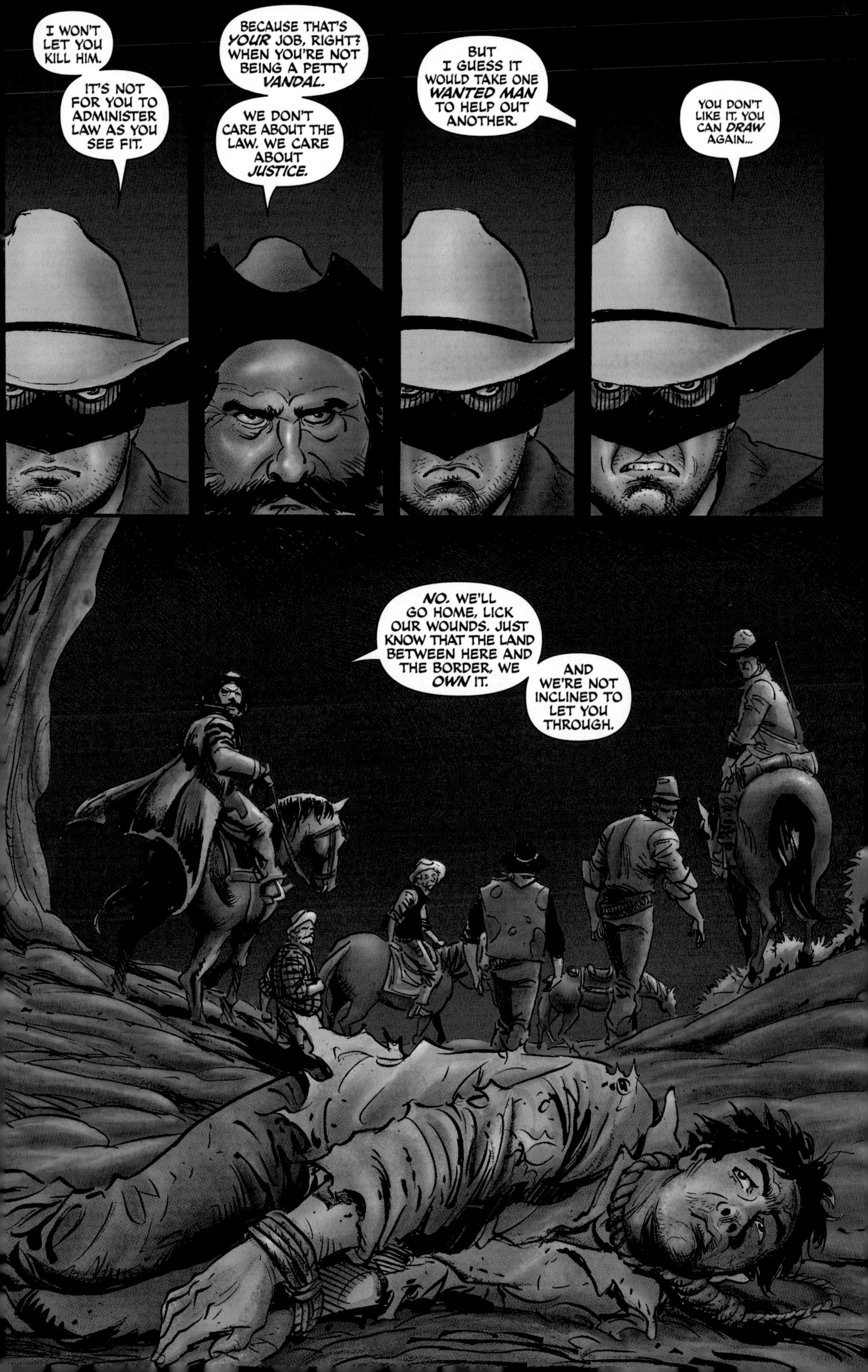
I WON'T LET YOU KILL HIM.
IT'S NOT FOR YOU TO ADMINISTER LAW AS YOU SEE FIT.
BECAUSE THAT'S YOUR JOB, RIGHT? WHEN YOU'RE NOT BEING A PETTY VANDAL.
WE DON'T CARE ABOUT THE LAW. WE CARE ABOUT JUSTICE.
BUT I GUESS IT WOULD TAKE ONE WANTED MAN TO HELP OUT ANOTHER.
YOU DON'T LIKE IT, YOU CAN DRAW AGAIN...
NO. WE'LL GO HOME, LICK OUR WOUNDS. JUST KNOW THAT THE LAND BETWEEN HERE AND THE BORDER, WE OWN IT.
AND WE'RE NOT INCLINED TO LET YOU THROUGH.

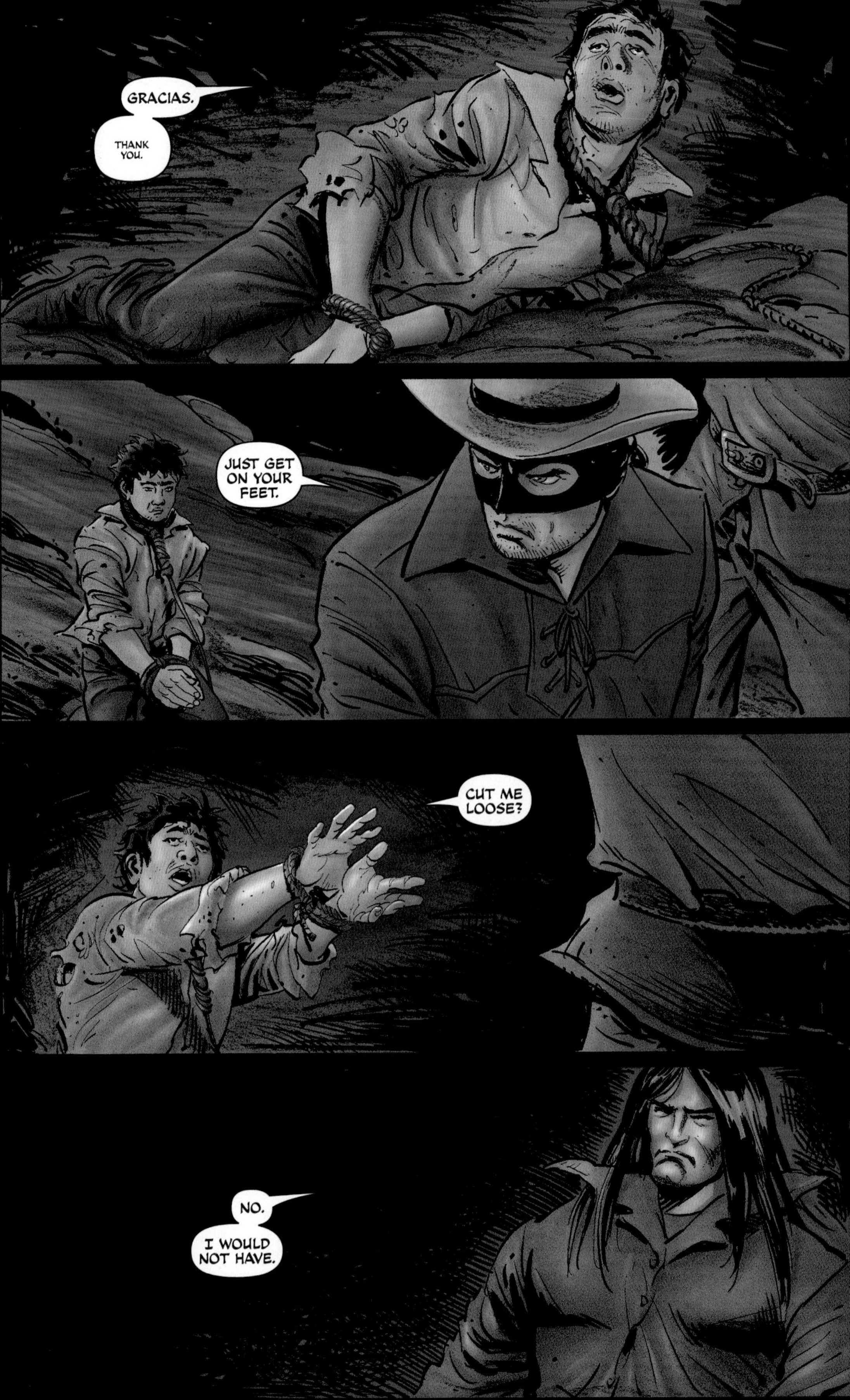
GRACIAS.
THANK YOU.
JUST GET ON YOUR FEET.
CUT ME LOOSE?
NO.
I WOULD NOT HAVE.

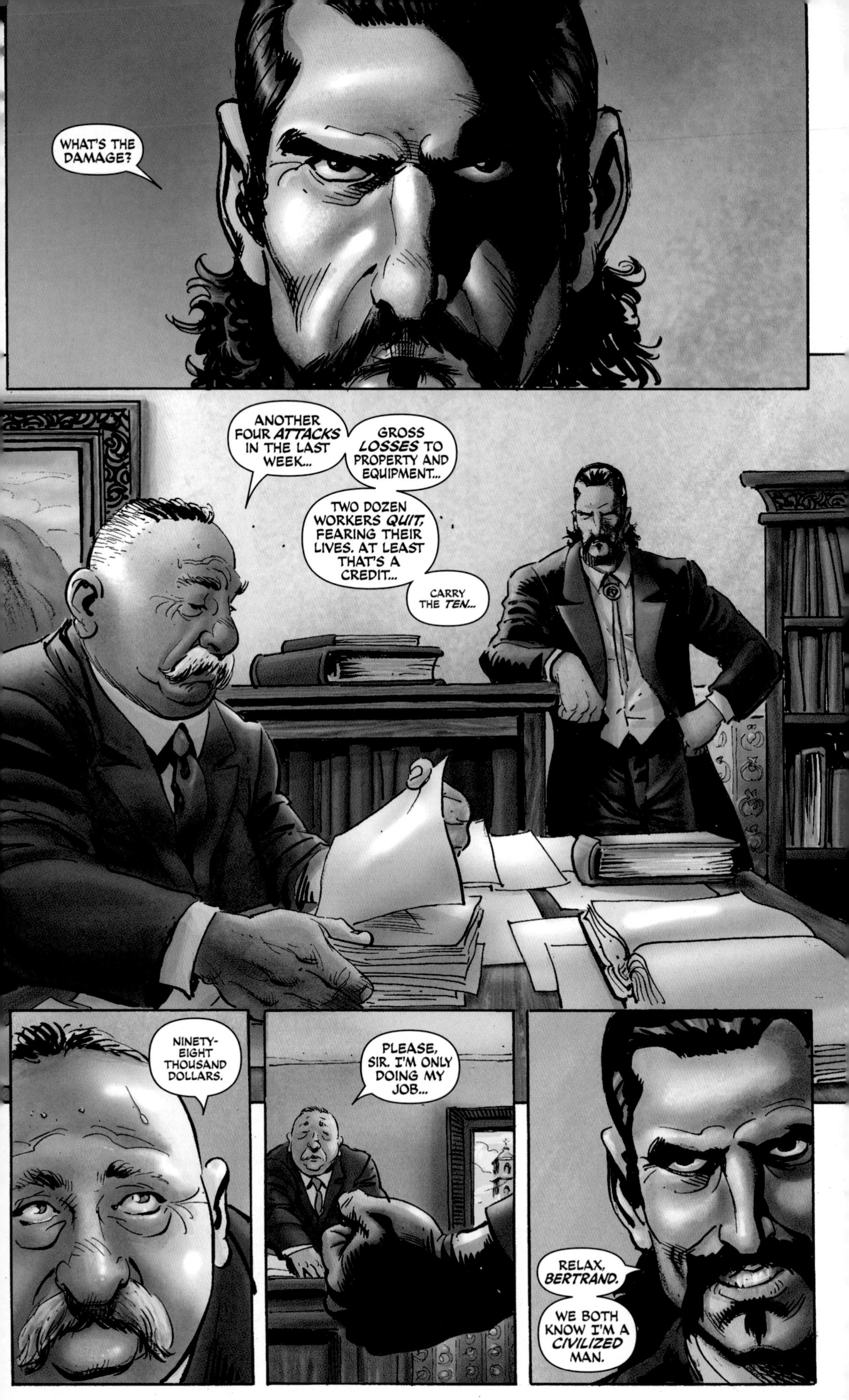
WHAT'S THE DAMAGE?
ANOTHER FOUR *ATTACKS* IN THE LAST WEEK...
GROSS *LOSSES* TO PROPERTY AND EQUIPMENT...
TWO DOZEN WORKERS *QUIT,* FEARING THEIR LIVES. AT LEAST THAT'S A CREDIT...
CARRY THE *TEN...*
NINETY-EIGHT THOUSAND DOLLARS.
PLEASE, SIR. I'M ONLY DOING MY JOB...
RELAX, *BERTRAND.*
WE BOTH KNOW I'M A *CIVILIZED* MAN.

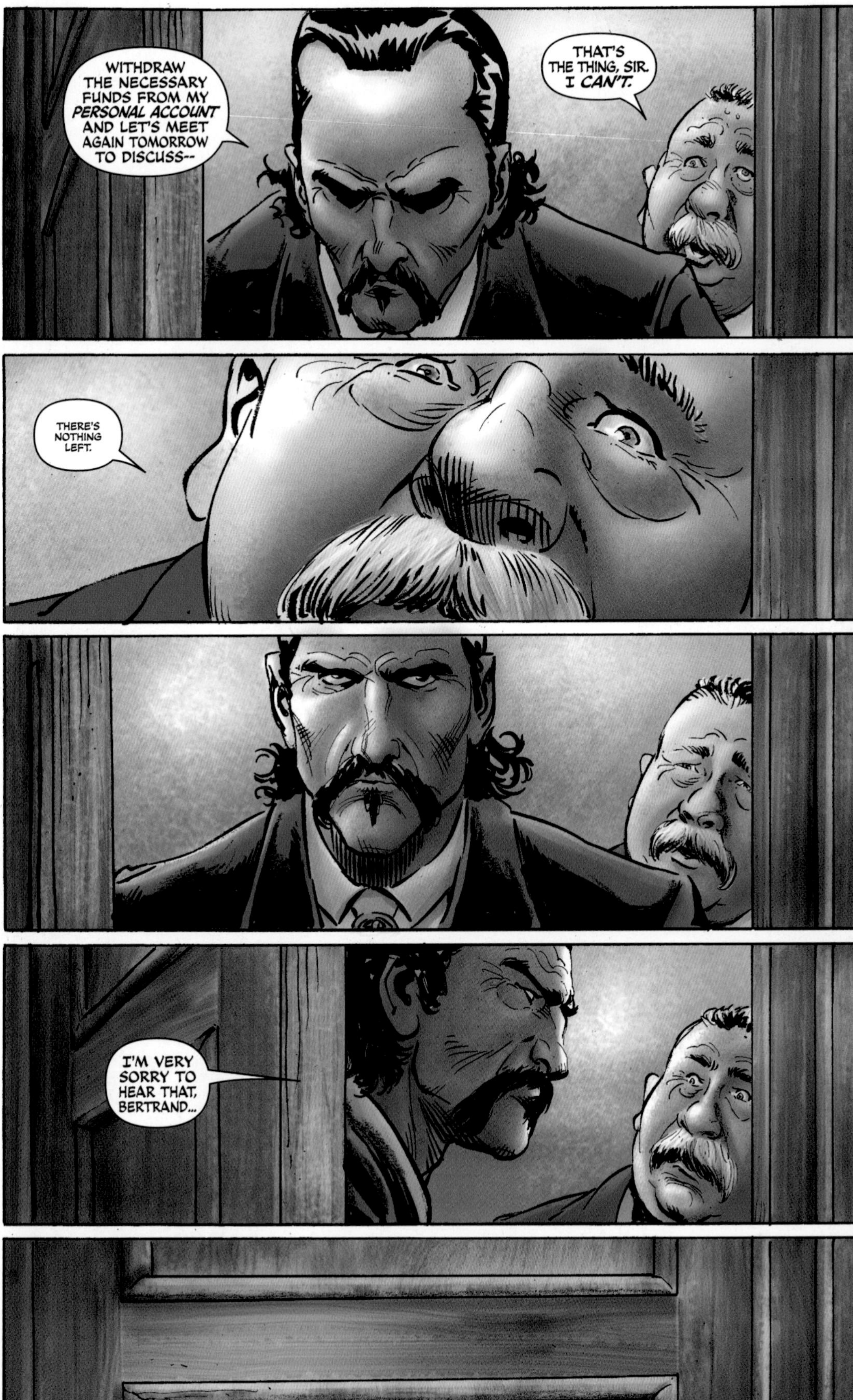
WITHDRAW THE NECESSARY FUNDS FROM MY *PERSONAL ACCOUNT* AND LET'S MEET AGAIN TOMORROW TO DISCUSS--
THAT'S THE THING, SIR. I *CAN'T.*
THERE'S NOTHING LEFT.
I'M VERY SORRY TO HEAR THAT, BERTRAND...

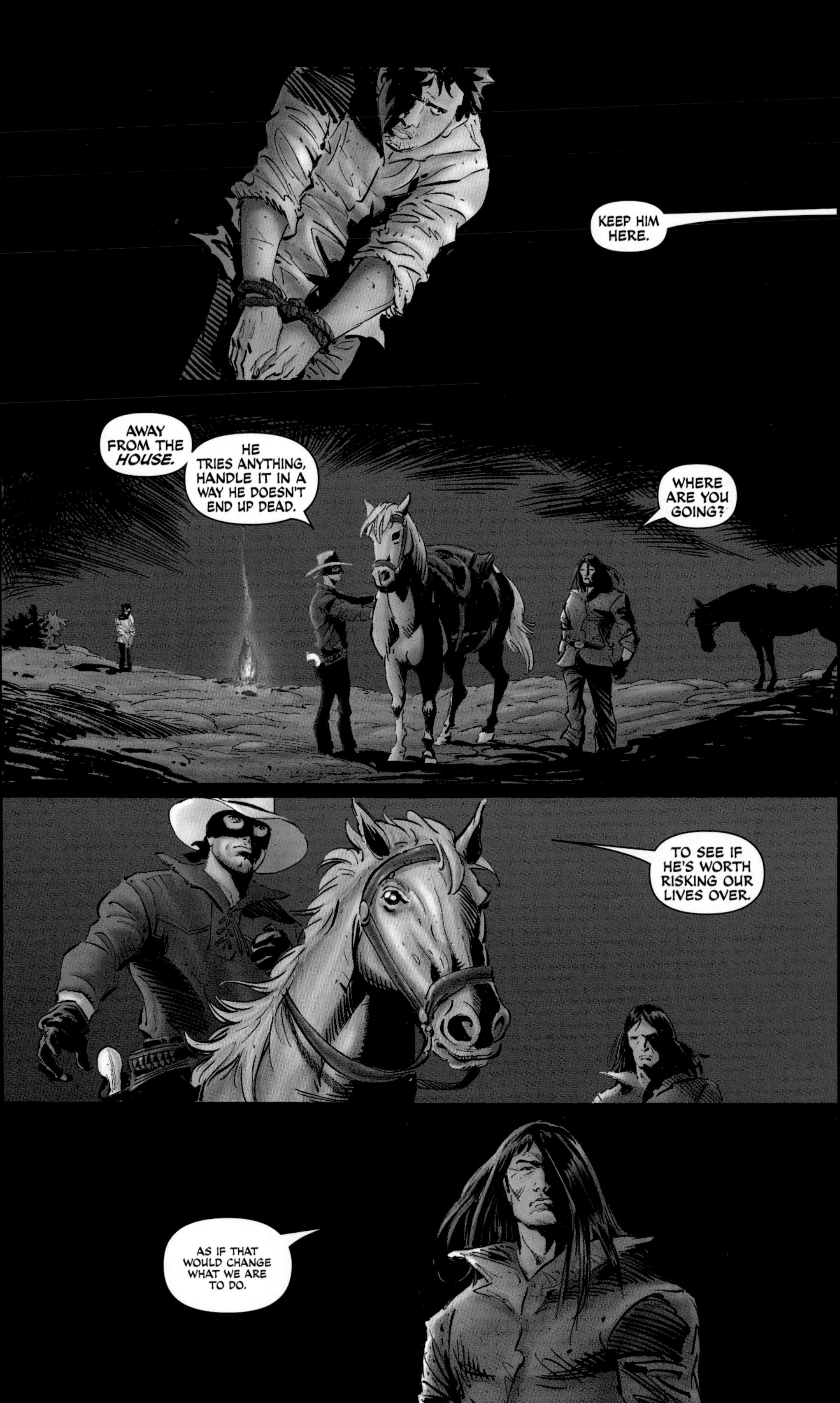
KEEP HIM HERE.
AWAY FROM THE HOUSE.
HE TRIES ANYTHING, HANDLE IT IN A WAY HE DOESN'T END UP DEAD.
WHERE ARE YOU GOING?
TO SEE IF HE'S WORTH RISKING OUR LIVES OVER.
AS IF THAT WOULD CHANGE WHAT WE ARE TO DO.

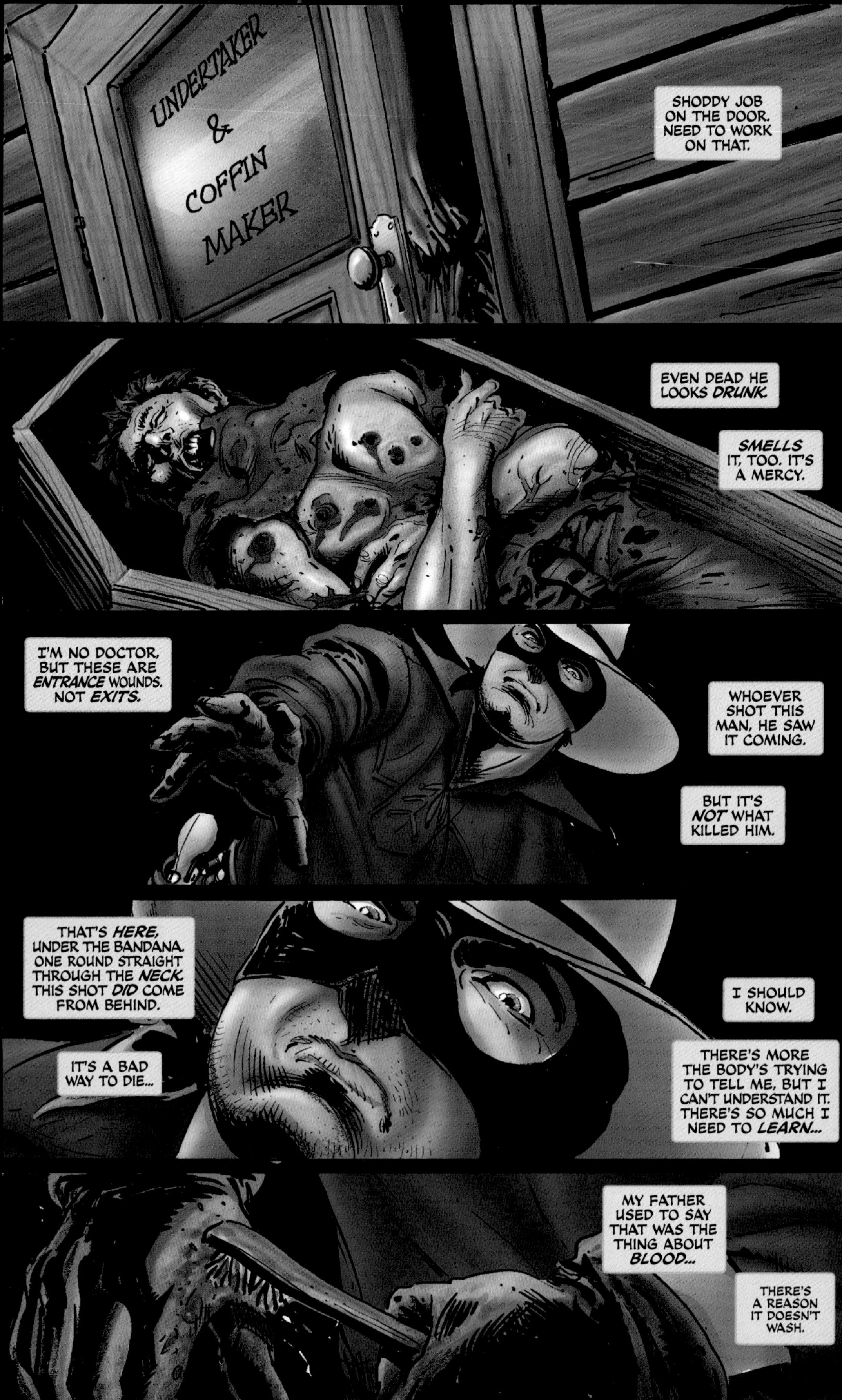
UNDERTAKER & COFFIN MAKER
SHODDY JOB ON THE DOOR. NEED TO WORK ON THAT.
EVEN DEAD HE LOOKS *DRUNK.*
SMELLS IT, TOO. IT'S A MERCY.
I'M NO DOCTOR, BUT THESE ARE *ENTRANCE* WOUNDS. NOT *EXITS.*
WHOEVER SHOT THIS MAN, HE SAW IT COMING.
BUT IT'S *NOT* WHAT KILLED HIM.
THAT'S *HERE,* UNDER THE BANDANA. ONE ROUND STRAIGHT THROUGH THE *NECK.* THIS SHOT *DID* COME FROM BEHIND.
IT'S A BAD WAY TO DIE...
I SHOULD KNOW.
THERE'S MORE THE BODY'S TRYING TO TELL ME, BUT I CAN'T UNDERSTAND IT. THERE'S SO MUCH I NEED TO *LEARN...*
MY FATHER USED TO SAY THAT WAS THE THING ABOUT *BLOOD...*
THERE'S A REASON IT DOESN'T WASH.

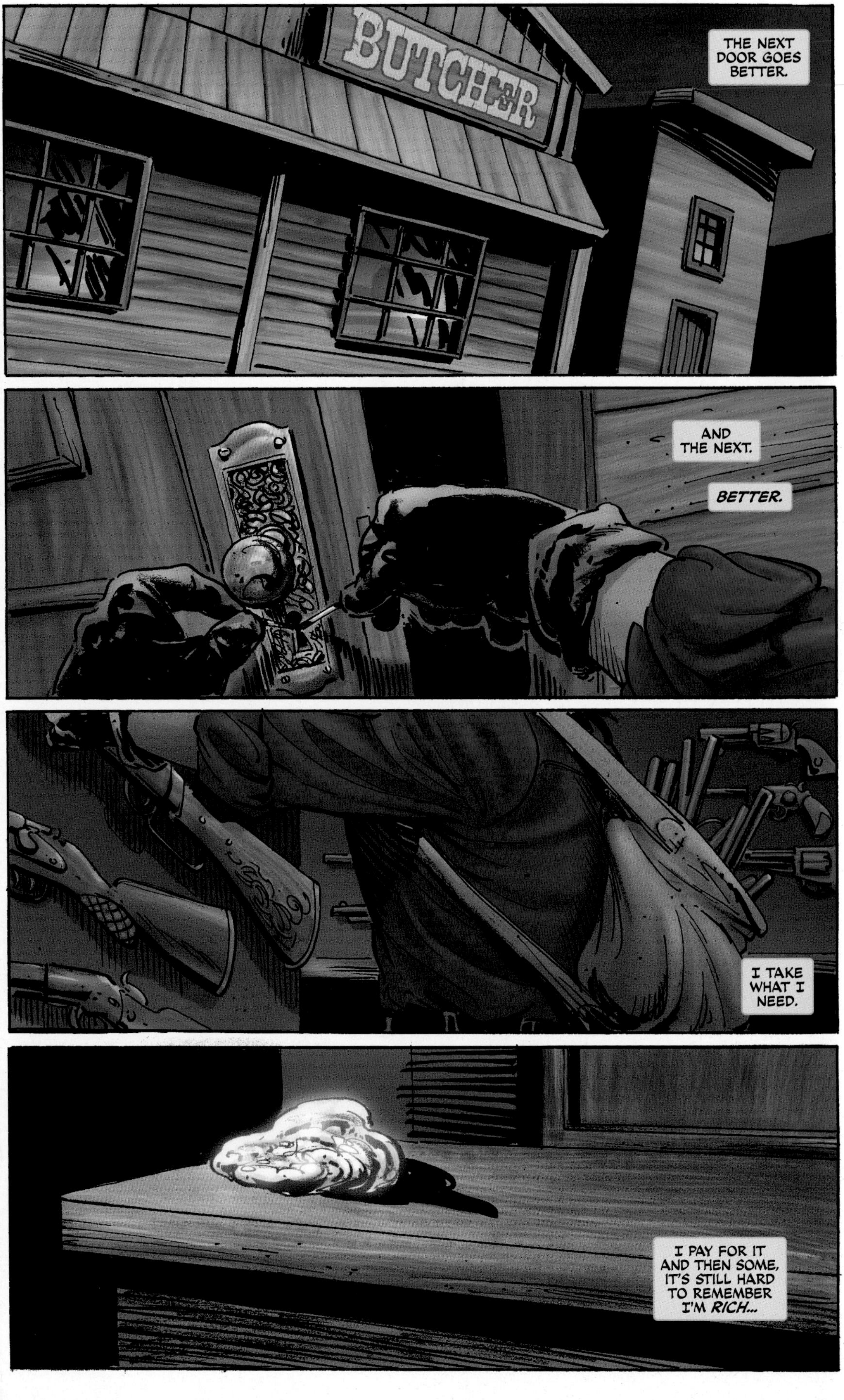
BUTCHER
THE NEXT DOOR GOES BETTER.
AND THE NEXT.
BETTER.
I TAKE WHAT I NEED.
I PAY FOR IT AND THEN SOME, IT'S STILL HARD TO REMEMBER I'M *RICH*...

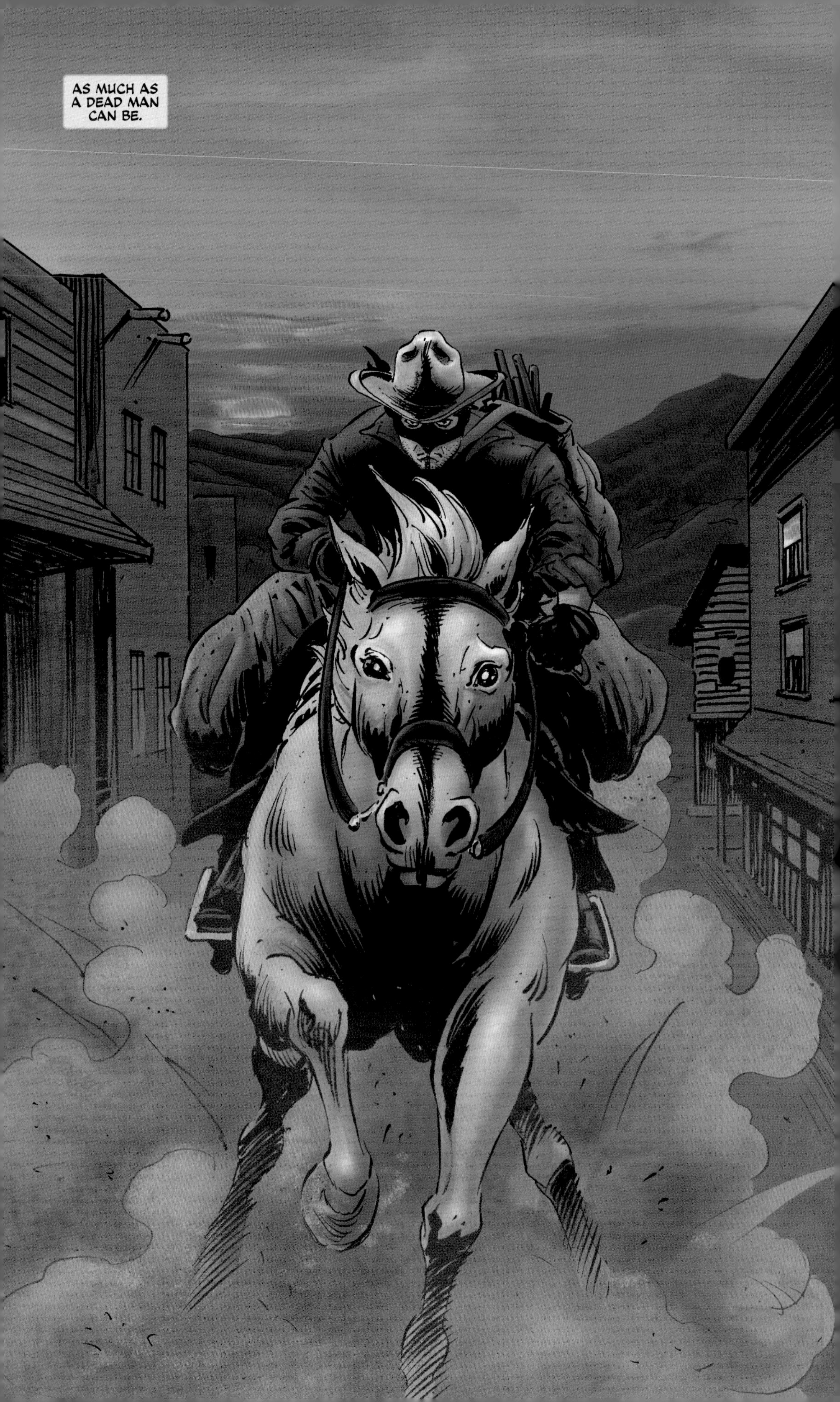
AS MUCH AS A DEAD MAN CAN BE.

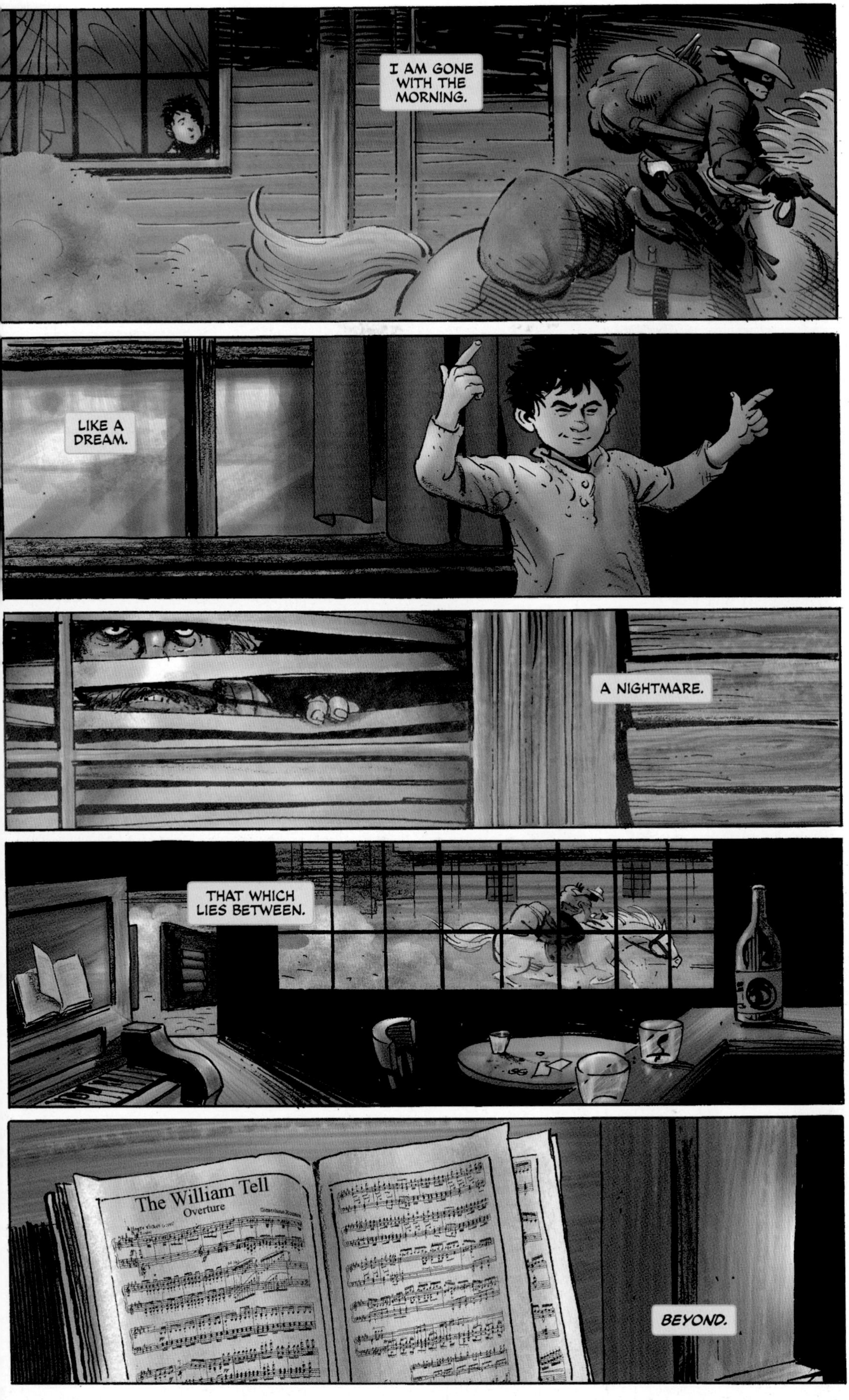
I AM GONE WITH THE MORNING.
LIKE A DREAM.
A NIGHTMARE.
THAT WHICH LIES BETWEEN.
The William Tell
Overture
BEYOND.

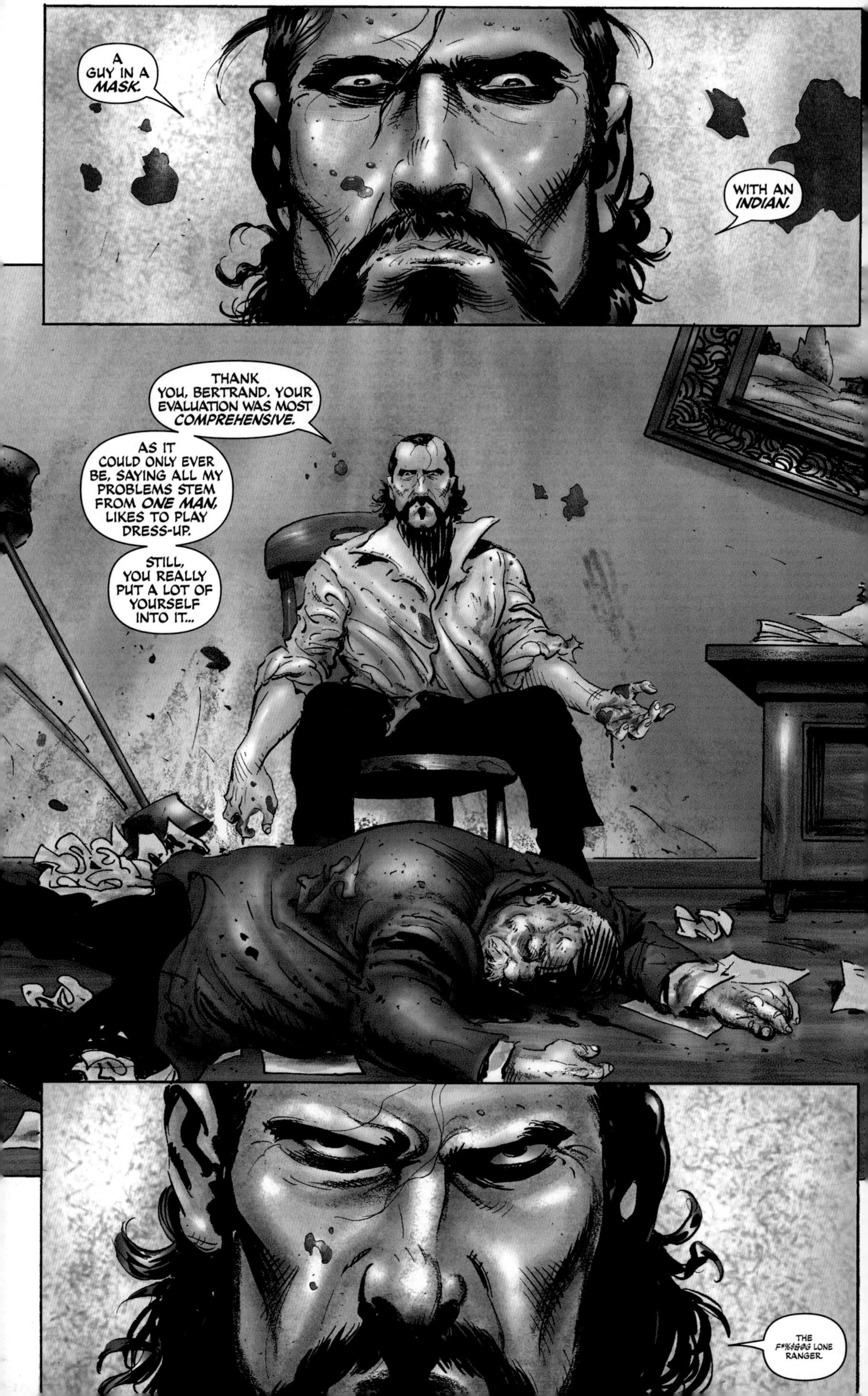
A GUY IN A MASK.
WITH AN INDIAN.
THANK YOU, BERTRAND. YOUR EVALUATION WAS MOST COMPREHENSIVE.
AS IT COULD ONLY EVER BE, SAYING ALL MY PROBLEMS STEM FROM ONE MAN, LIKES TO PLAY DRESS-UP.
STILL, YOU REALLY PUT A LOT OF YOURSELF INTO IT...
THE F*%$&@G LONE RANGER.

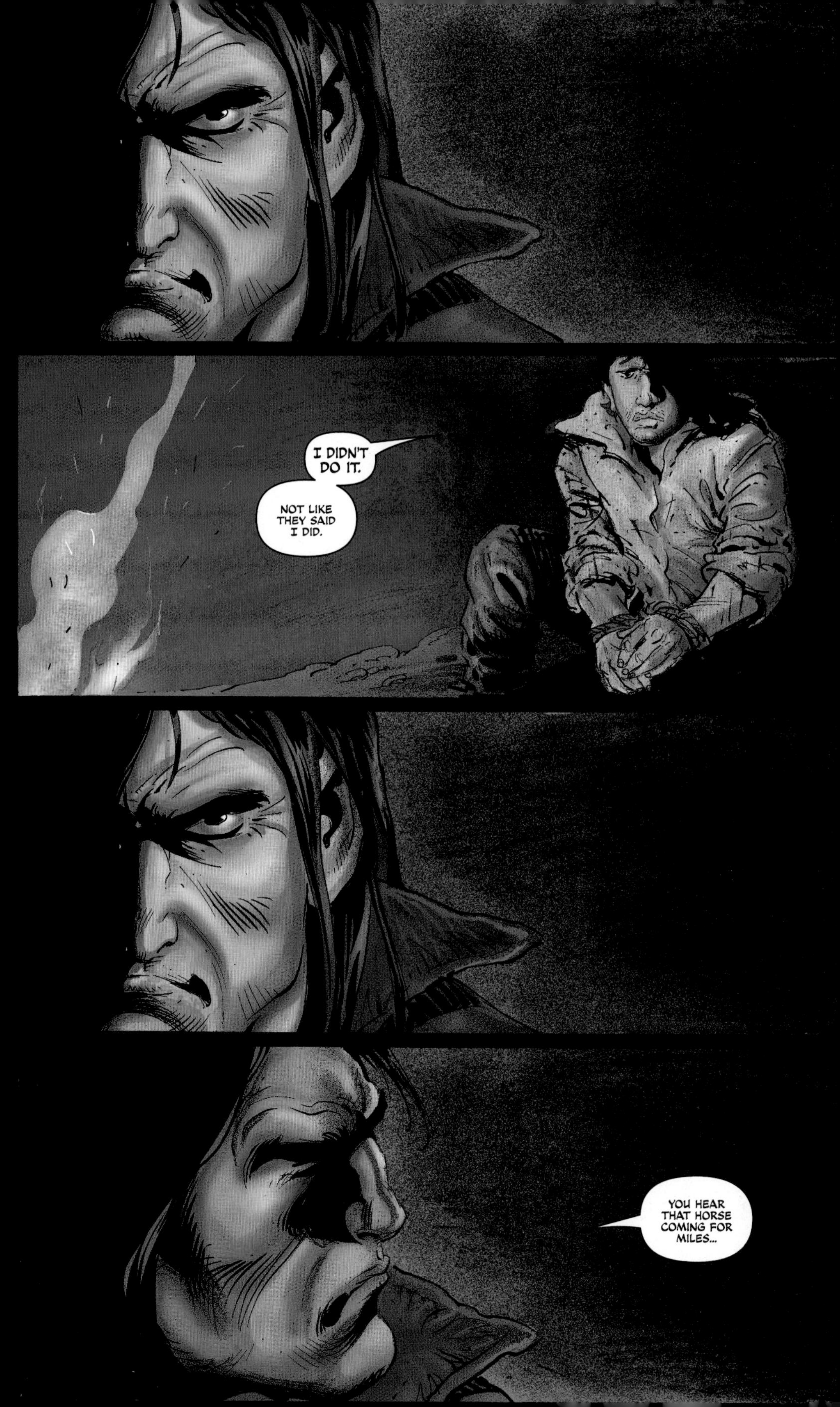
I DIDN'T DO IT.
NOT LIKE THEY SAID I DID.
YOU HEAR THAT HORSE COMING FOR MILES...

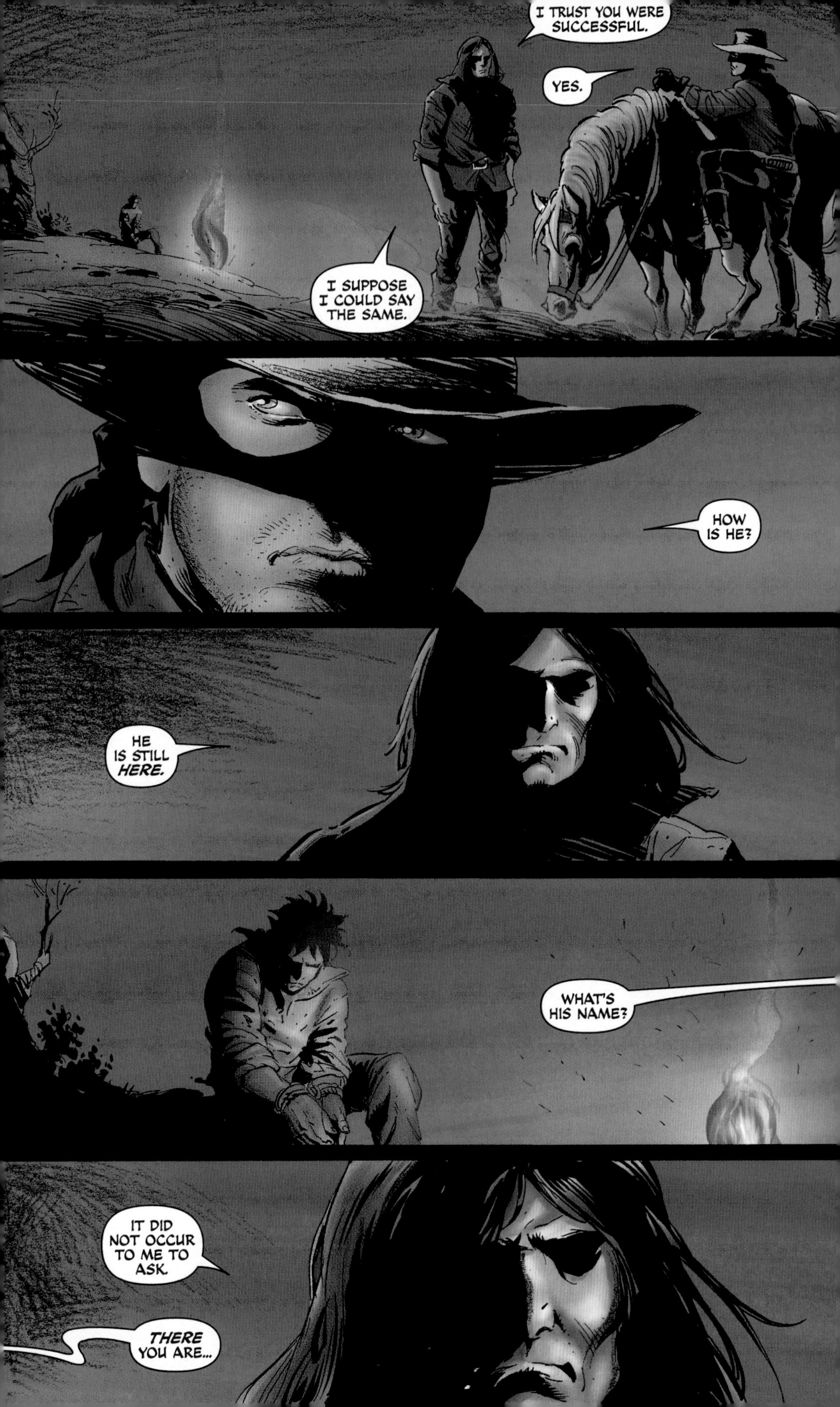
I TRUST YOU WERE SUCCESSFUL.
YES.
I SUPPOSE I COULD SAY THE SAME.
HOW IS HE?
HE IS STILL *HERE.*
WHAT'S HIS NAME?
IT DID NOT OCCUR TO ME TO ASK.
THERE YOU ARE...

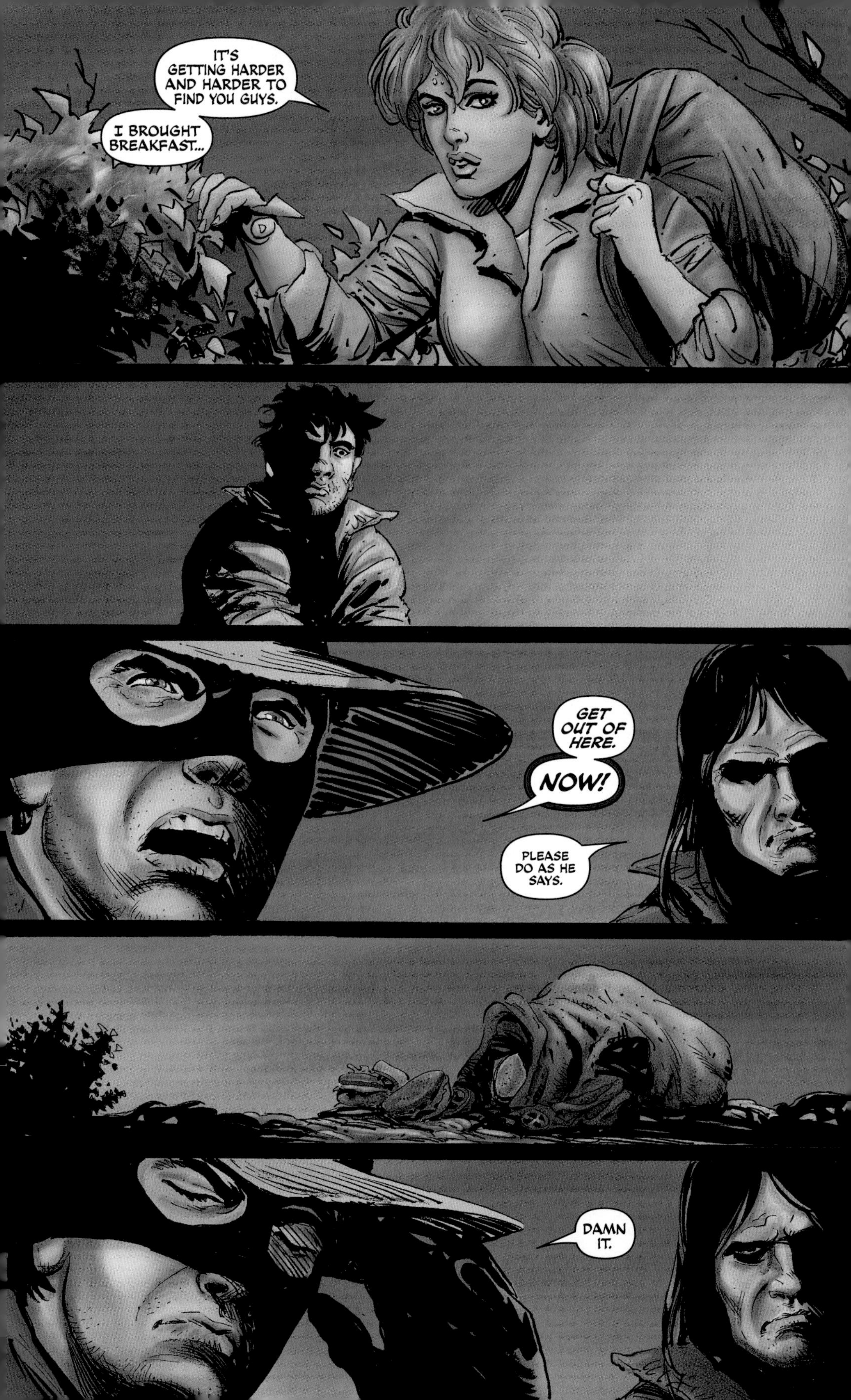
IT'S GETTING HARDER AND HARDER TO FIND YOU GUYS.
I BROUGHT BREAKFAST...
GET OUT OF HERE.
NOW!
PLEASE DO AS HE SAYS.
DAMN IT.

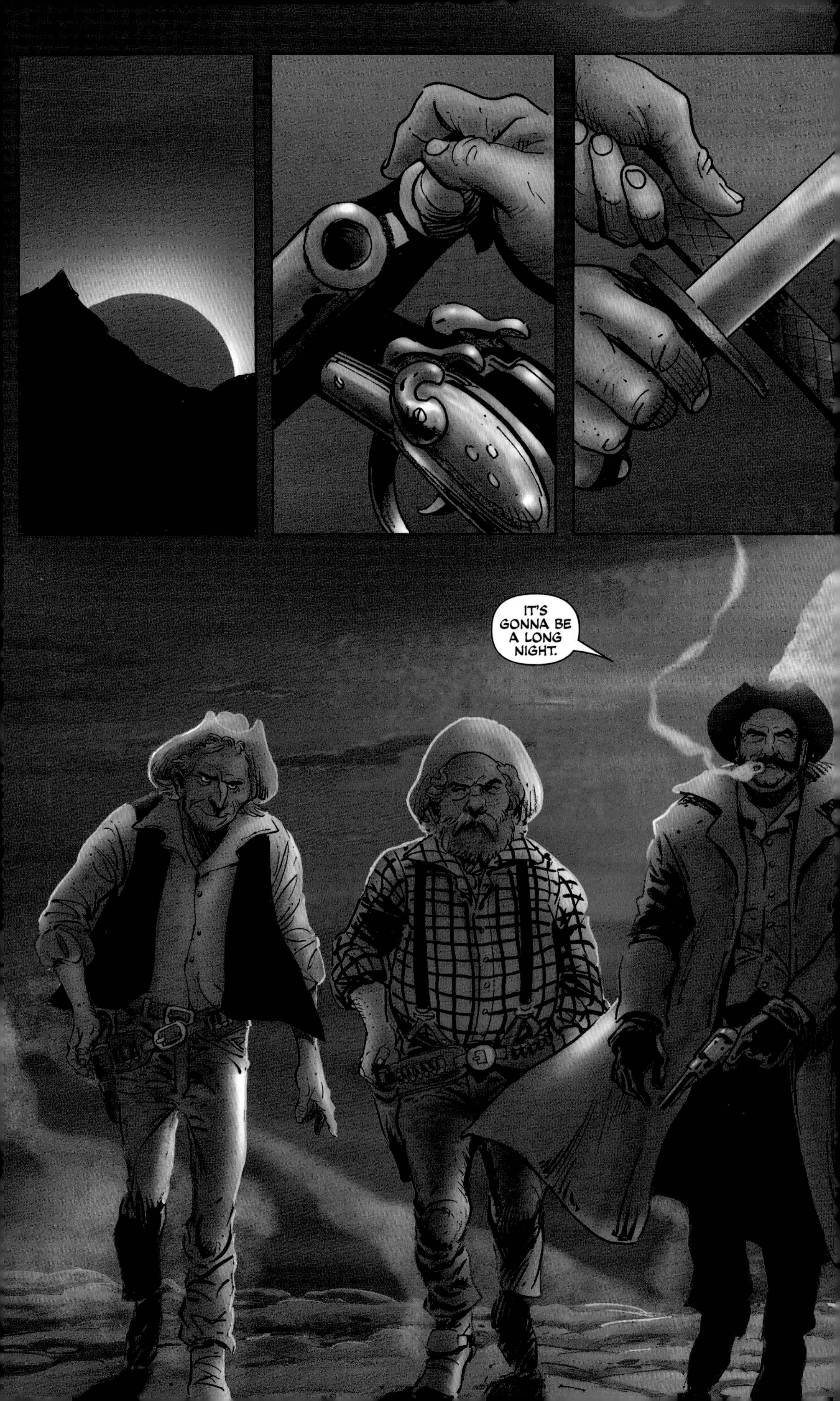
IT'S GONNA BE A LONG NIGHT.

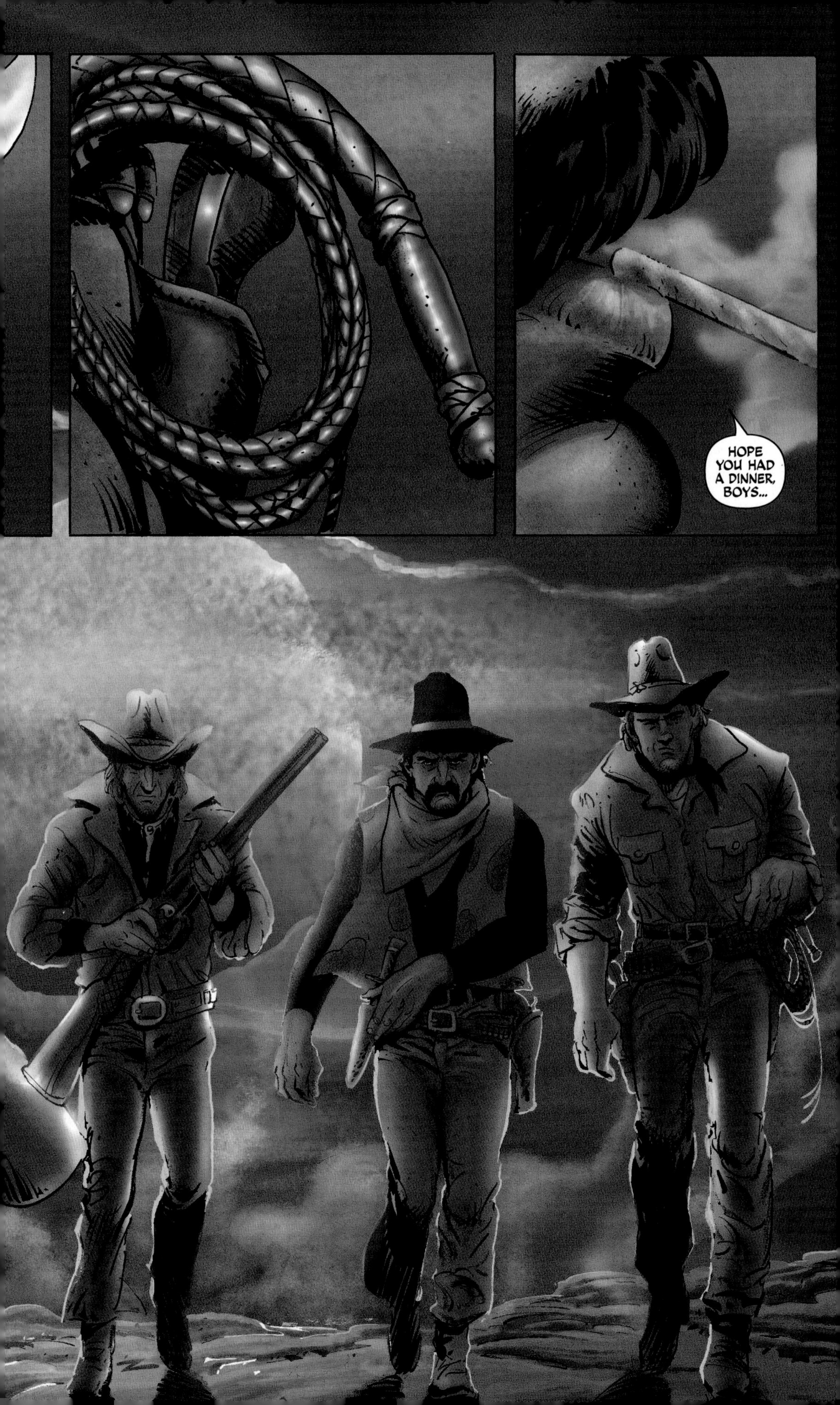
HOPE YOU HAD A DINNER, BOYS...

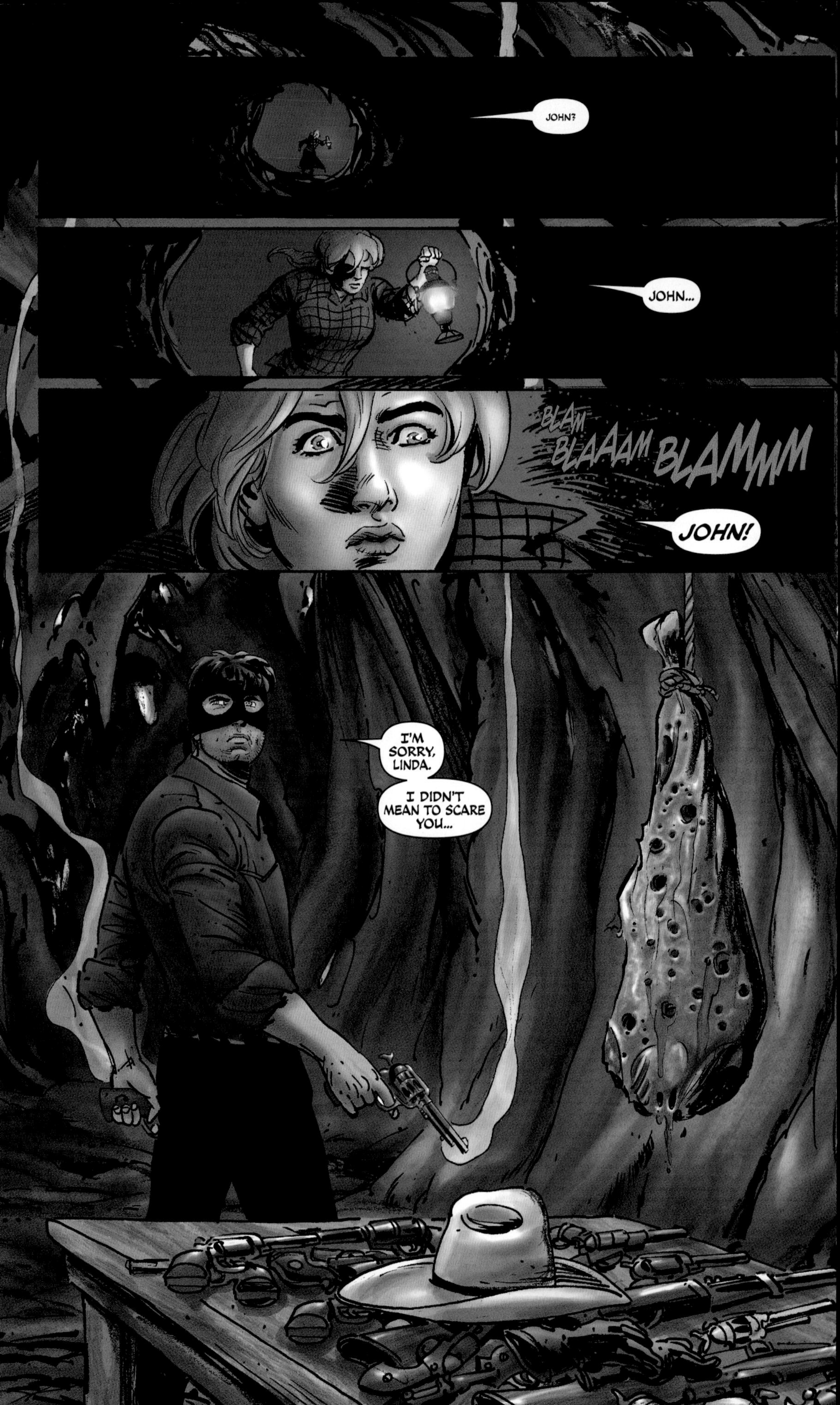
JOHN?
JOHN...
BLAM BLAAAM BLAMMM
JOHN!
I'M SORRY, LINDA.
I DIDN'T MEAN TO SCARE YOU...

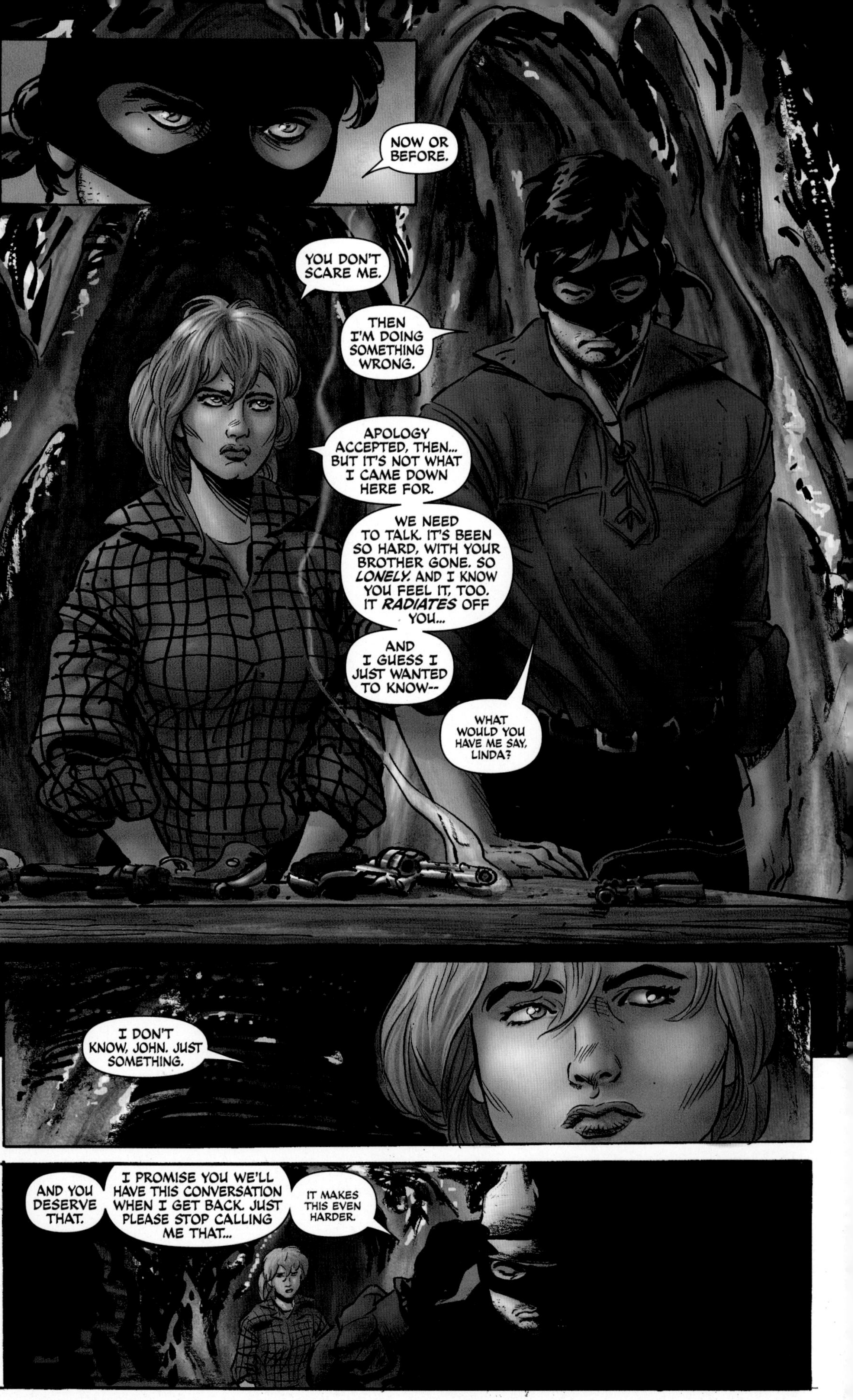
NOW OR BEFORE.
YOU DON'T SCARE ME.
THEN I'M DOING SOMETHING WRONG.
APOLOGY ACCEPTED, THEN... BUT IT'S NOT WHAT I CAME DOWN HERE FOR.
WE NEED TO TALK. IT'S BEEN SO HARD, WITH YOUR BROTHER GONE. SO *LONELY.* AND I KNOW YOU FEEL IT, TOO. IT *RADIATES* OFF YOU...
AND I GUESS I JUST WANTED TO KNOW--
WHAT WOULD YOU HAVE ME SAY, LINDA?
I DON'T KNOW, JOHN. JUST SOMETHING.
AND YOU DESERVE THAT.
I PROMISE YOU WE'LL HAVE THIS CONVERSATION WHEN I GET BACK. JUST PLEASE STOP CALLING ME THAT...
IT MAKES THIS EVEN HARDER.

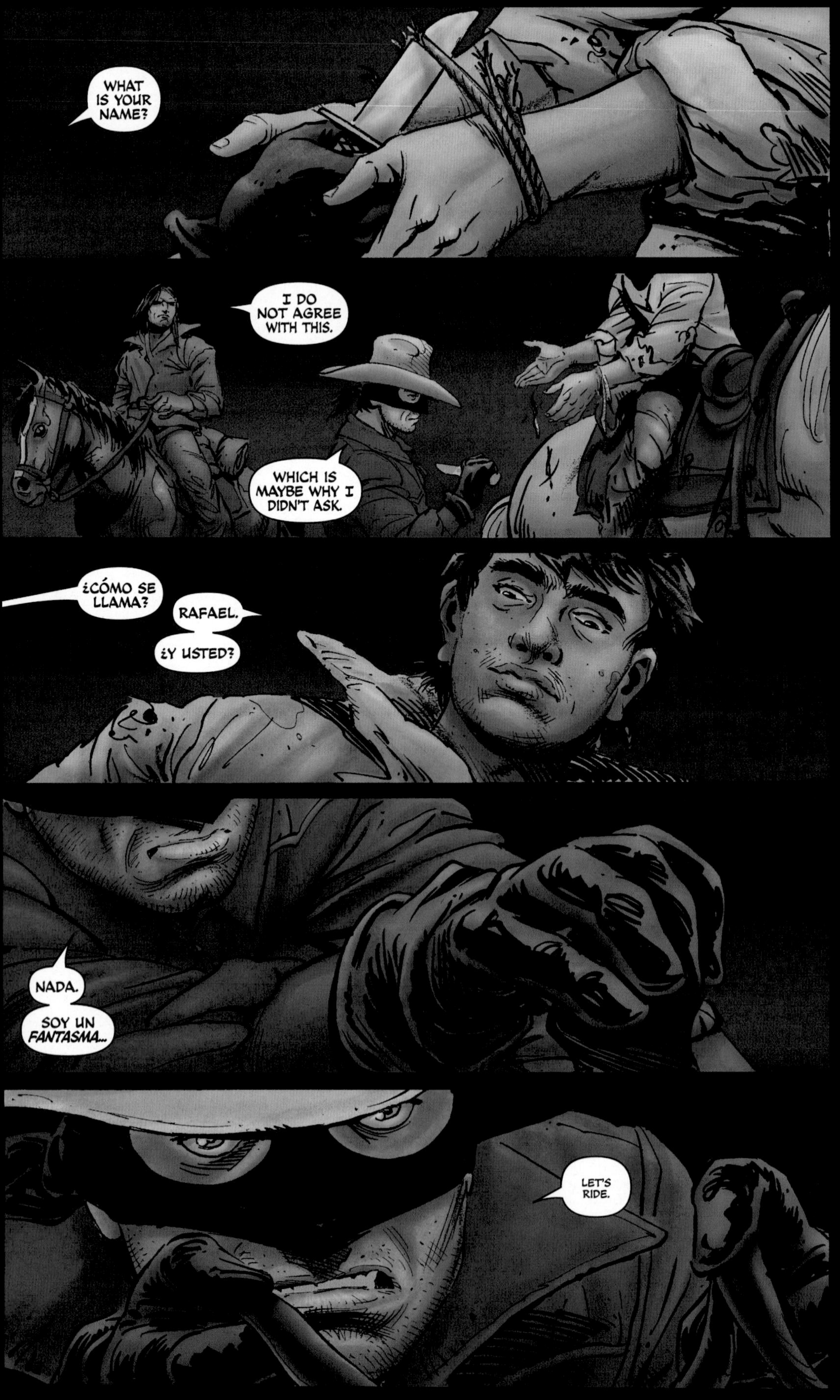

WHAT IS YOUR NAME?
I DO NOT AGREE WITH THIS.
WHICH IS MAYBE WHY I DIDN'T ASK.
¿CÓMO SE LLAMA?
RAFAEL.
¿Y USTED?
NADA.
SOY UN *FANTASMA...*
LET'S RIDE.

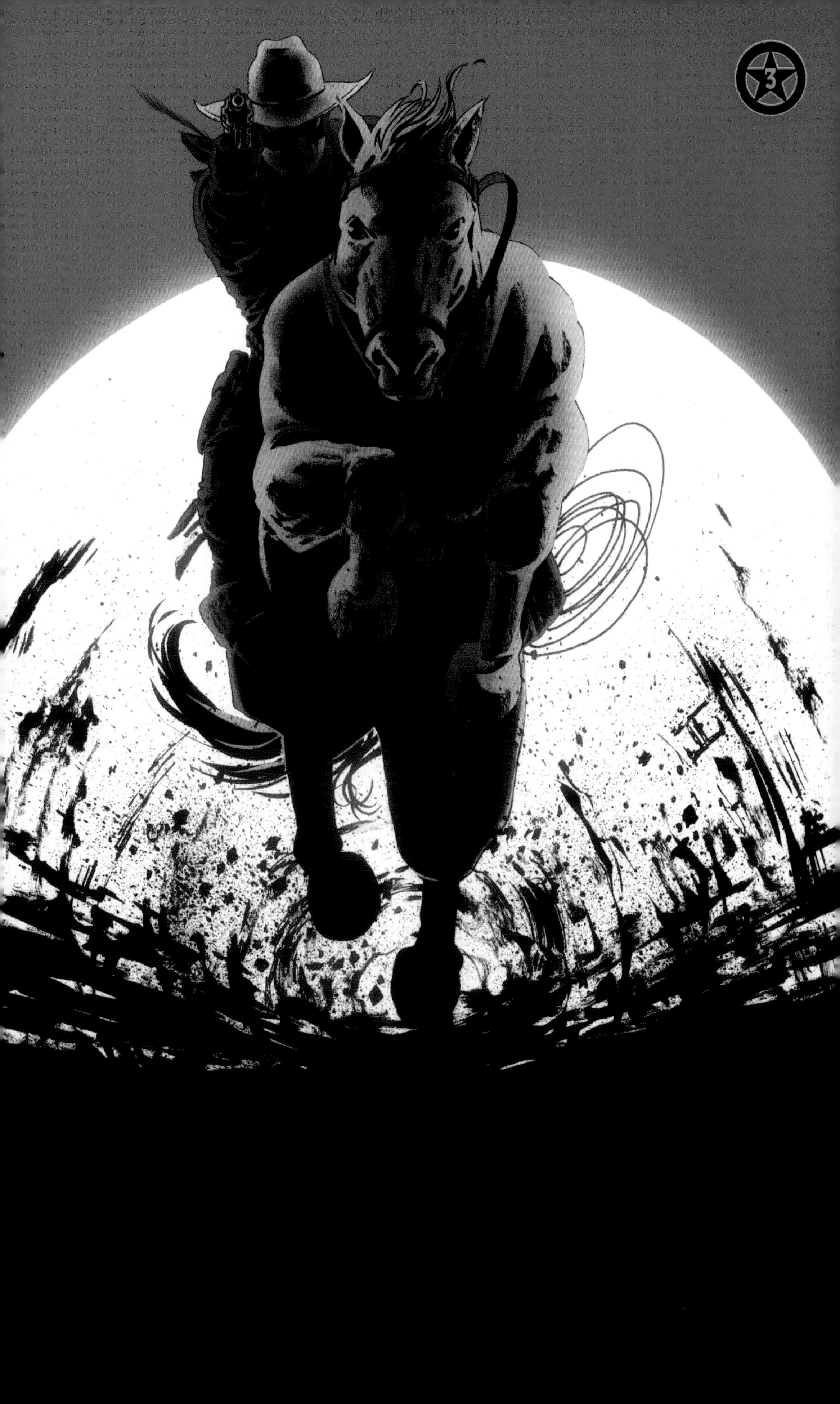
3

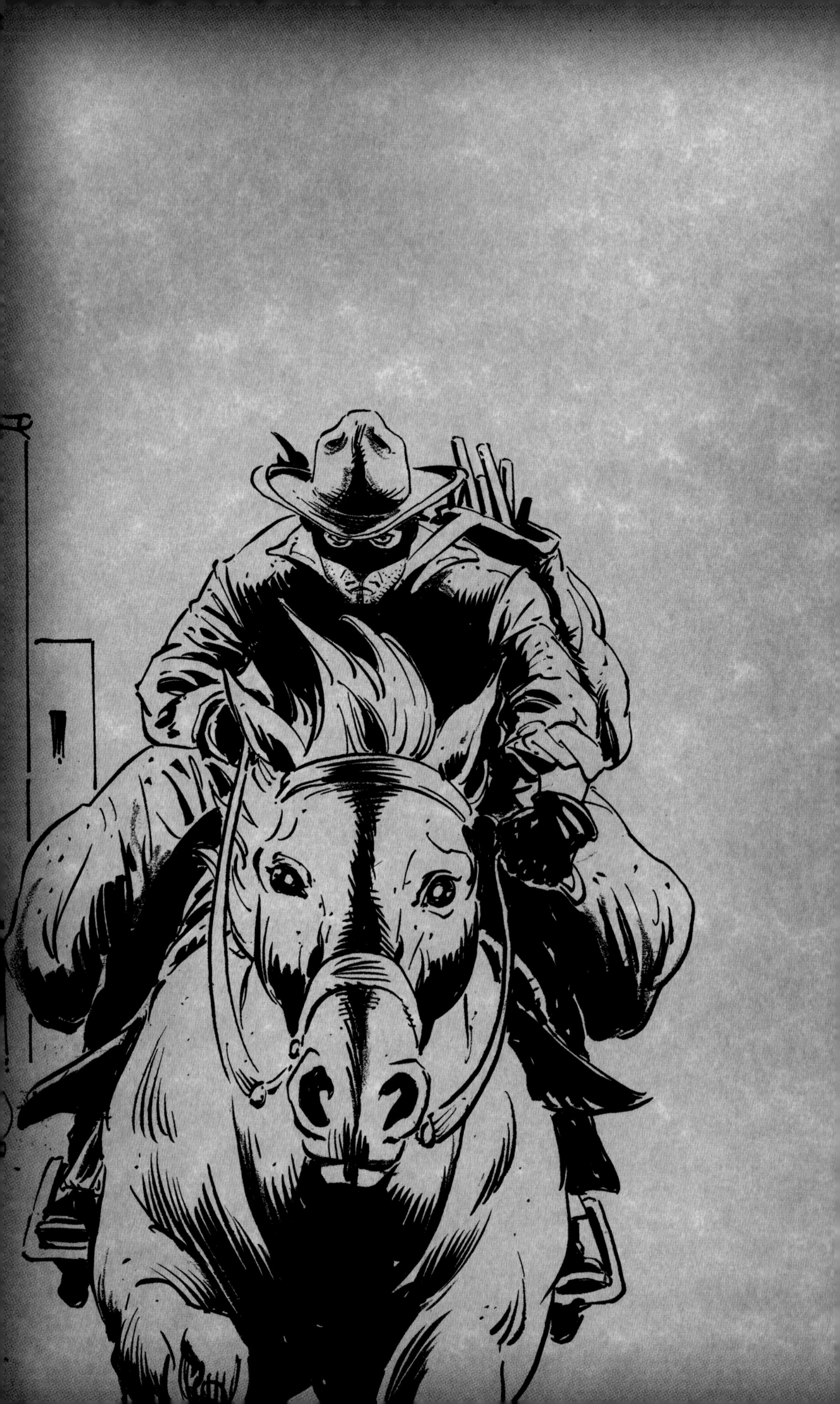

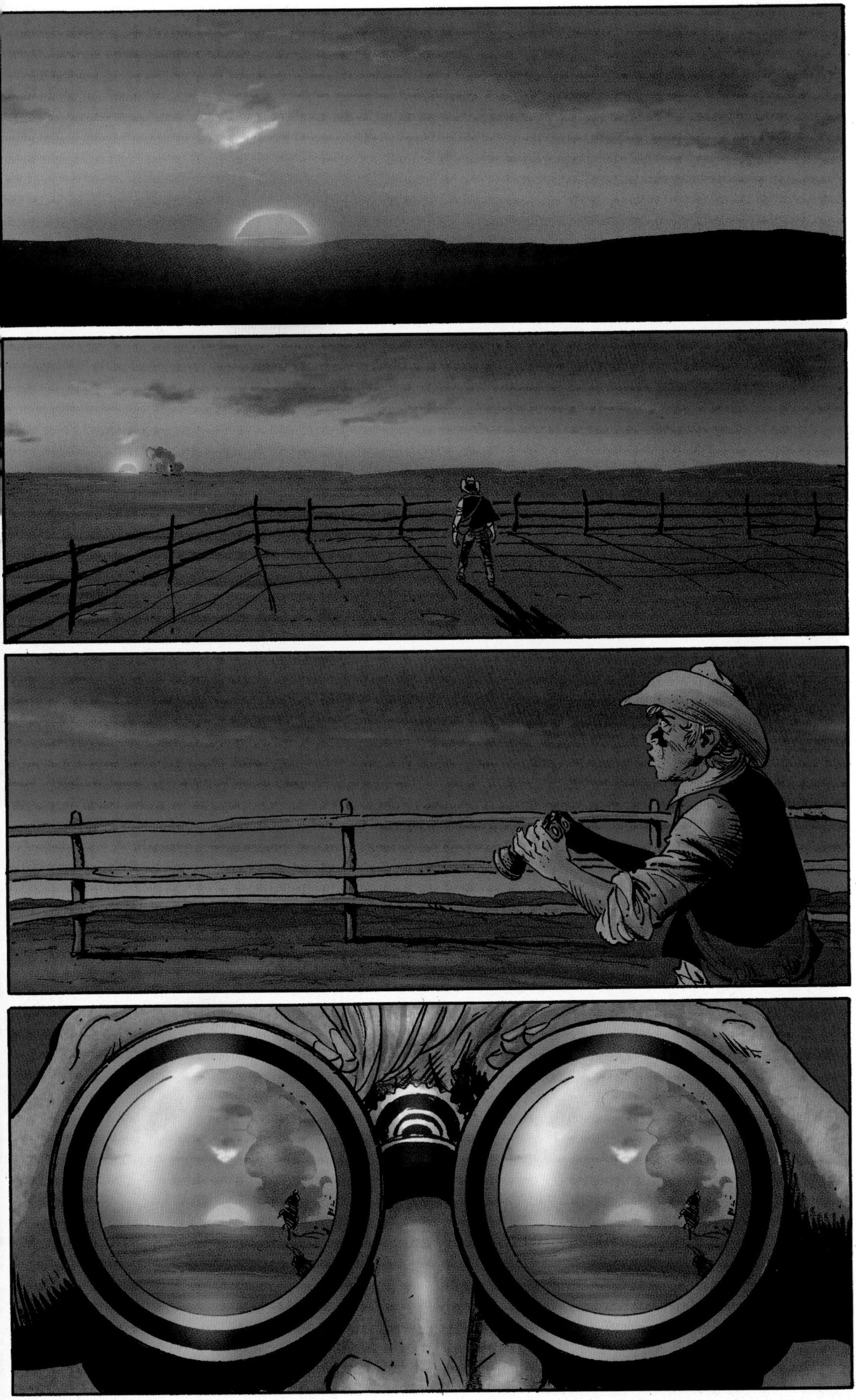

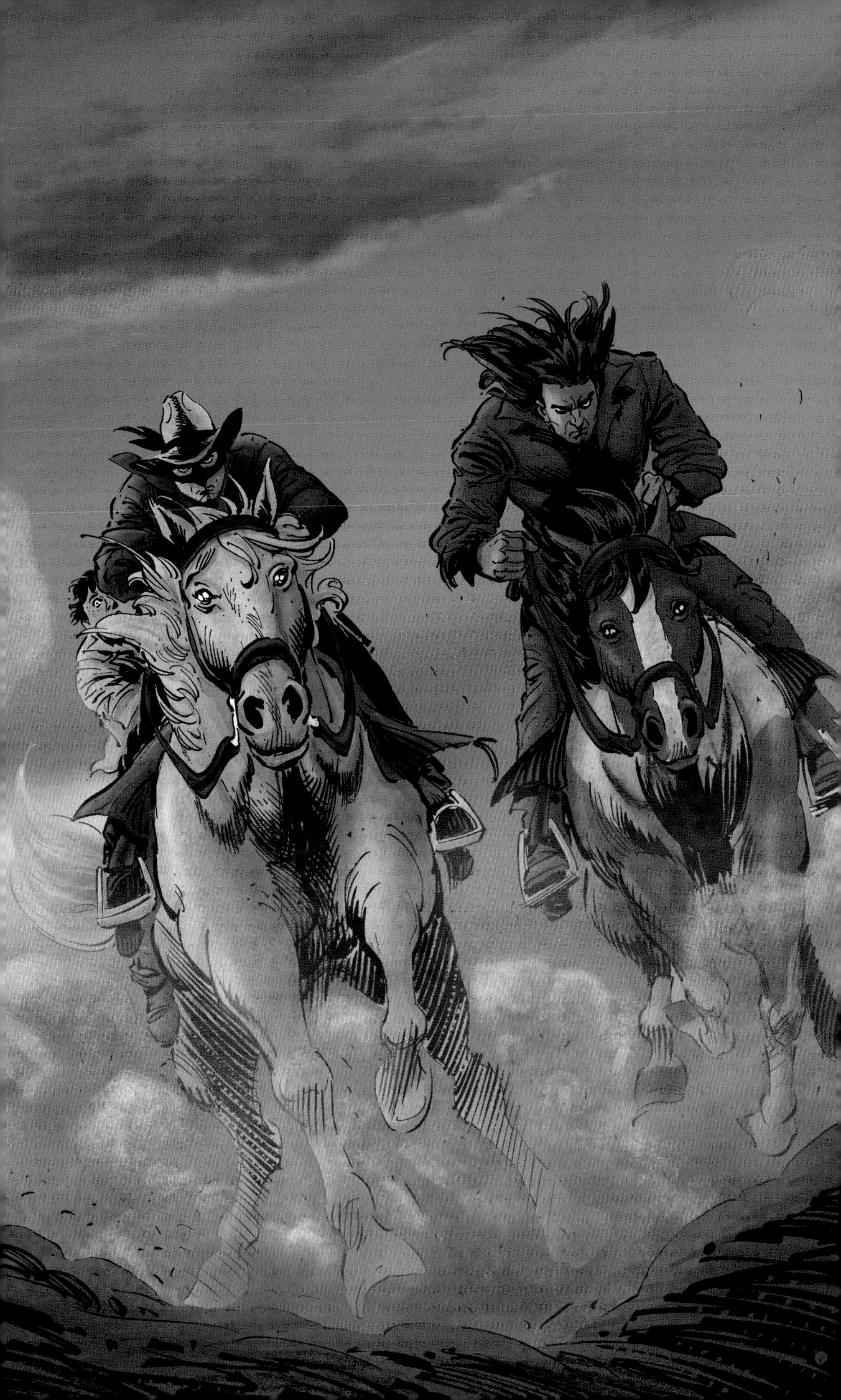

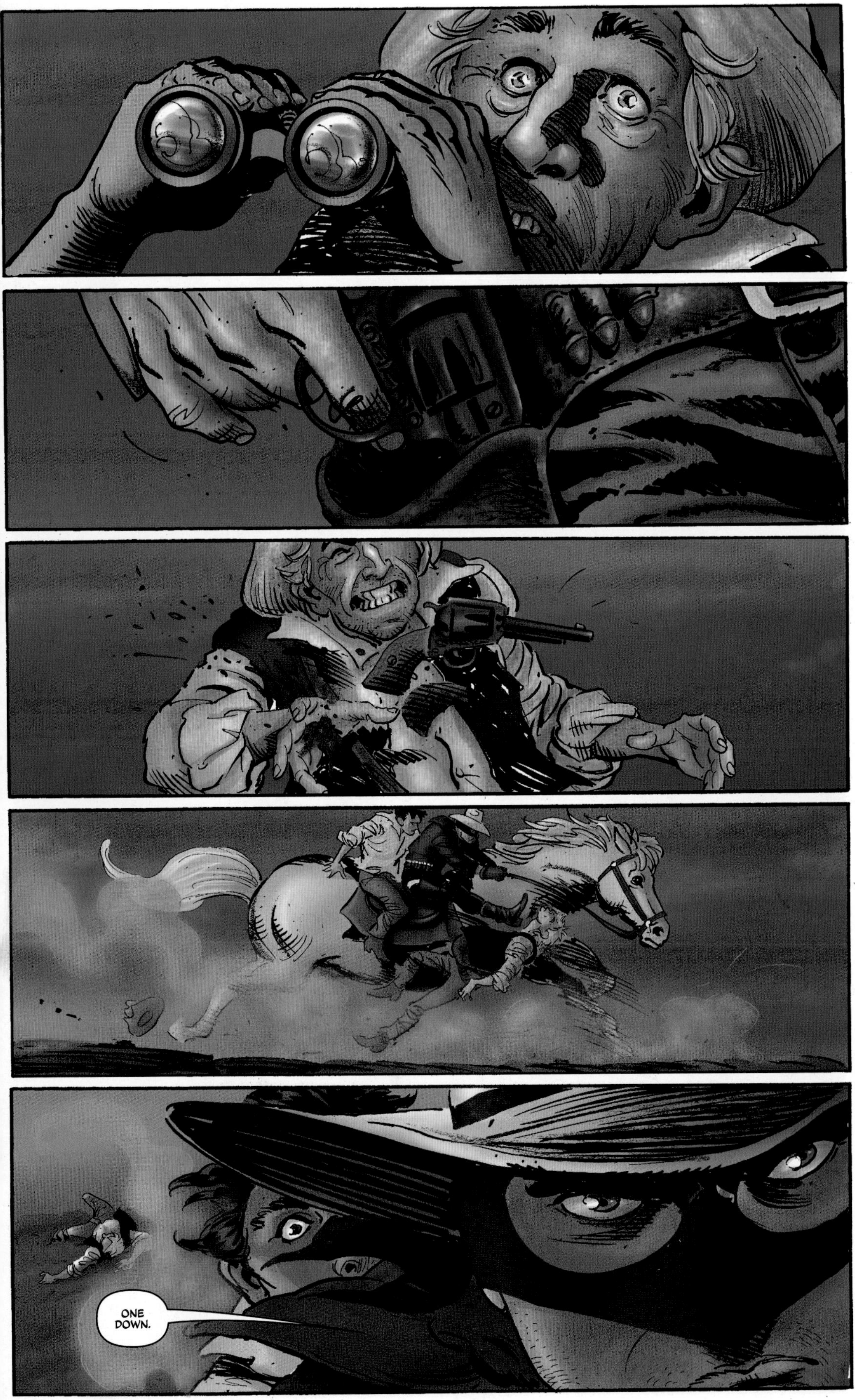
ONE DOWN.

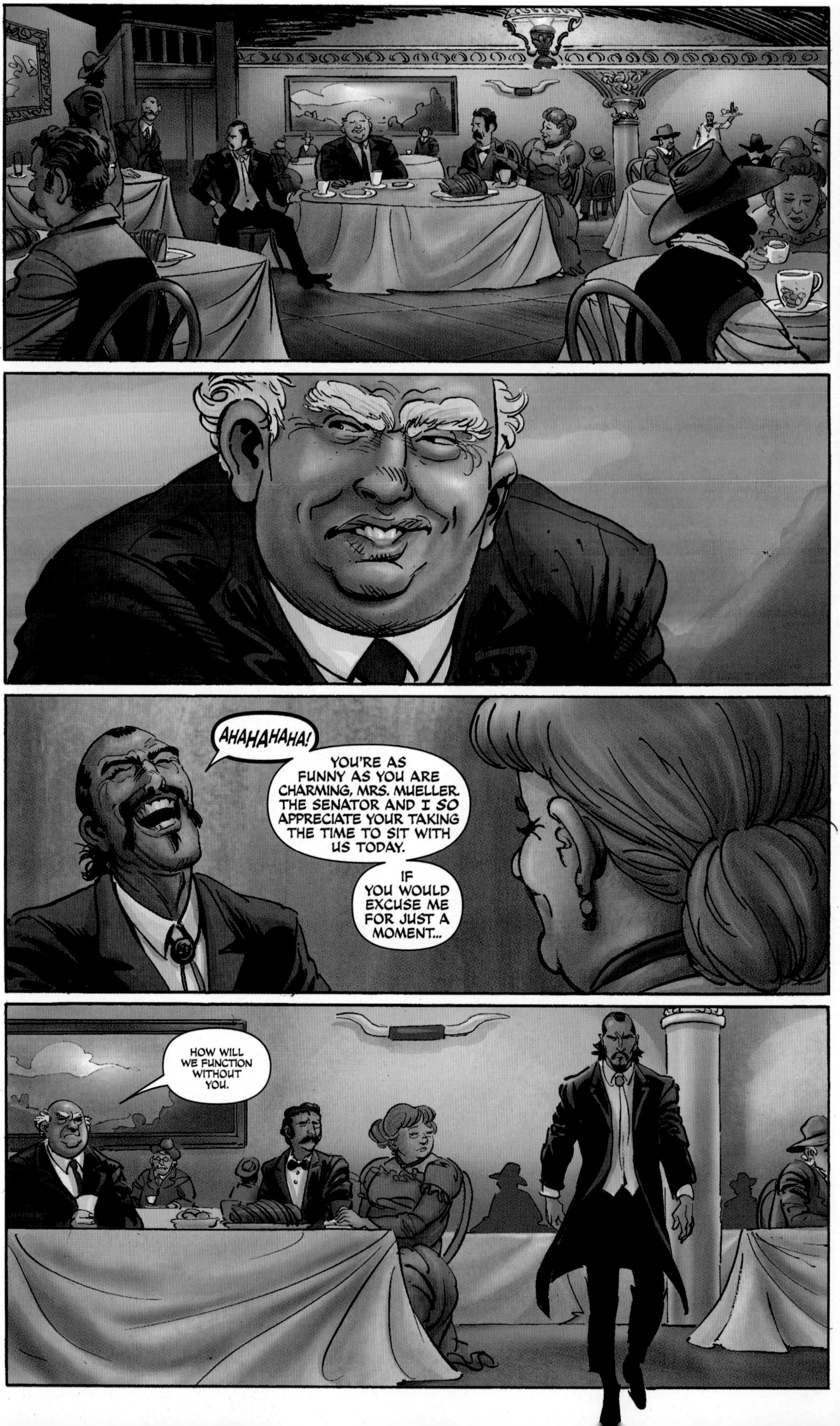
AHAHAHAHA!
YOU'RE AS FUNNY AS YOU ARE CHARMING, MRS. MUELLER. THE SENATOR AND I SO APPRECIATE YOUR TAKING THE TIME TO SIT WITH US TODAY.
IF YOU WOULD EXCUSE ME FOR JUST A MOMENT...
HOW WILL WE FUNCTION WITHOUT YOU.

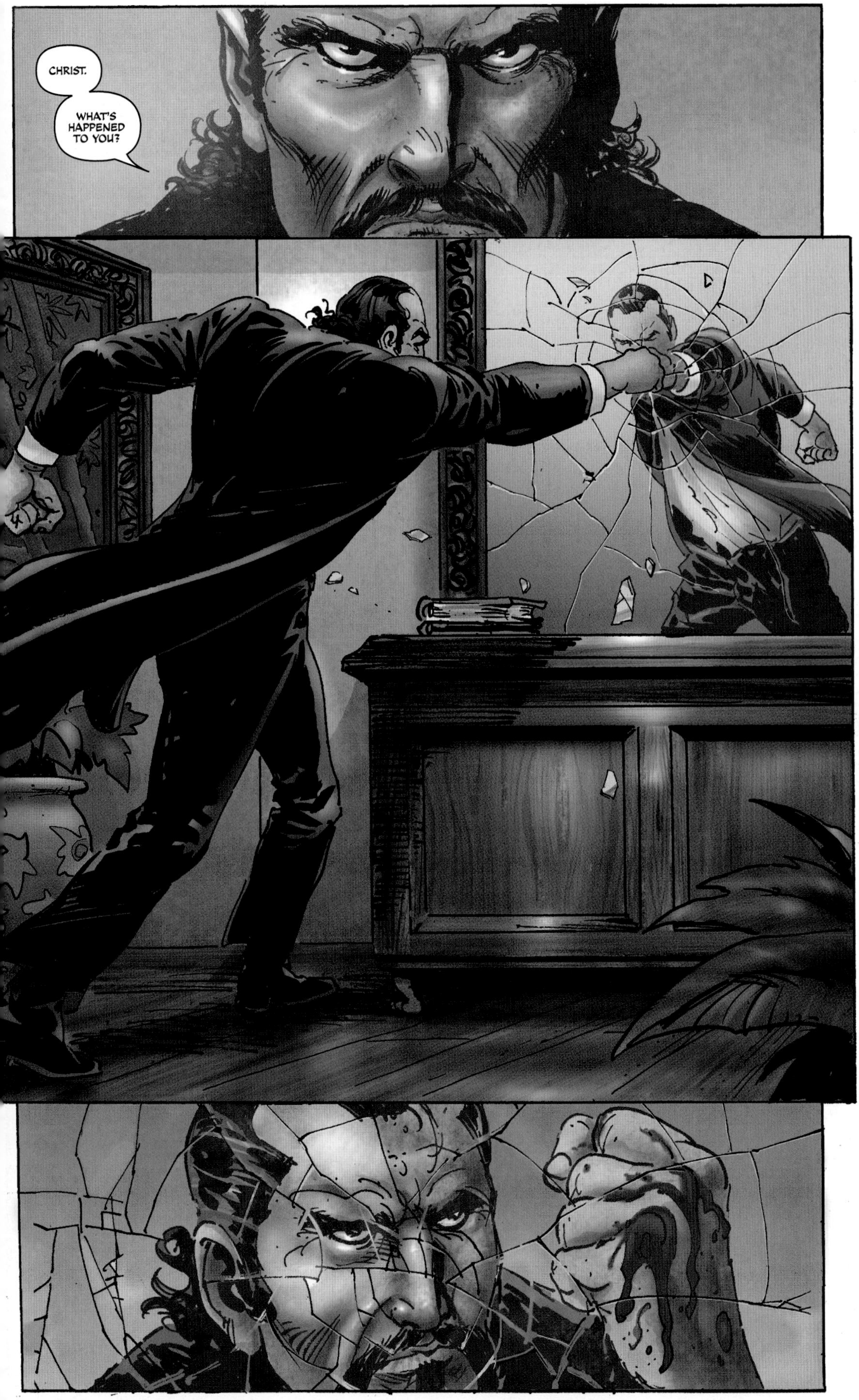
CHRIST.
WHAT'S HAPPENED TO YOU?

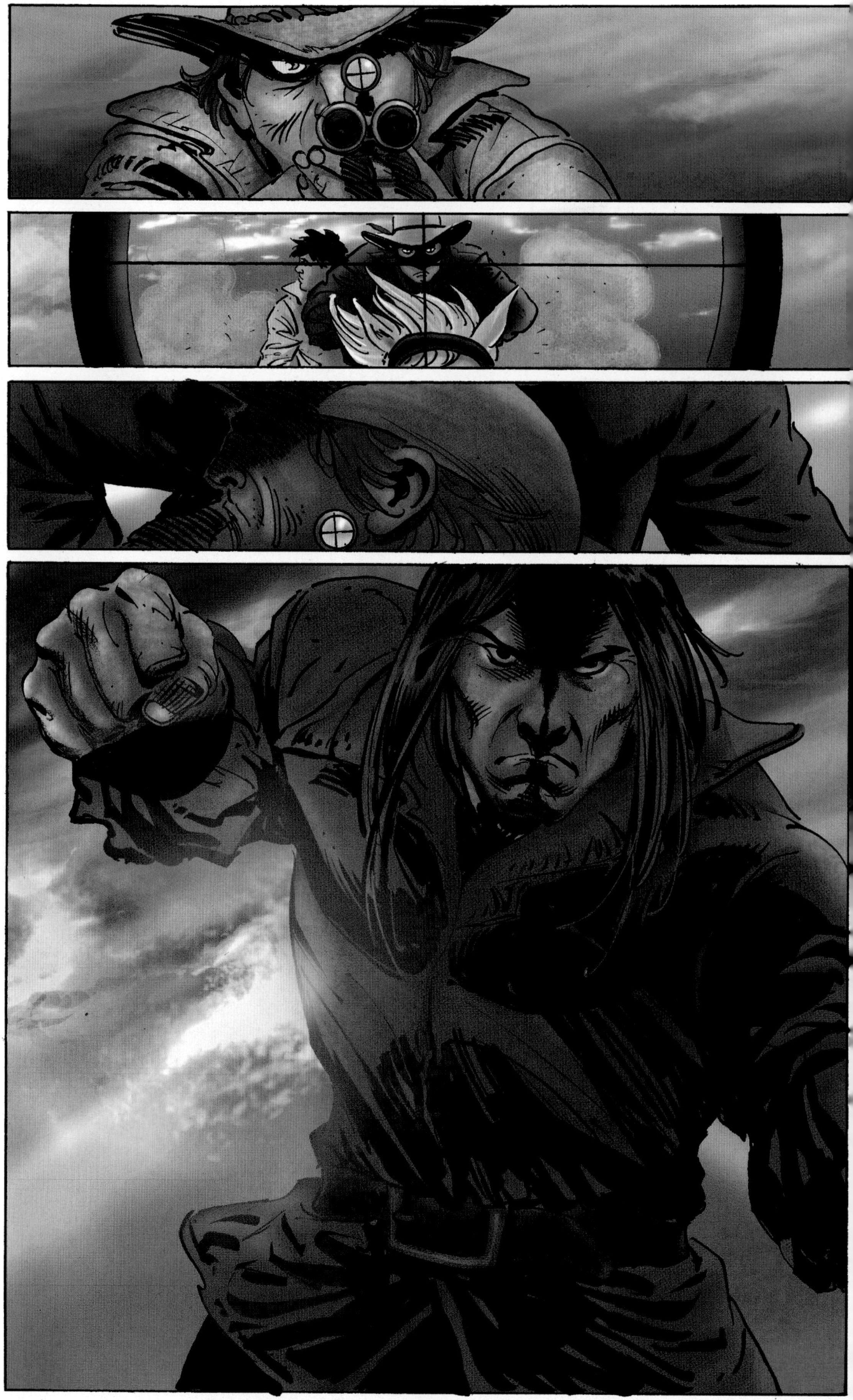

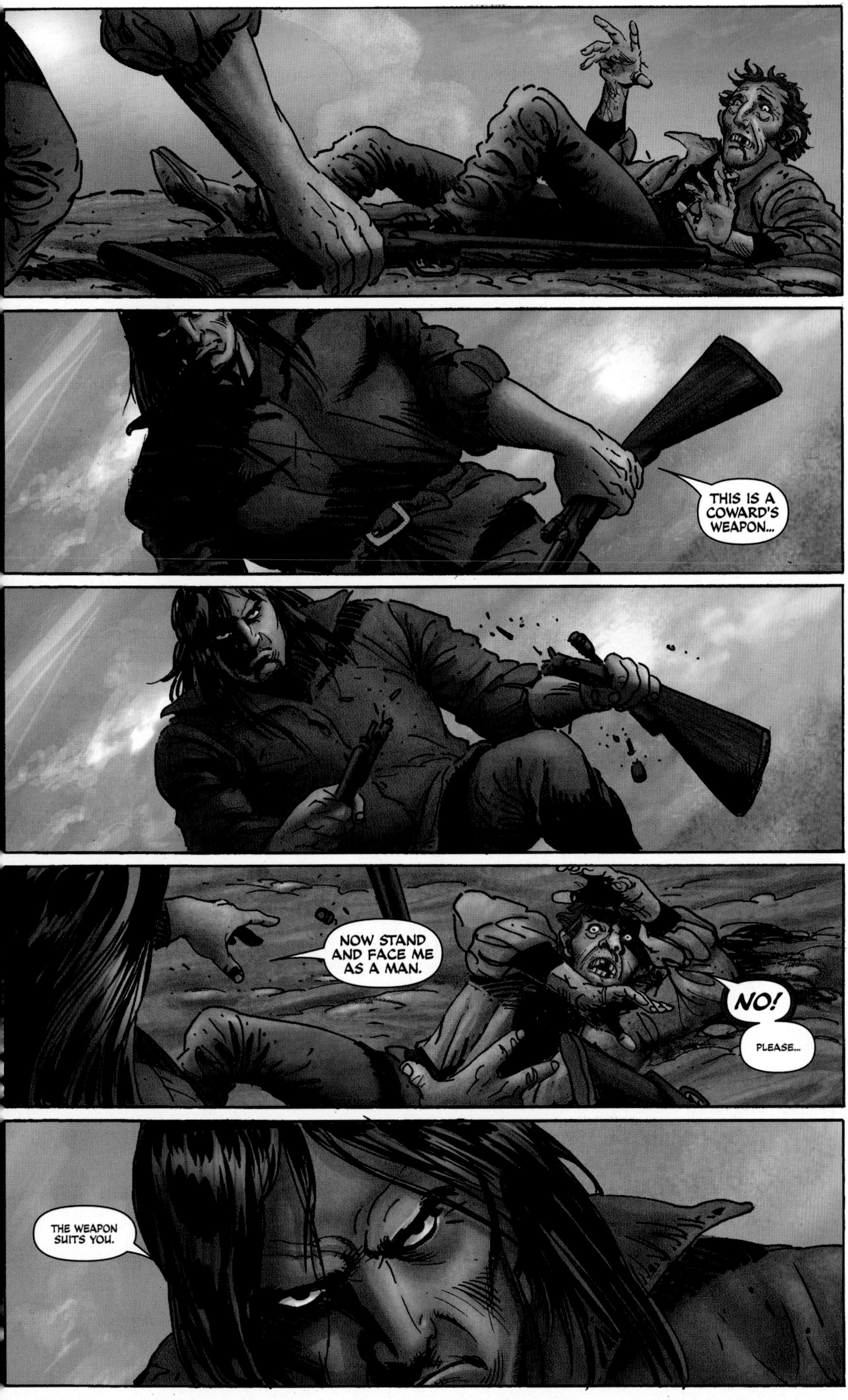
THIS IS A COWARD'S WEAPON...
NOW STAND AND FACE ME AS A MAN.
NO!
PLEASE...
THE WEAPON SUITS YOU.

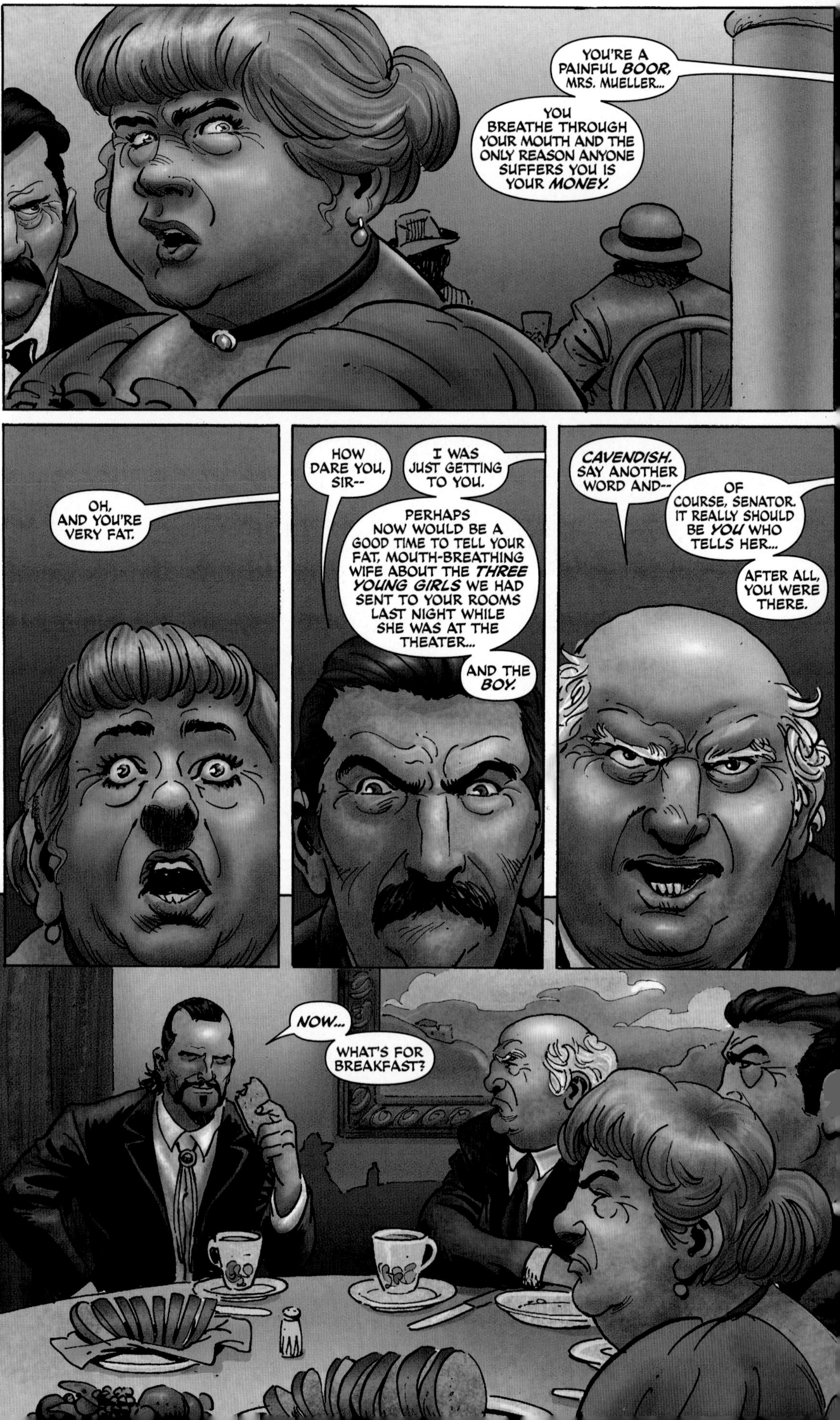

YOU'RE A PAINFUL BOOR, MRS. MUELLER...
YOU BREATHE THROUGH YOUR MOUTH AND THE ONLY REASON ANYONE SUFFERS YOU IS YOUR MONEY.
OH, AND YOU'RE VERY FAT.
HOW DARE YOU, SIR--
I WAS JUST GETTING TO YOU.
PERHAPS NOW WOULD BE A GOOD TIME TO TELL YOUR FAT, MOUTH-BREATHING WIFE ABOUT THE THREE YOUNG GIRLS WE HAD SENT TO YOUR ROOMS LAST NIGHT WHILE SHE WAS AT THE THEATER...
AND THE BOY.
CAVENDISH. SAY ANOTHER WORD AND--
OF COURSE, SENATOR. IT REALLY SHOULD BE YOU WHO TELLS HER...
AFTER ALL, YOU WERE THERE.
NOW...
WHAT'S FOR BREAKFAST?

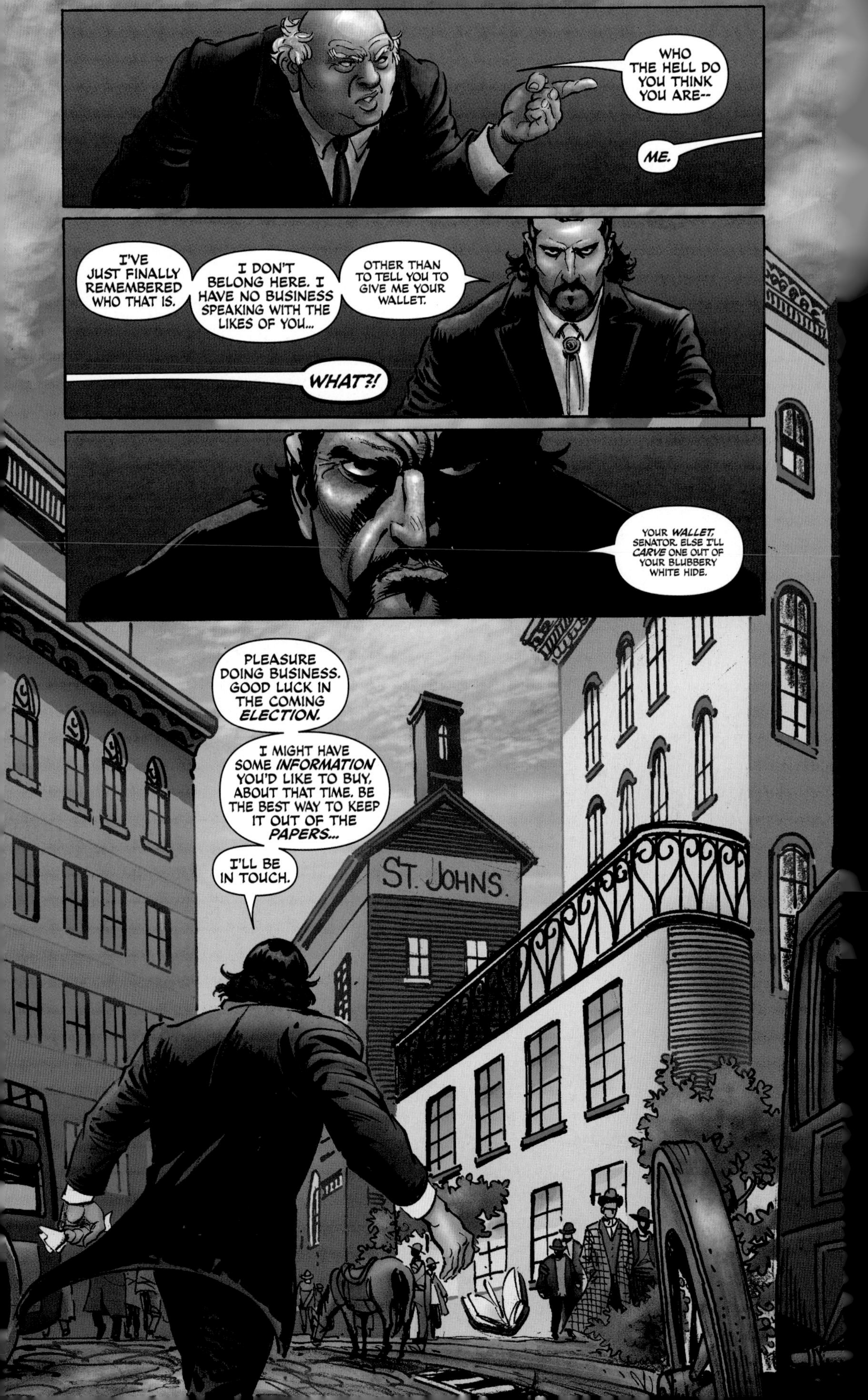

WHO THE HELL DO YOU THINK YOU ARE--
ME.
I'VE JUST FINALLY REMEMBERED WHO THAT IS.
I DON'T BELONG HERE. I HAVE NO BUSINESS SPEAKING WITH THE LIKES OF YOU...
OTHER THAN TO TELL YOU TO GIVE ME YOUR WALLET.
WHAT?!
YOUR WALLET, SENATOR. ELSE I'LL CARVE ONE OUT OF YOUR BLUBBERY WHITE HIDE.
PLEASURE DOING BUSINESS. GOOD LUCK IN THE COMING ELECTION.
I MIGHT HAVE SOME INFORMATION YOU'D LIKE TO BUY, ABOUT THAT TIME. BE THE BEST WAY TO KEEP IT OUT OF THE PAPERS...
I'LL BE IN TOUCH.
ST. JOHNS.

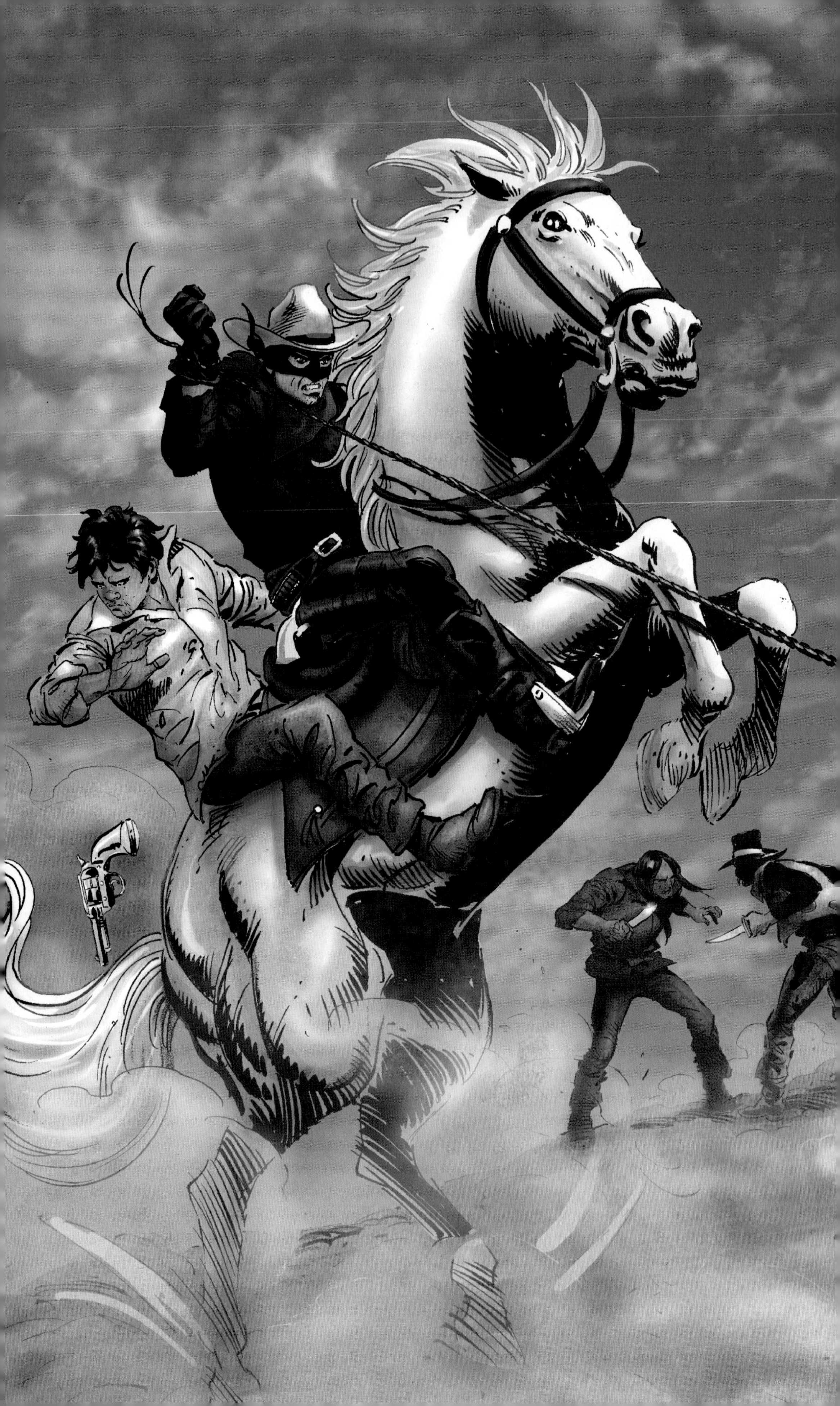

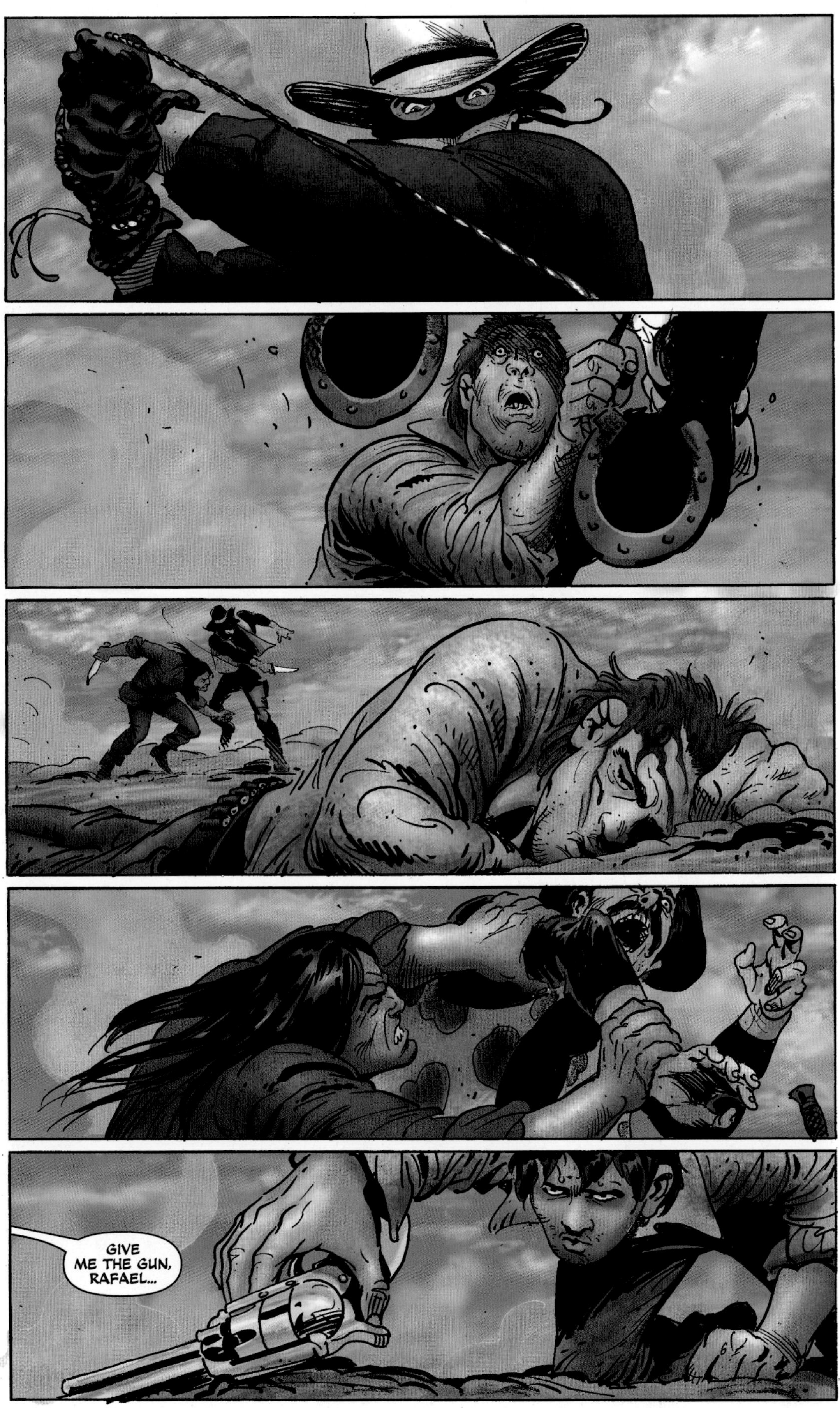
GIVE ME THE GUN, RAFAEL...

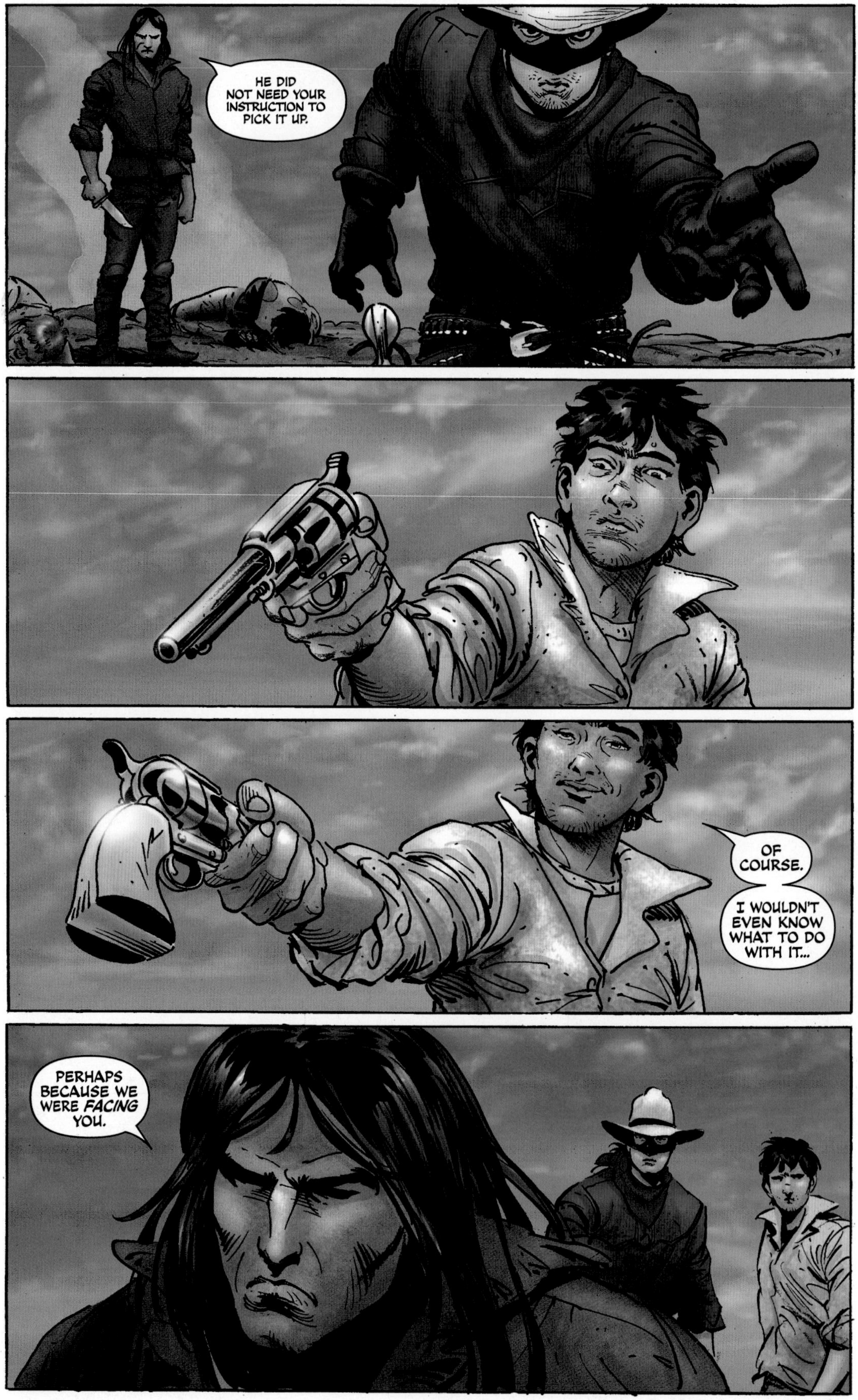
HE DID NOT NEED YOUR INSTRUCTION TO PICK IT UP.
OF COURSE.
I WOULDN'T EVEN KNOW WHAT TO DO WITH IT...
PERHAPS BECAUSE WE WERE *FACING* YOU.

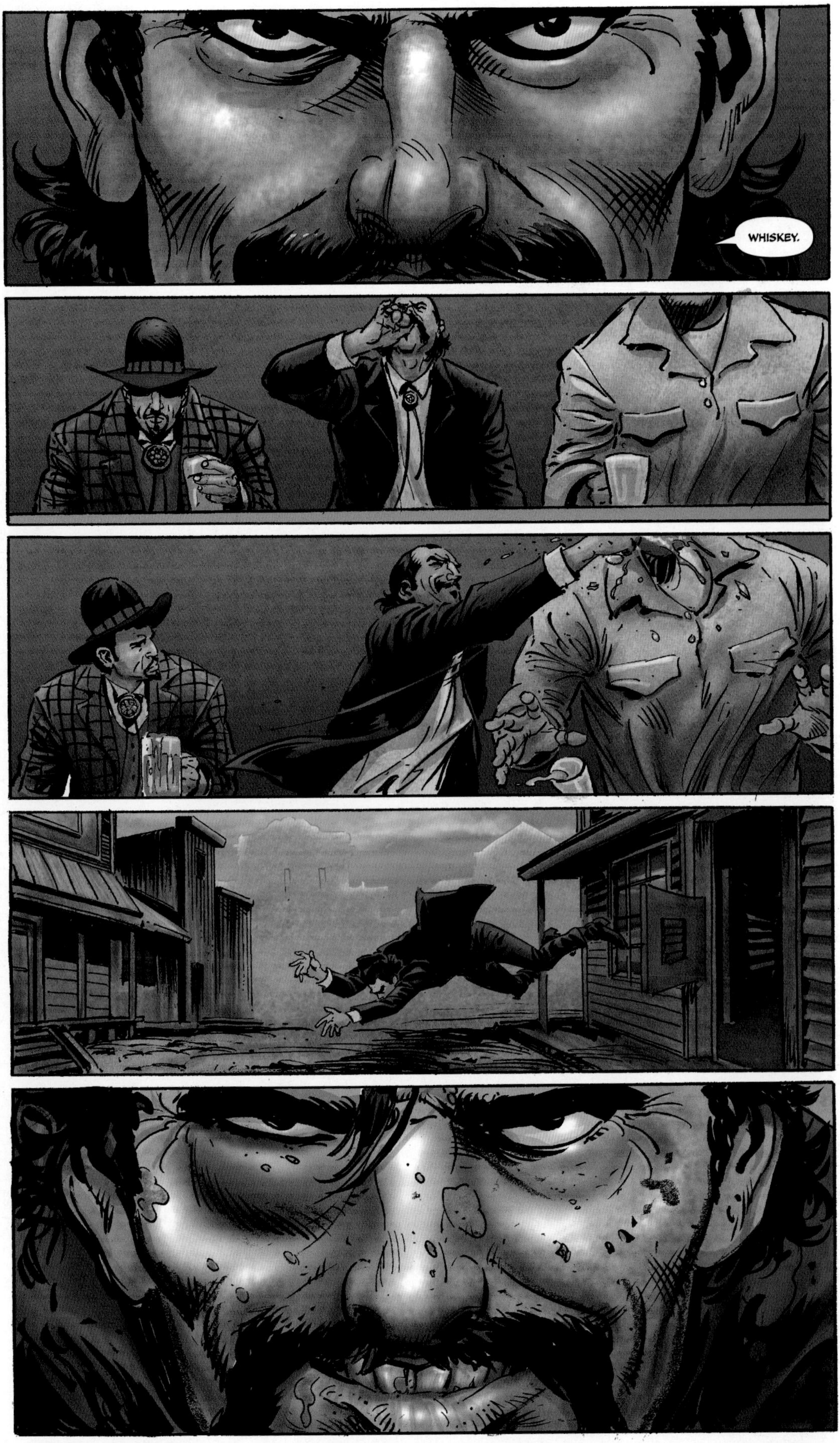
WHISKEY.

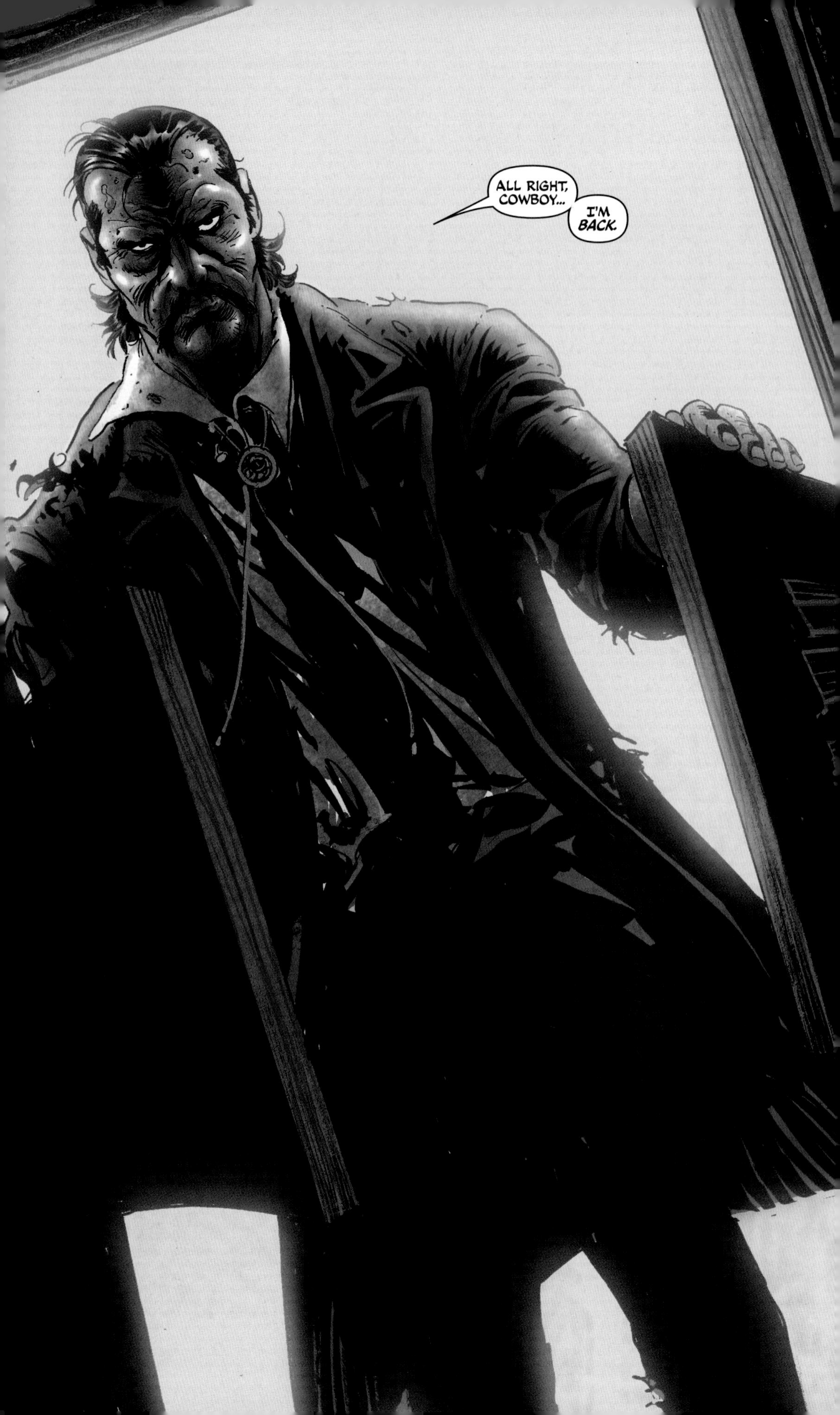
ALL RIGHT, COWBOY...
I'M BACK.

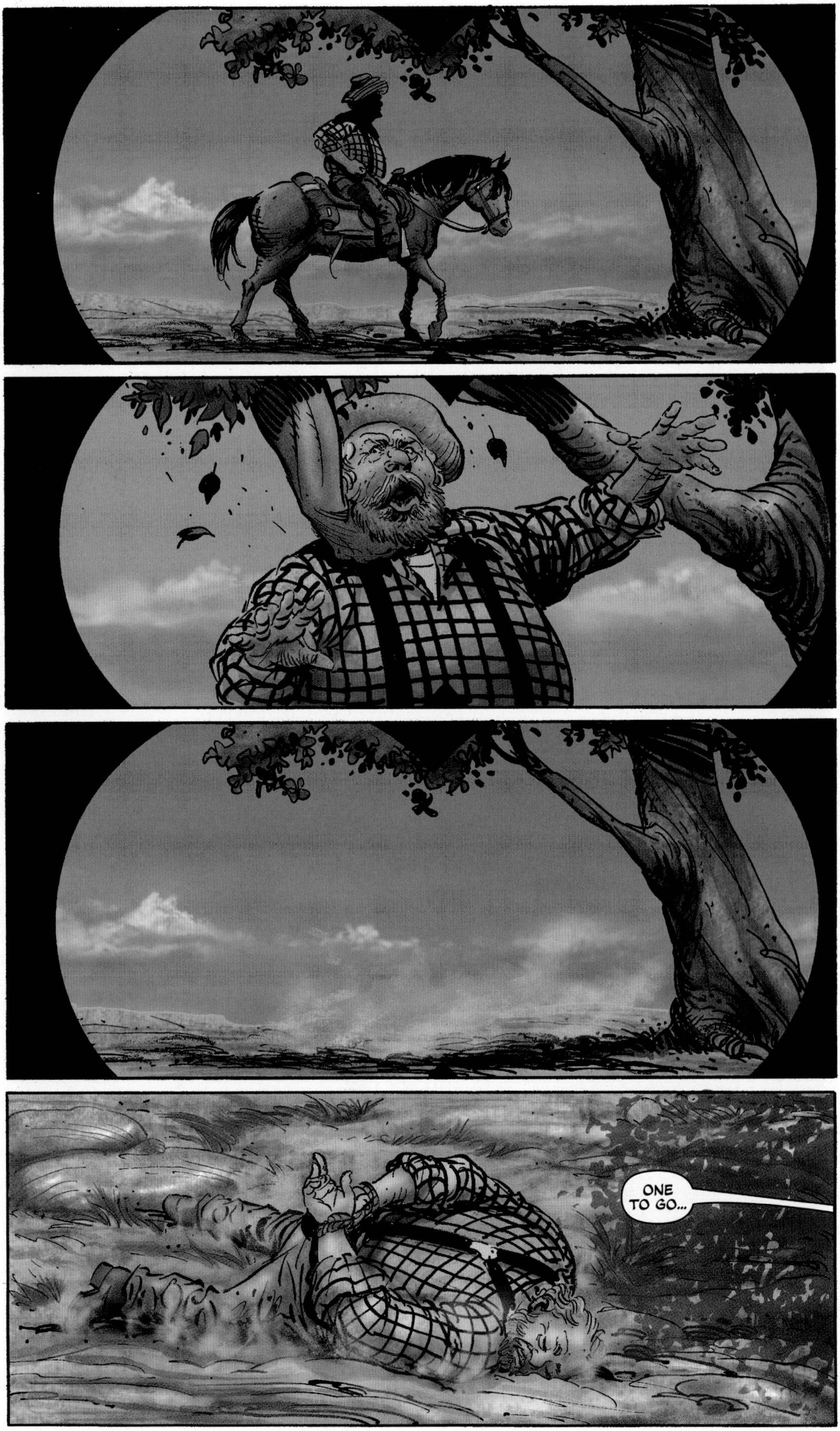
ONE TO GO...

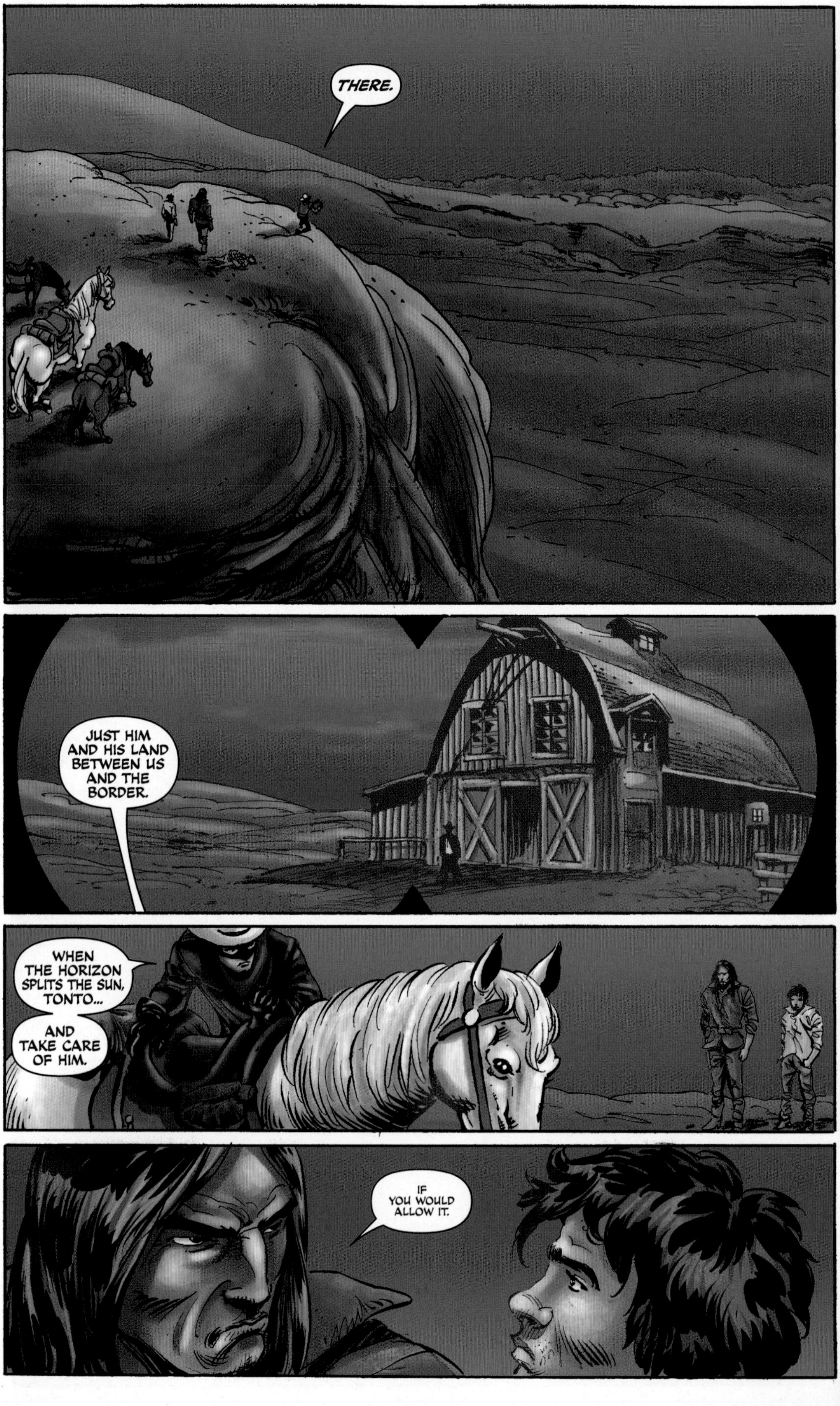
THERE.
JUST HIM AND HIS LAND BETWEEN US AND THE BORDER.
WHEN THE HORIZON SPLITS THE SUN, TONTO...
AND TAKE CARE OF HIM.
IF YOU WOULD ALLOW IT.

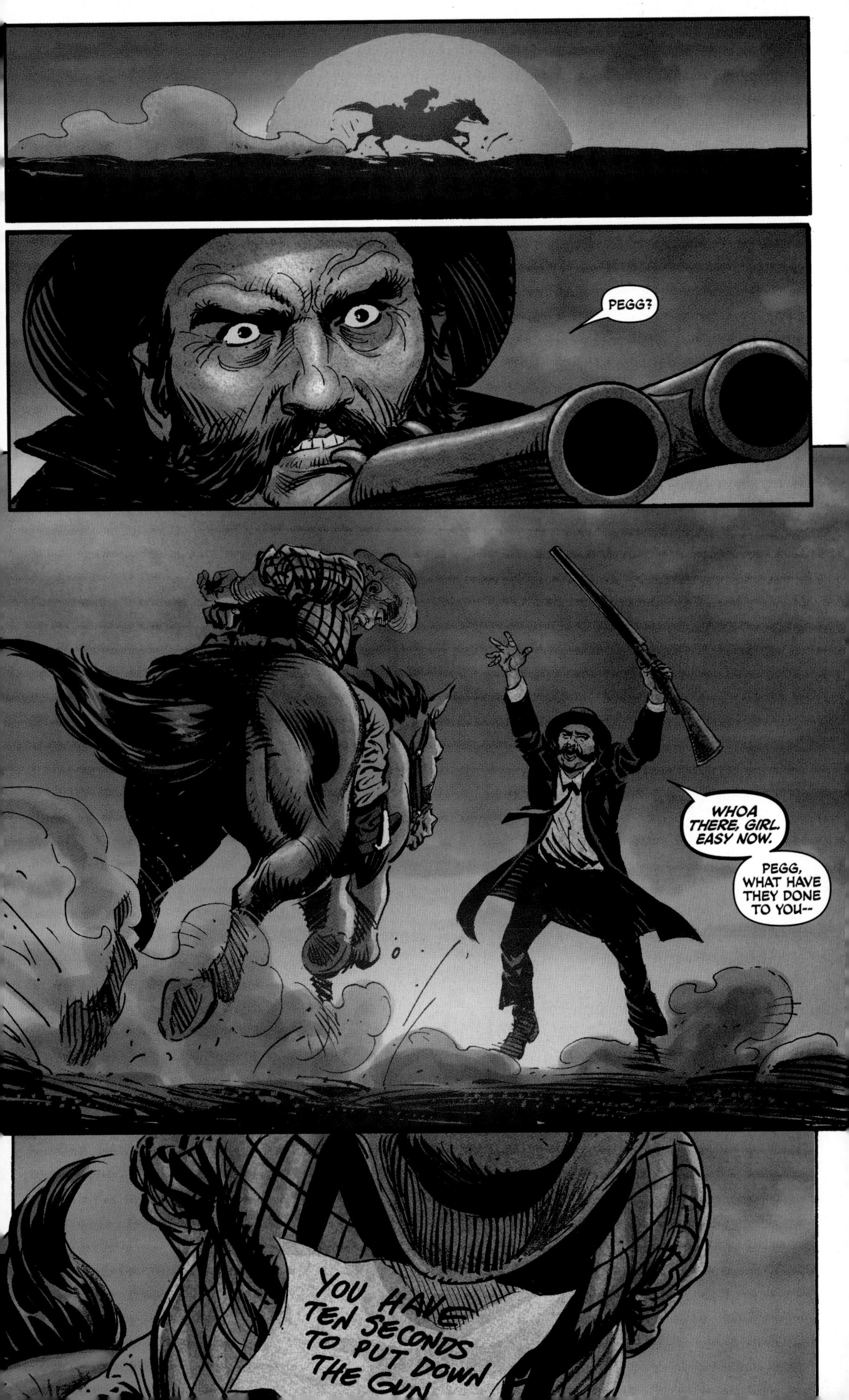
PEGG?
WHOA THERE, GIRL. EASY NOW.
PEGG, WHAT HAVE THEY DONE TO YOU--
YOU HAVE TEN SECONDS TO PUT DOWN THE GUN

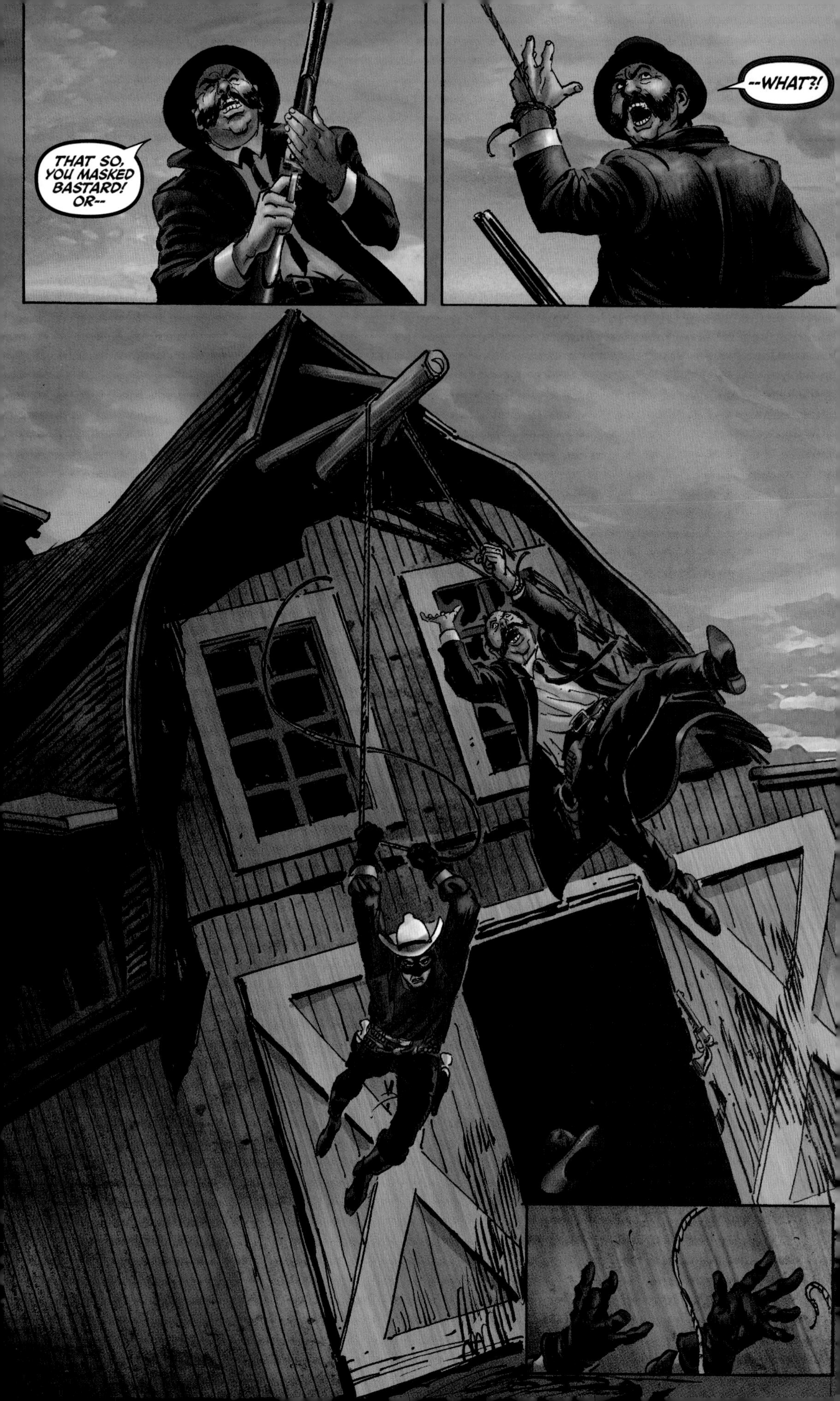
THAT SO, YOU MASKED BASTARD! OR--
--WHAT?!

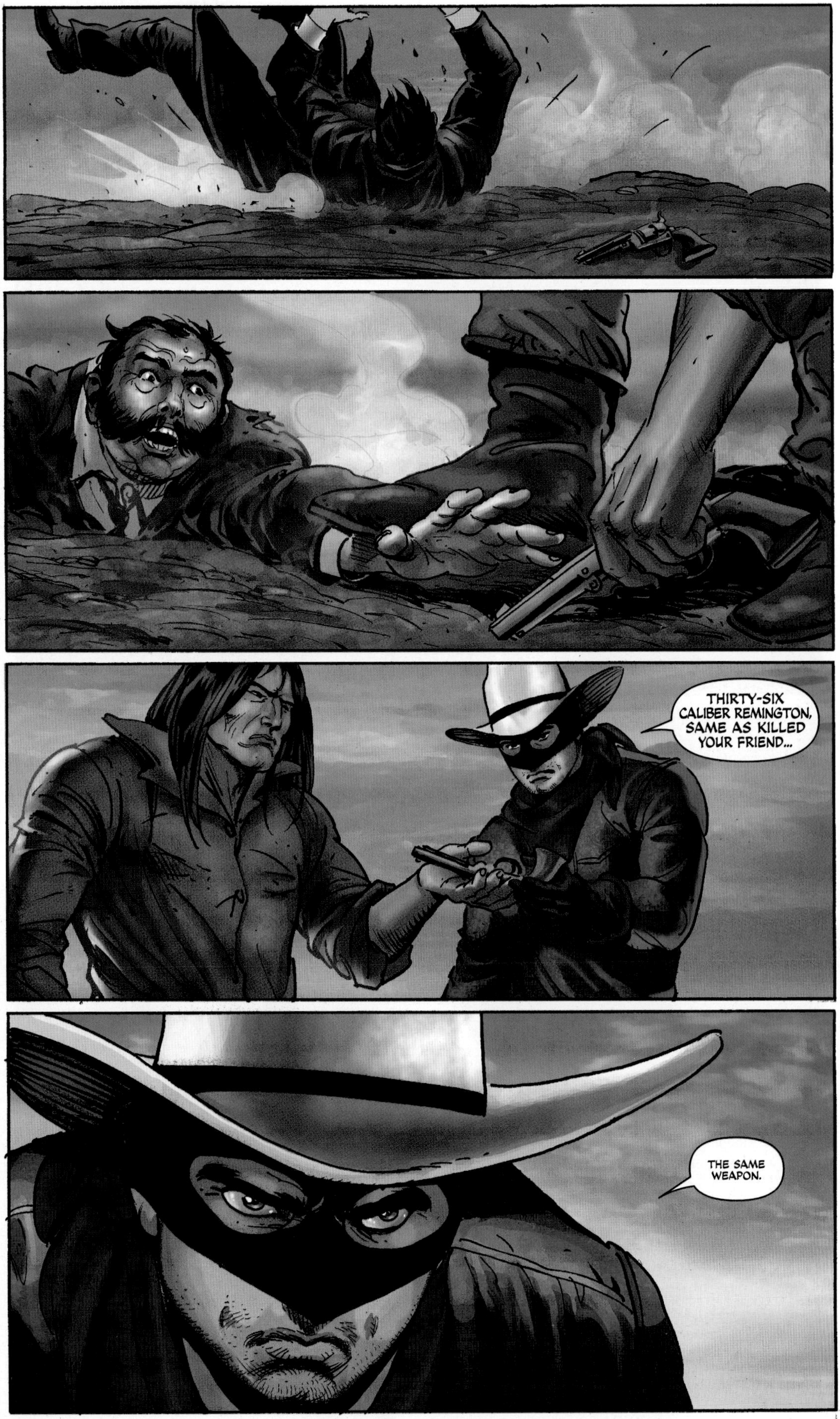
THIRTY-SIX CALIBER REMINGTON, SAME AS KILLED YOUR FRIEND...
THE SAME WEAPON.

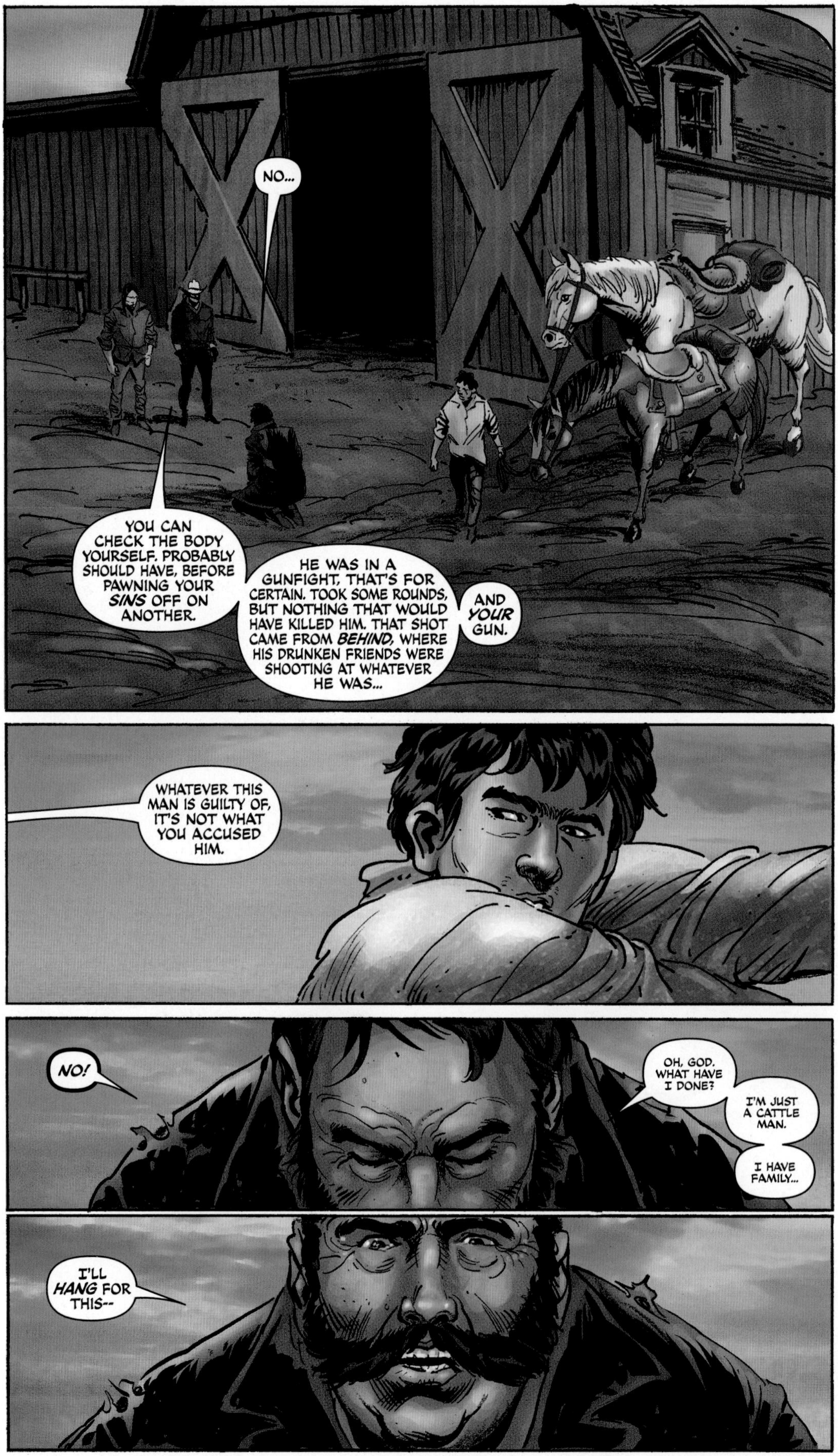
NO...
YOU CAN CHECK THE BODY YOURSELF. PROBABLY SHOULD HAVE, BEFORE PAWNING YOUR *SINS* OFF ON ANOTHER.
HE WAS IN A GUNFIGHT, THAT'S FOR CERTAIN. TOOK SOME ROUNDS, BUT NOTHING THAT WOULD HAVE KILLED HIM. THAT SHOT CAME FROM *BEHIND,* WHERE HIS DRUNKEN FRIENDS WERE SHOOTING AT WHATEVER HE WAS...
AND *YOUR* GUN.
WHATEVER THIS MAN IS GUILTY OF, IT'S NOT WHAT YOU ACCUSED HIM.
NO!
OH, GOD. WHAT HAVE I DONE?
I'M JUST A CATTLE MAN.
I HAVE FAMILY...
I'LL *HANG* FOR THIS--

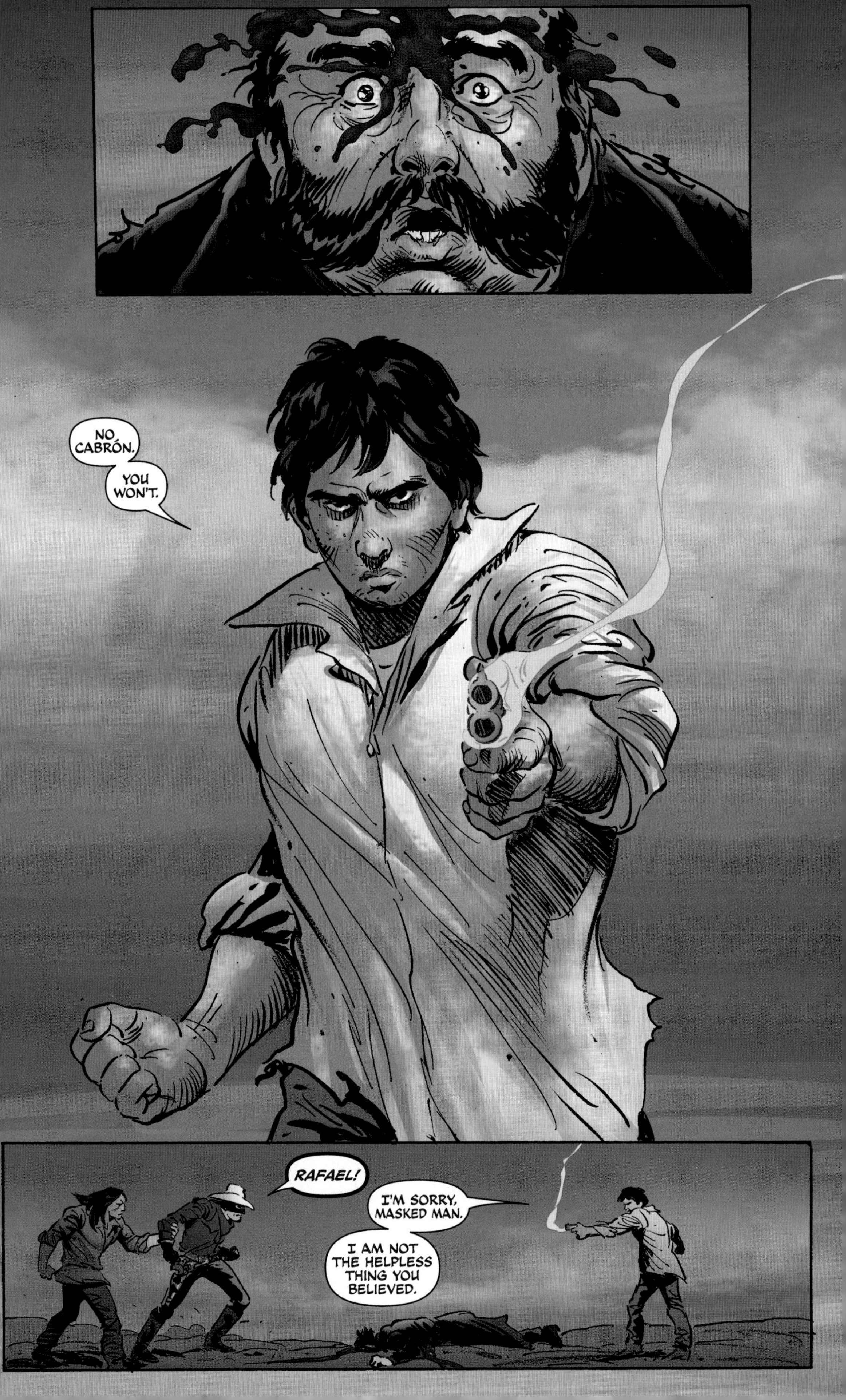
NO, CABRÓN.
YOU WON'T.
RAFAEL!
I'M SORRY, MASKED MAN.
I AM NOT THE HELPLESS THING YOU BELIEVED.

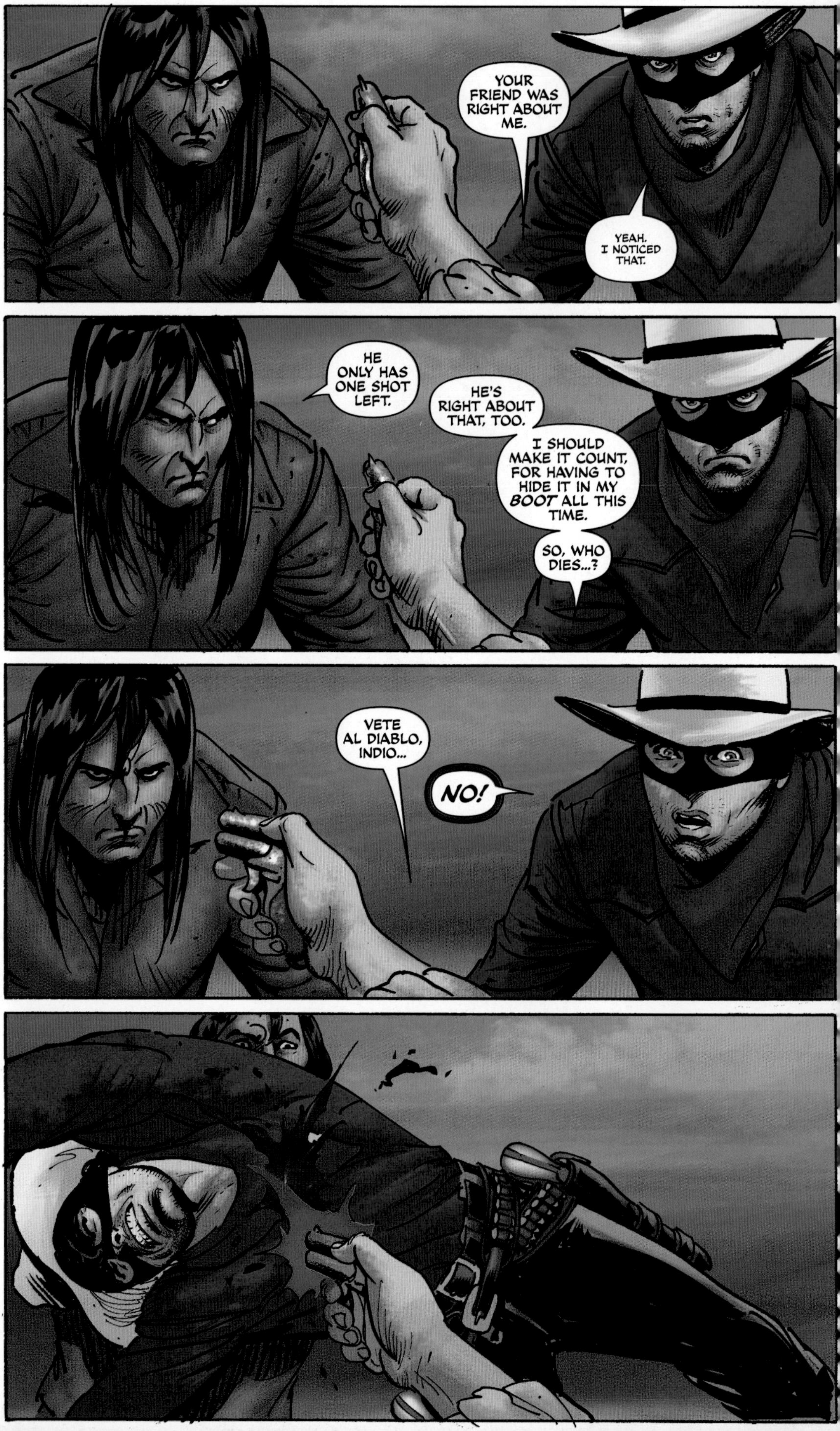

YOUR FRIEND WAS RIGHT ABOUT ME.
YEAH. I NOTICED THAT.
HE ONLY HAS ONE SHOT LEFT.
HE'S RIGHT ABOUT THAT, TOO.
I SHOULD MAKE IT COUNT, FOR HAVING TO HIDE IT IN MY BOOT ALL THIS TIME.
SO, WHO DIES...?
VETE AL DIABLO, INDIO...
NO!

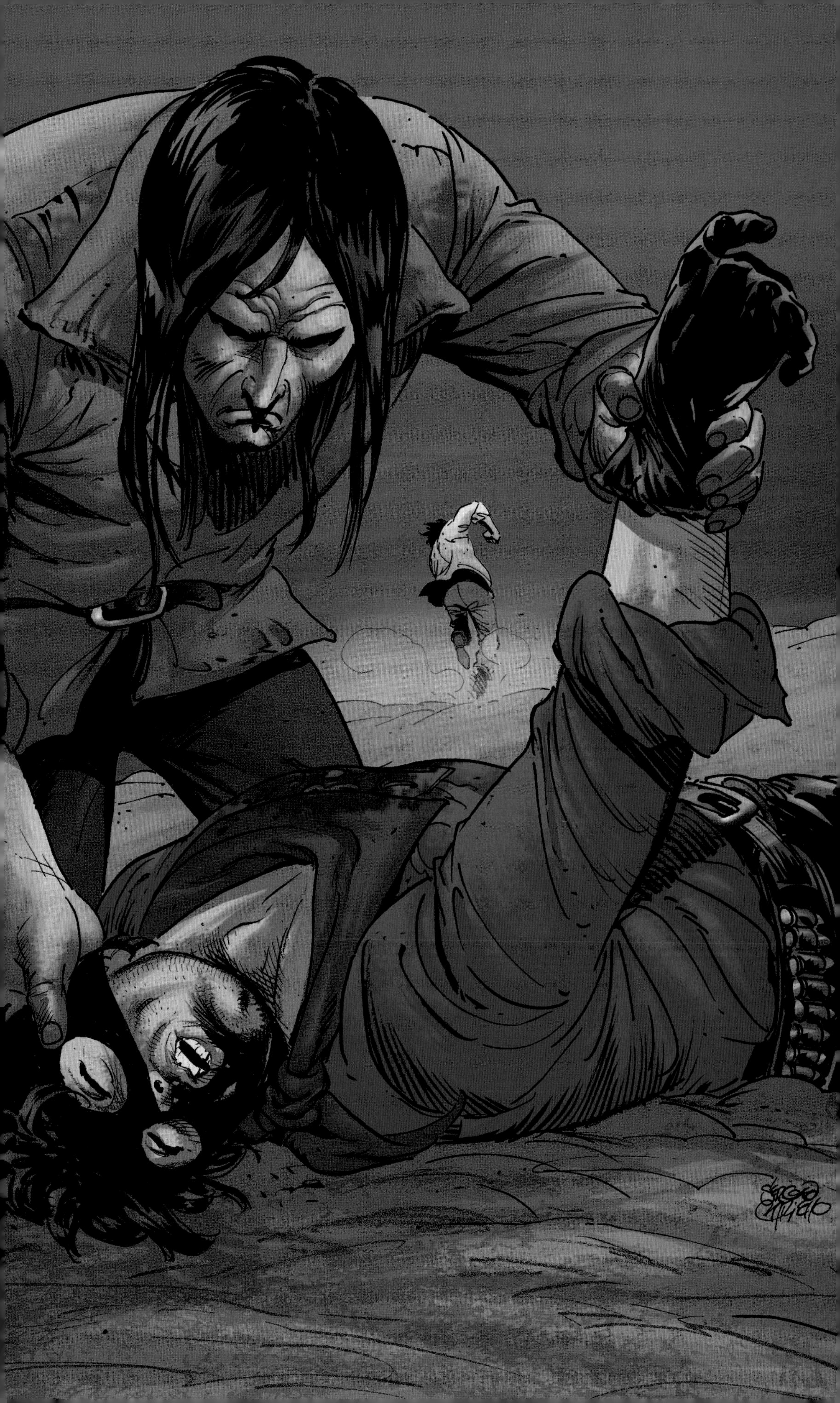

4

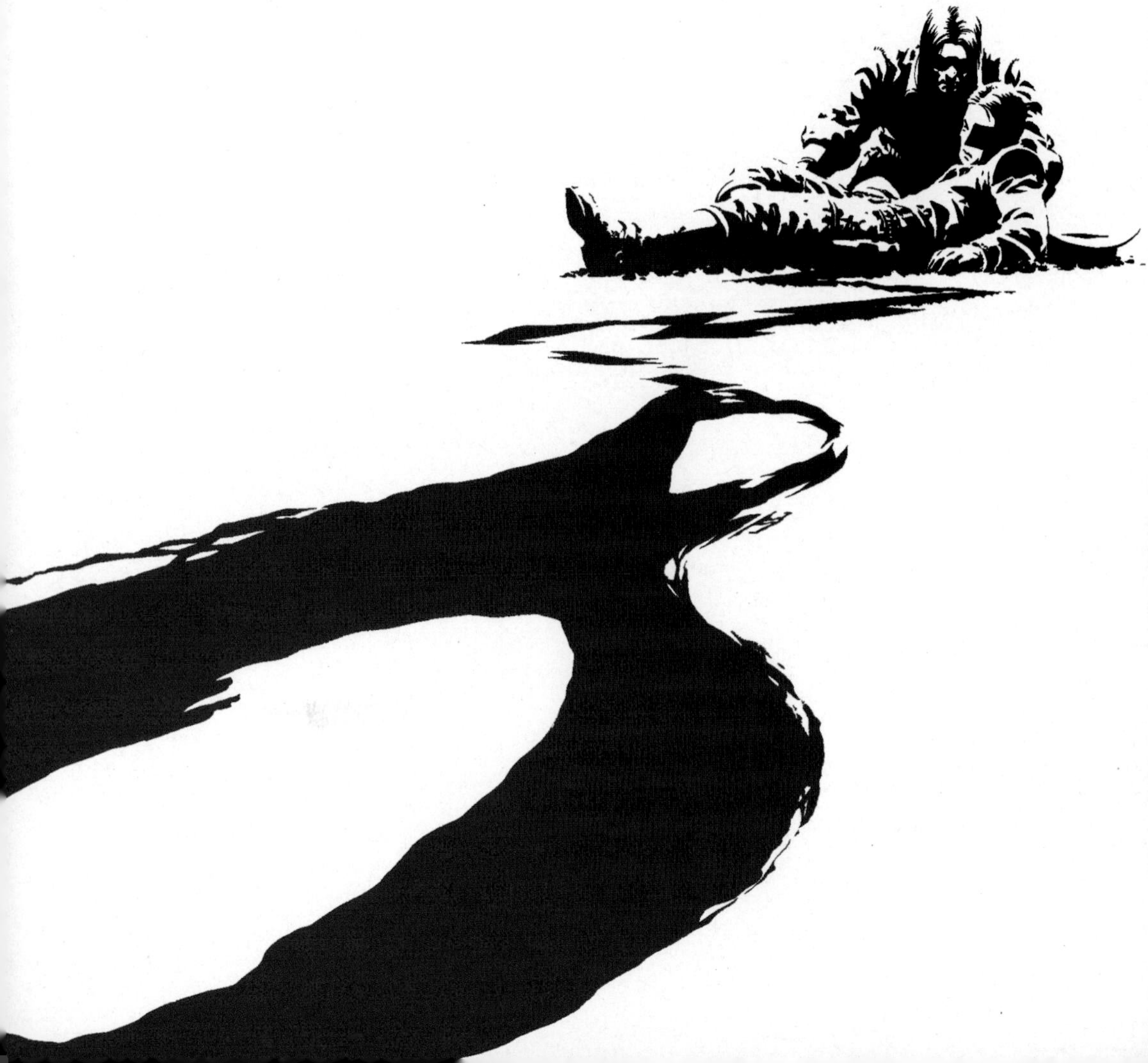

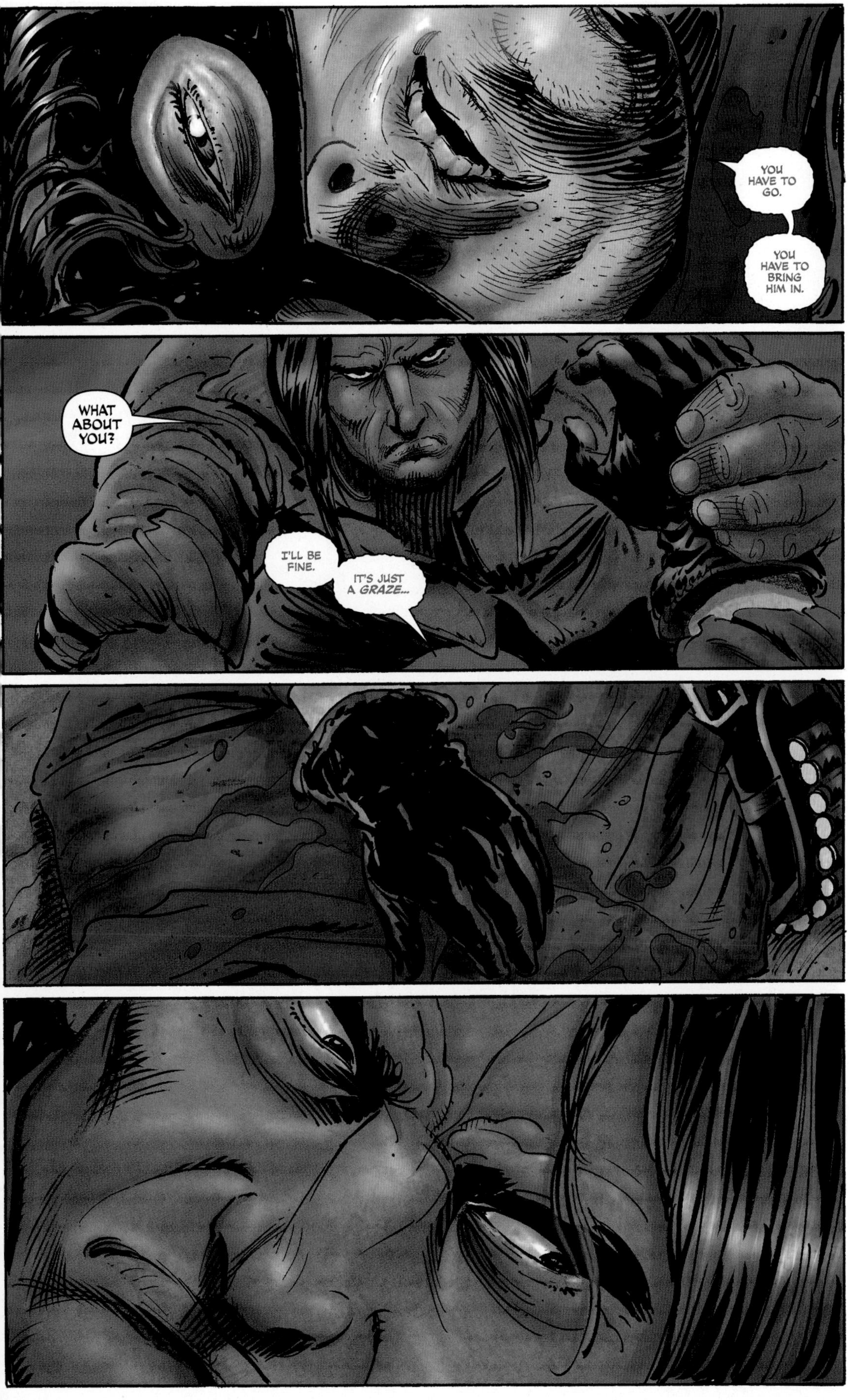

YOU HAVE TO GO.
YOU HAVE TO BRING HIM IN.
WHAT ABOUT YOU?
I'LL BE FINE.
IT'S JUST A *GRAZE...*

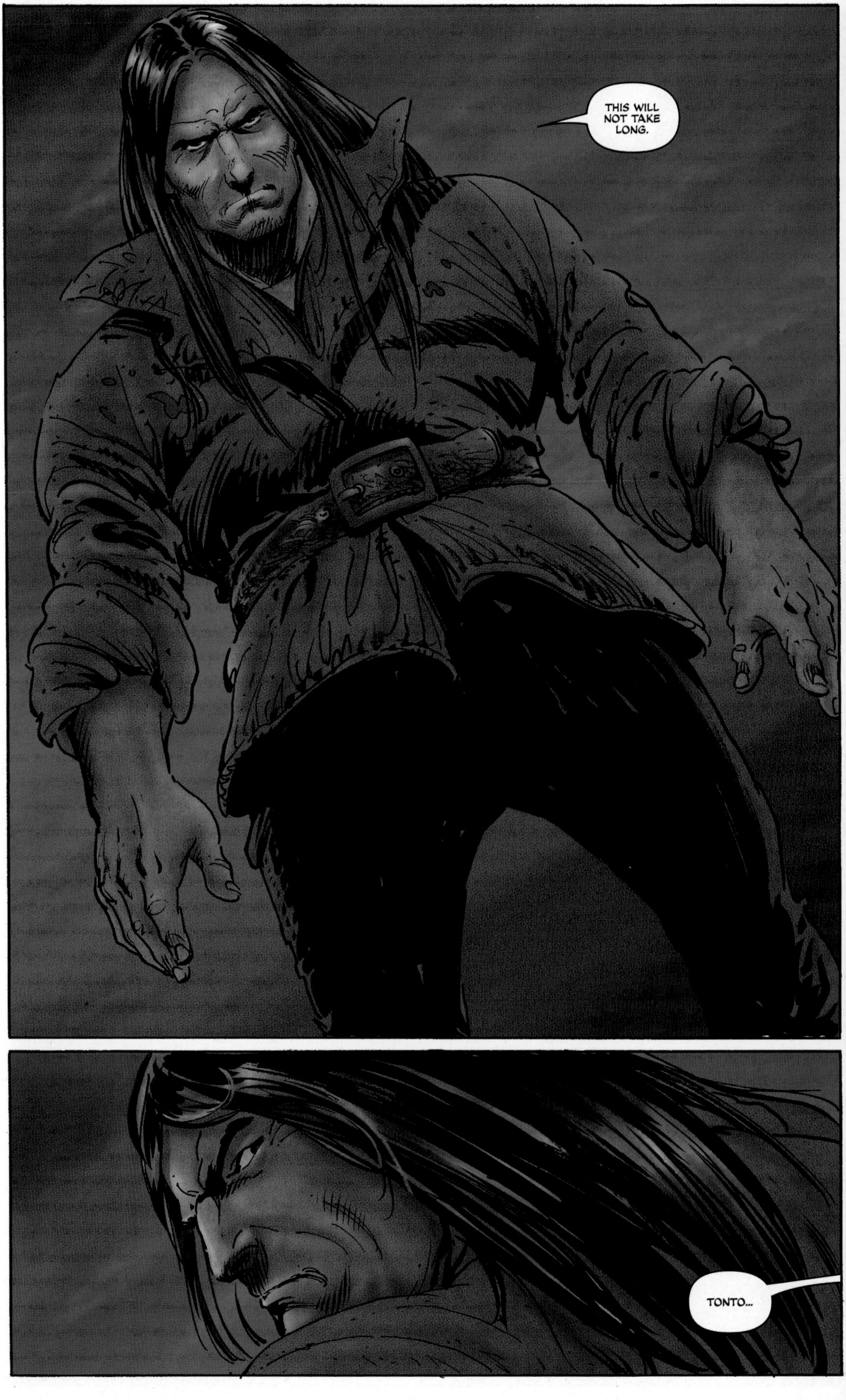
THIS WILL NOT TAKE LONG.
TONTO...

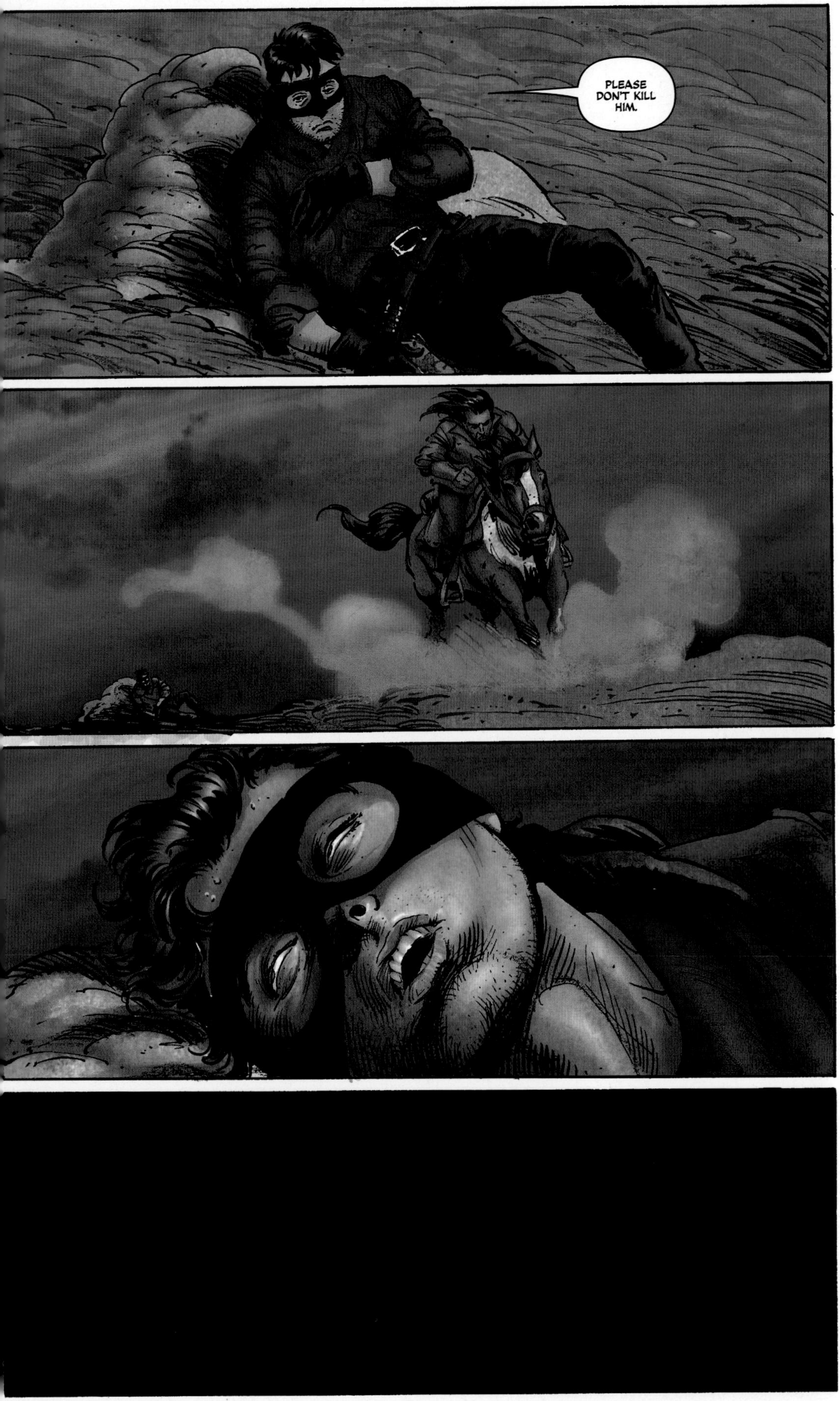
PLEASE DON'T KILL HIM.

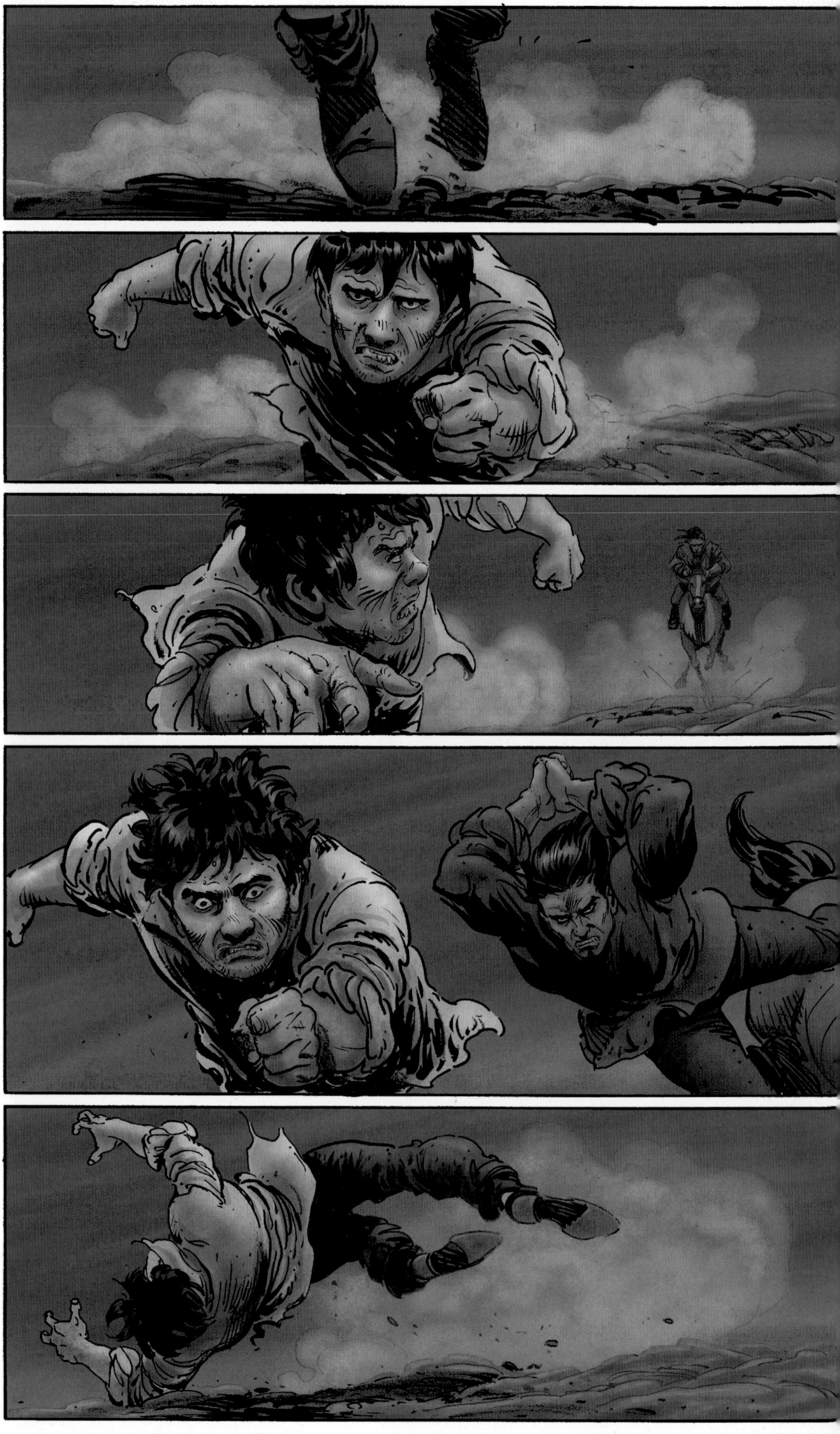

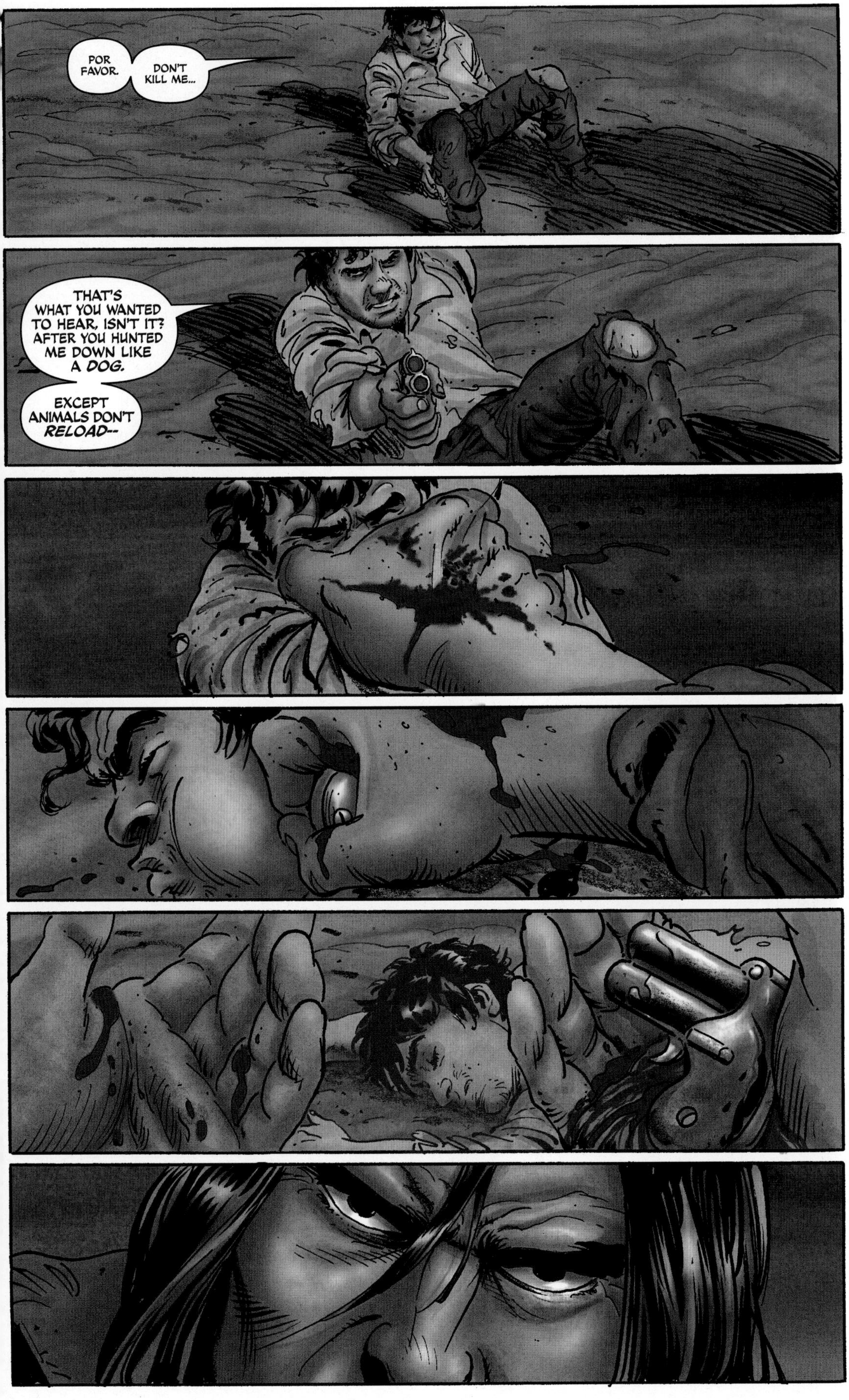
POR FAVOR.
DON'T KILL ME...
THAT'S WHAT YOU WANTED TO HEAR, ISN'T IT? AFTER YOU HUNTED ME DOWN LIKE A *DOG.*
EXCEPT ANIMALS DON'T *RELOAD--*

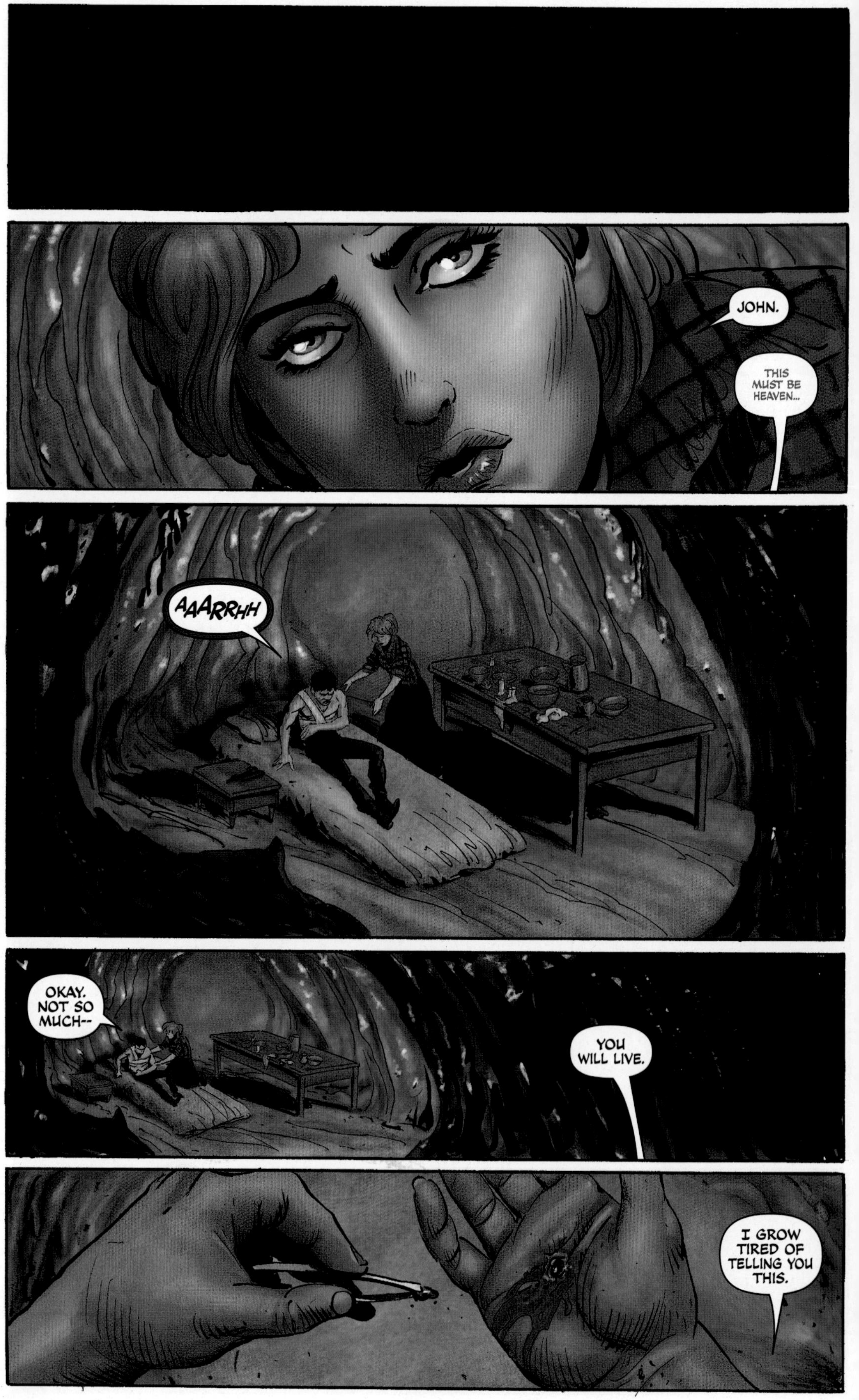

JOHN.
THIS MUST BE HEAVEN...
AAARRHH
OKAY. NOT SO MUCH--
YOU WILL LIVE.
I GROW TIRED OF TELLING YOU THIS.

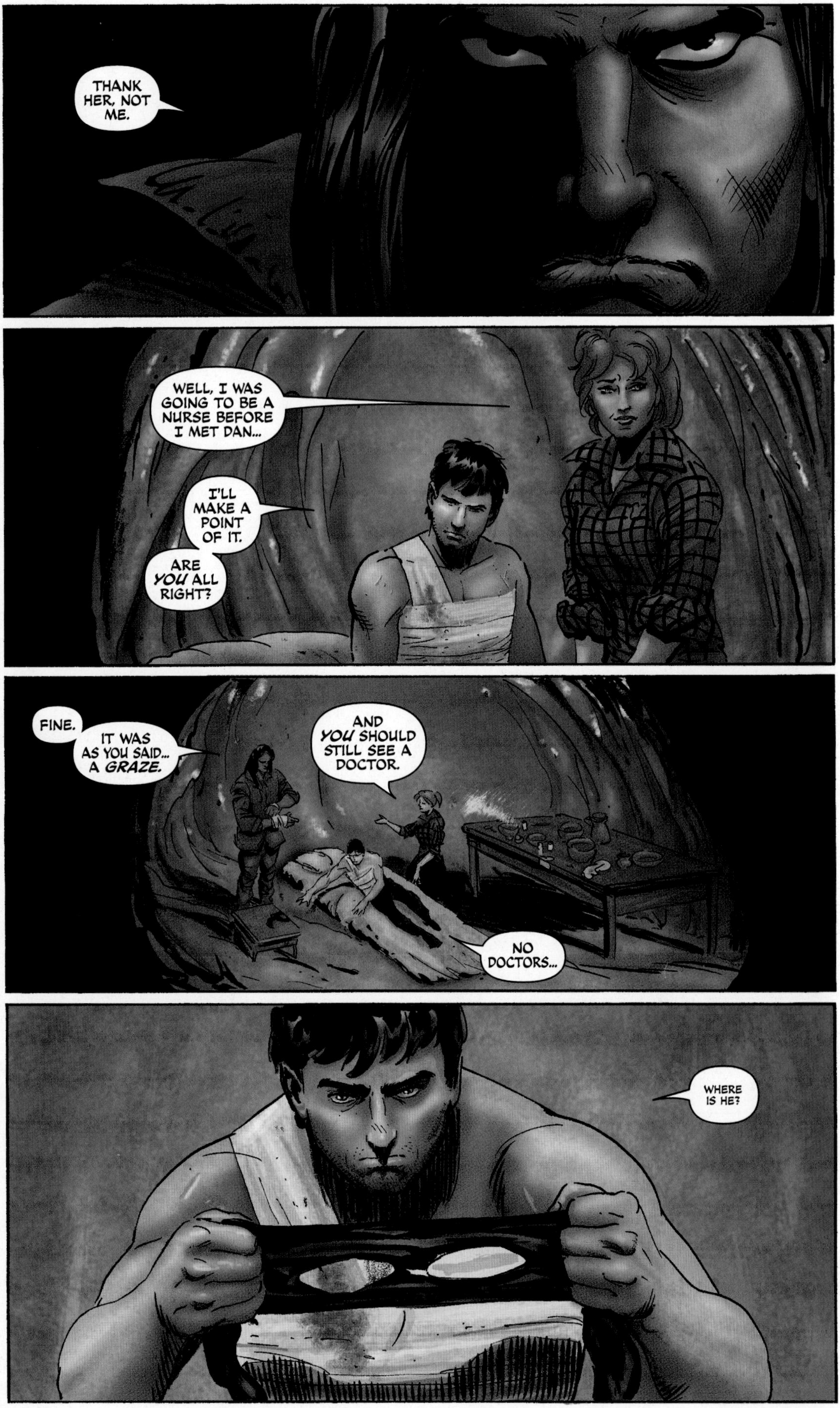
THANK HER, NOT ME.
WELL, I WAS GOING TO BE A NURSE BEFORE I MET DAN...
I'LL MAKE A POINT OF IT.
ARE *YOU* ALL RIGHT?
FINE.
IT WAS AS YOU SAID... A *GRAZE.*
AND *YOU* SHOULD STILL SEE A DOCTOR.
NO DOCTORS...
WHERE IS HE?

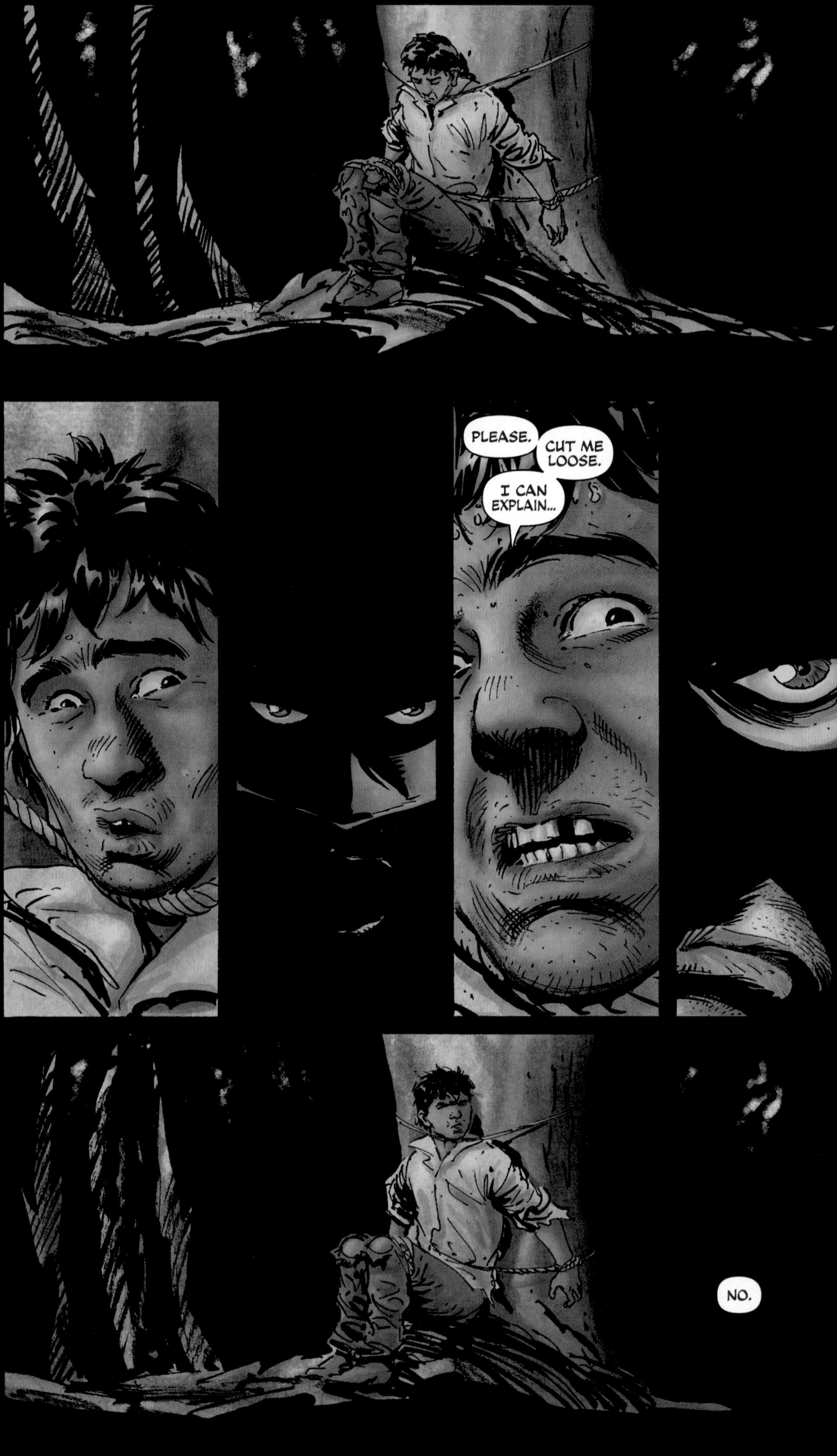
PLEASE.
CUT ME LOOSE.
I CAN EXPLAIN...
NO.

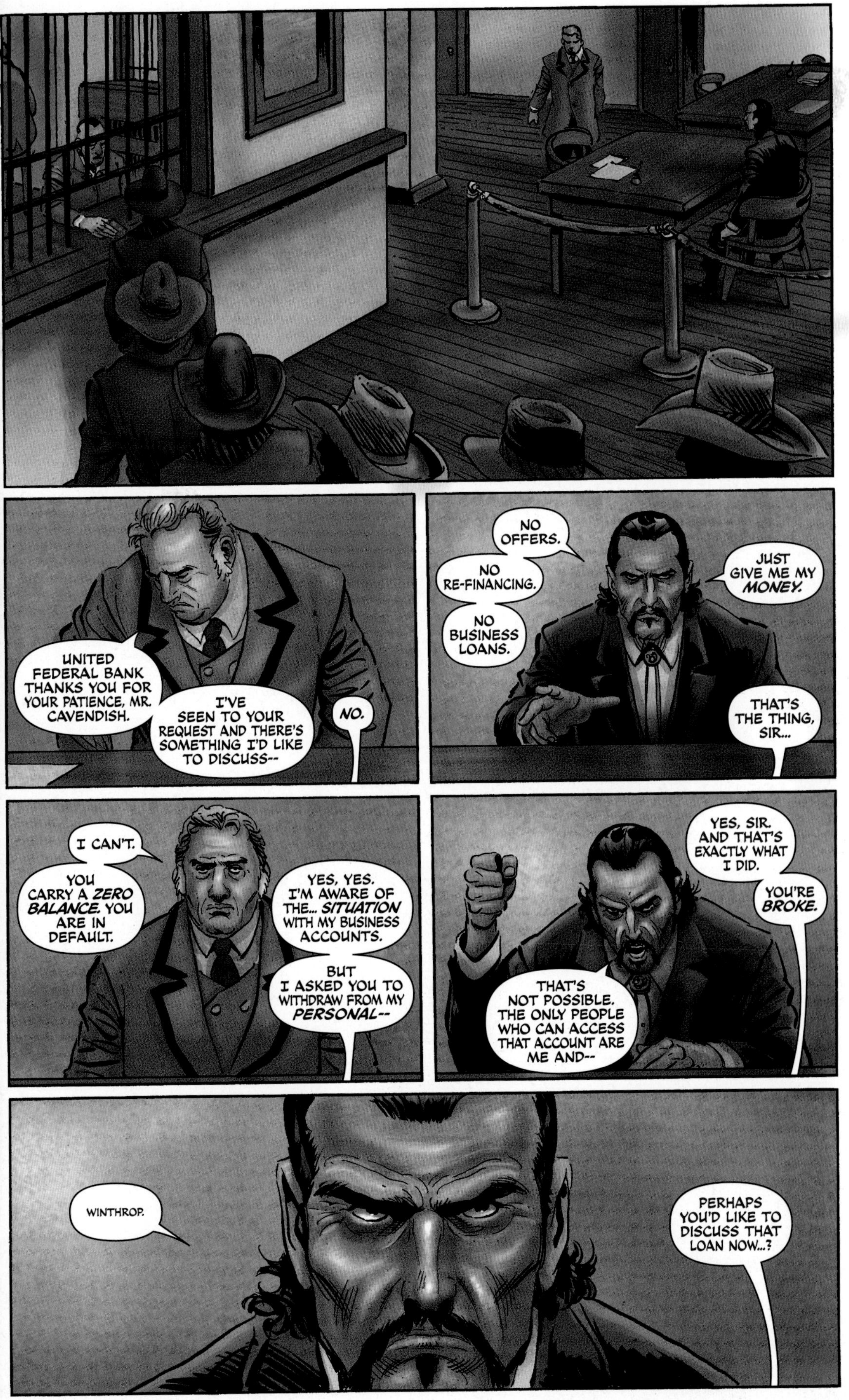
UNITED FEDERAL BANK THANKS YOU FOR YOUR PATIENCE, MR. CAVENDISH.
I'VE SEEN TO YOUR REQUEST AND THERE'S SOMETHING I'D LIKE TO DISCUSS--
NO.
NO OFFERS.
NO RE-FINANCING.
NO BUSINESS LOANS.
JUST GIVE ME MY *MONEY.*
THAT'S THE THING, SIR...
I CAN'T.
YOU CARRY A *ZERO BALANCE.* YOU ARE IN DEFAULT.
YES, YES. I'M AWARE OF THE... *SITUATION* WITH MY BUSINESS ACCOUNTS.
BUT I ASKED YOU TO WITHDRAW FROM MY *PERSONAL--*
YES, SIR. AND THAT'S EXACTLY WHAT I DID.
YOU'RE *BROKE.*
THAT'S NOT POSSIBLE. THE ONLY PEOPLE WHO CAN ACCESS THAT ACCOUNT ARE ME AND--
WINTHROP.
PERHAPS YOU'D LIKE TO DISCUSS THAT LOAN NOW...?

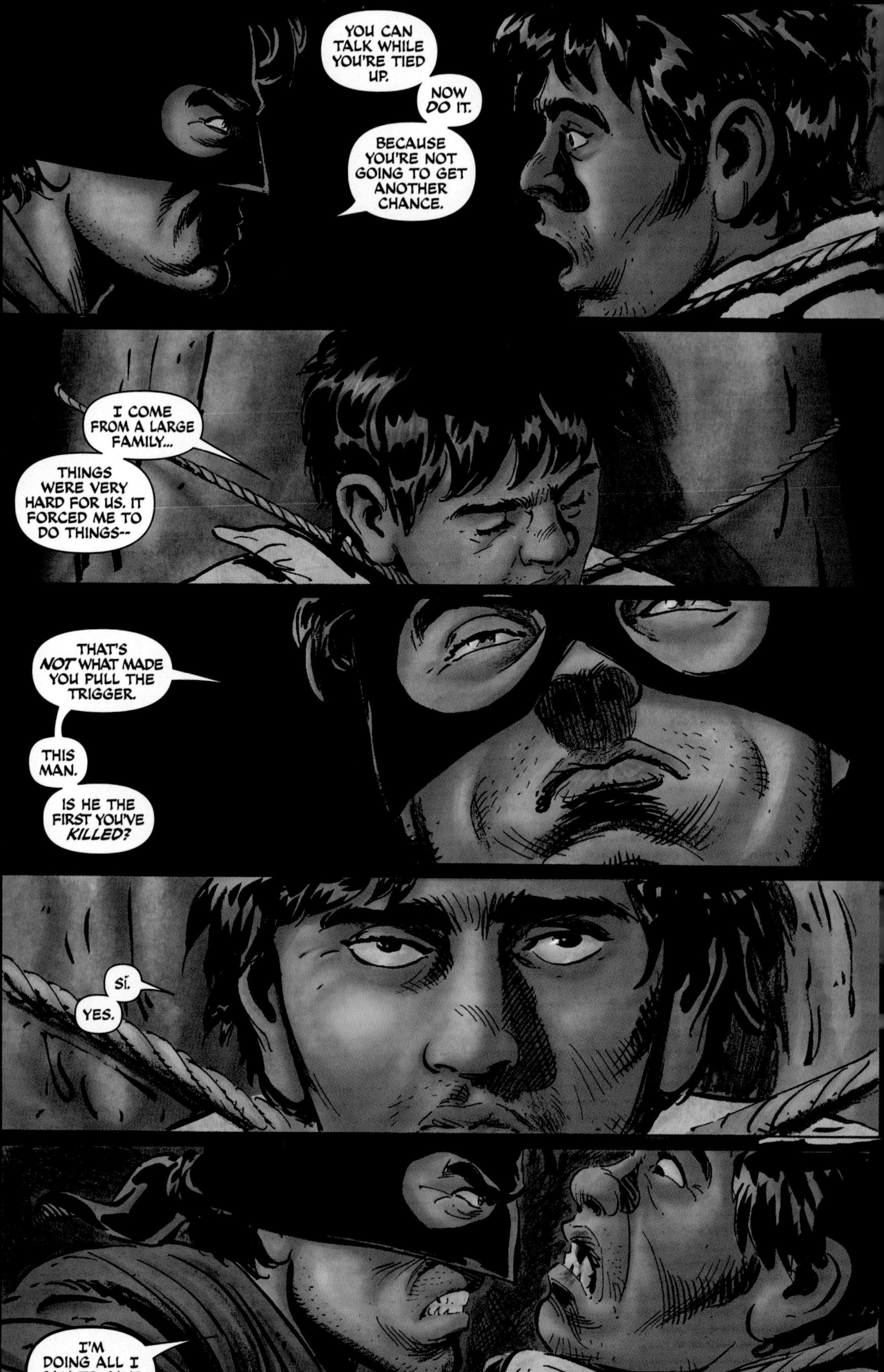
YOU CAN TALK WHILE YOU'RE TIED UP.
NOW DO IT.
BECAUSE YOU'RE NOT GOING TO GET ANOTHER CHANCE.
I COME FROM A LARGE FAMILY...
THINGS WERE VERY HARD FOR US. IT FORCED ME TO DO THINGS--
THAT'S NOT WHAT MADE YOU PULL THE TRIGGER.
THIS MAN.
IS HE THE FIRST YOU'VE KILLED?
SÍ.
YES.
I'M DOING ALL I CAN TO SAVE YOU AND YOU LIE TO ME?

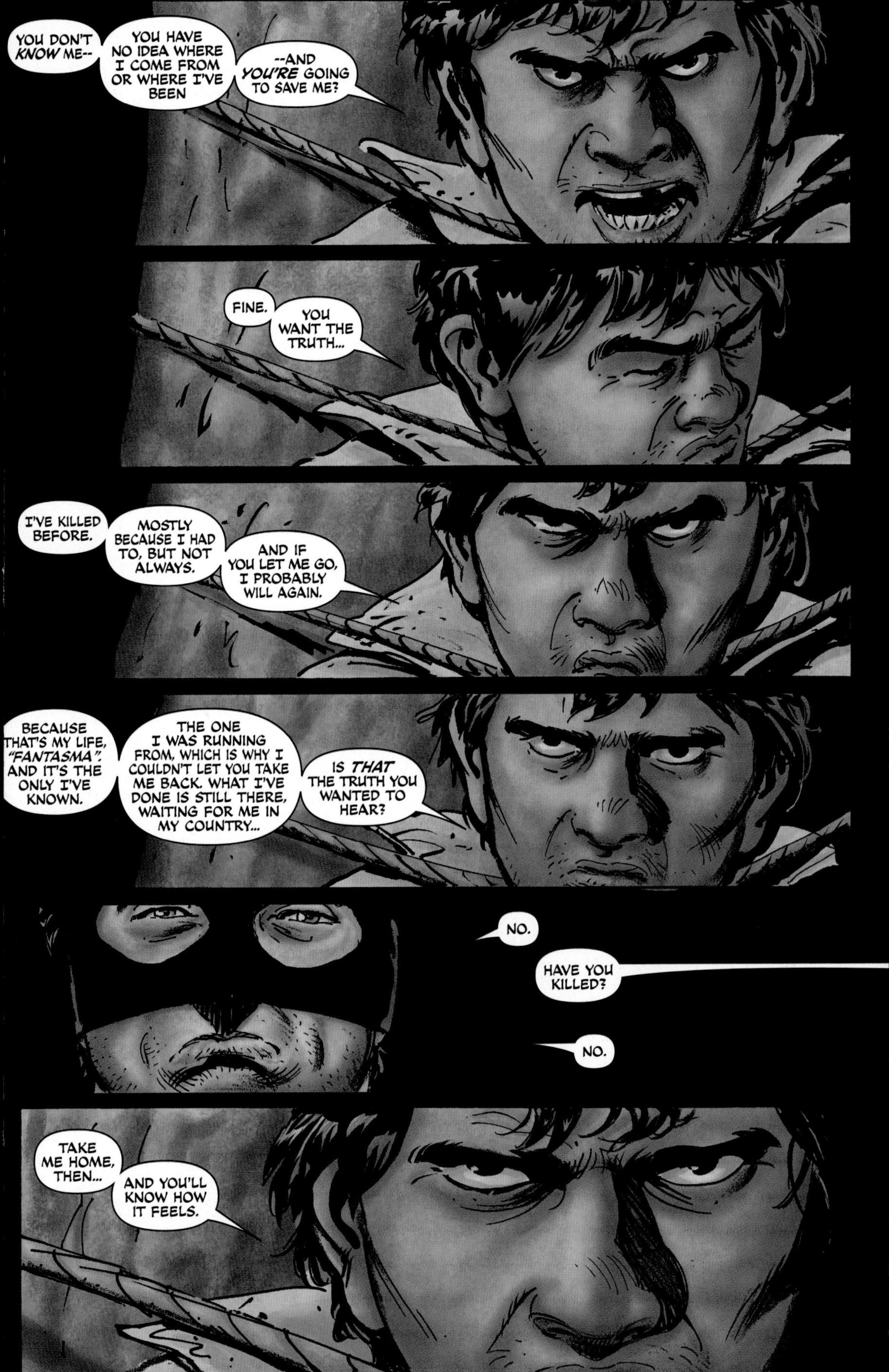
YOU DON'T KNOW ME--
YOU HAVE NO IDEA WHERE I COME FROM OR WHERE I'VE BEEN
--AND YOU'RE GOING TO SAVE ME?
FINE.
YOU WANT THE TRUTH...
I'VE KILLED BEFORE.
MOSTLY BECAUSE I HAD TO, BUT NOT ALWAYS.
AND IF YOU LET ME GO, I PROBABLY WILL AGAIN.
BECAUSE THAT'S MY LIFE, "FANTASMA". AND IT'S THE ONLY I'VE KNOWN.
THE ONE I WAS RUNNING FROM, WHICH IS WHY I COULDN'T LET YOU TAKE ME BACK. WHAT I'VE DONE IS STILL THERE, WAITING FOR ME IN MY COUNTRY...
IS THAT THE TRUTH YOU WANTED TO HEAR?
NO.
HAVE YOU KILLED?
NO.
TAKE ME HOME, THEN...
AND YOU'LL KNOW HOW IT FEELS.

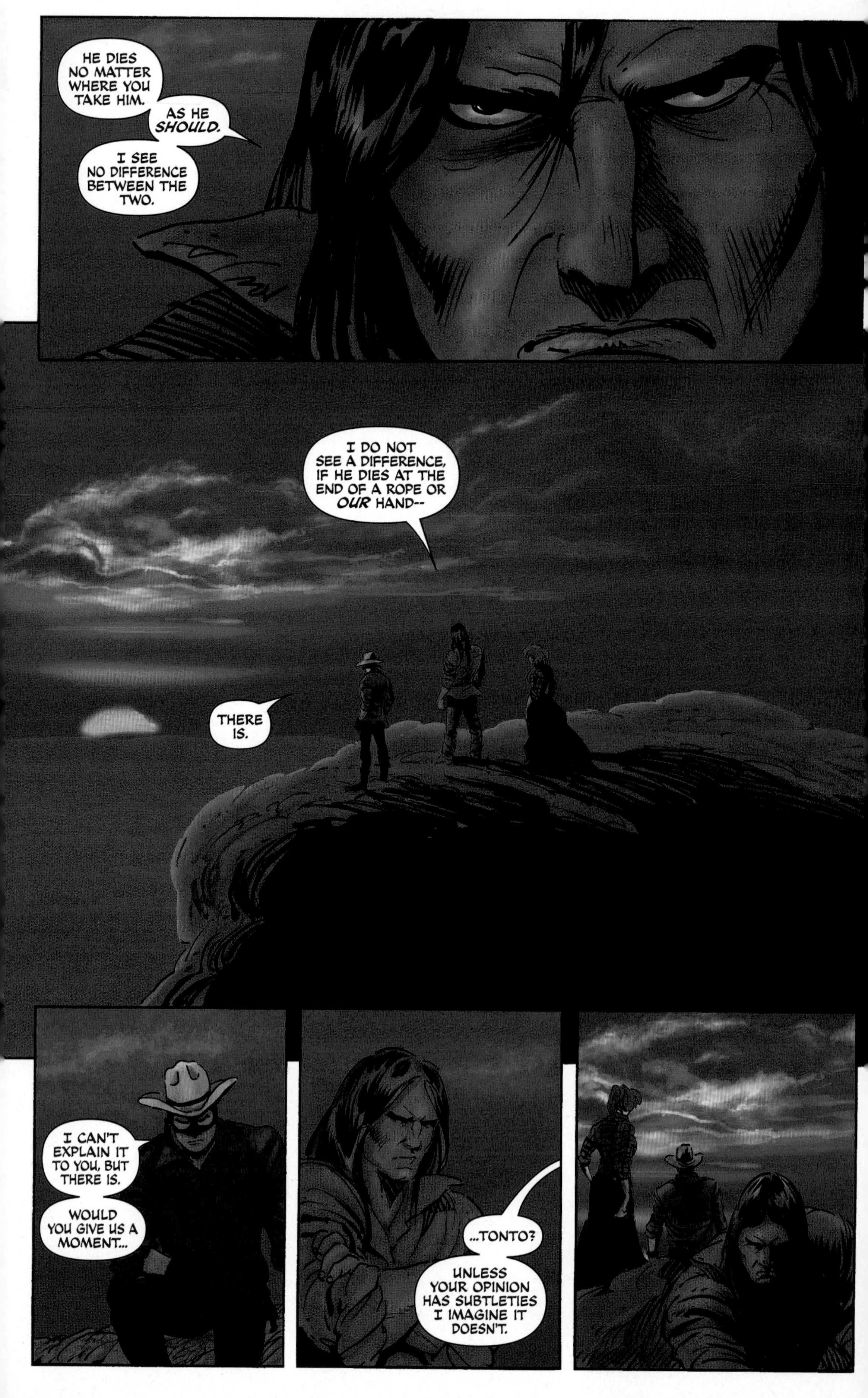
HE DIES NO MATTER WHERE YOU TAKE HIM.
AS HE SHOULD.
I SEE NO DIFFERENCE BETWEEN THE TWO.
I DO NOT SEE A DIFFERENCE, IF HE DIES AT THE END OF A ROPE OR OUR HAND--
THERE IS.
I CAN'T EXPLAIN IT TO YOU, BUT THERE IS.
WOULD YOU GIVE US A MOMENT...
...TONTO?
UNLESS YOUR OPINION HAS SUBTLETIES I IMAGINE IT DOESN'T.

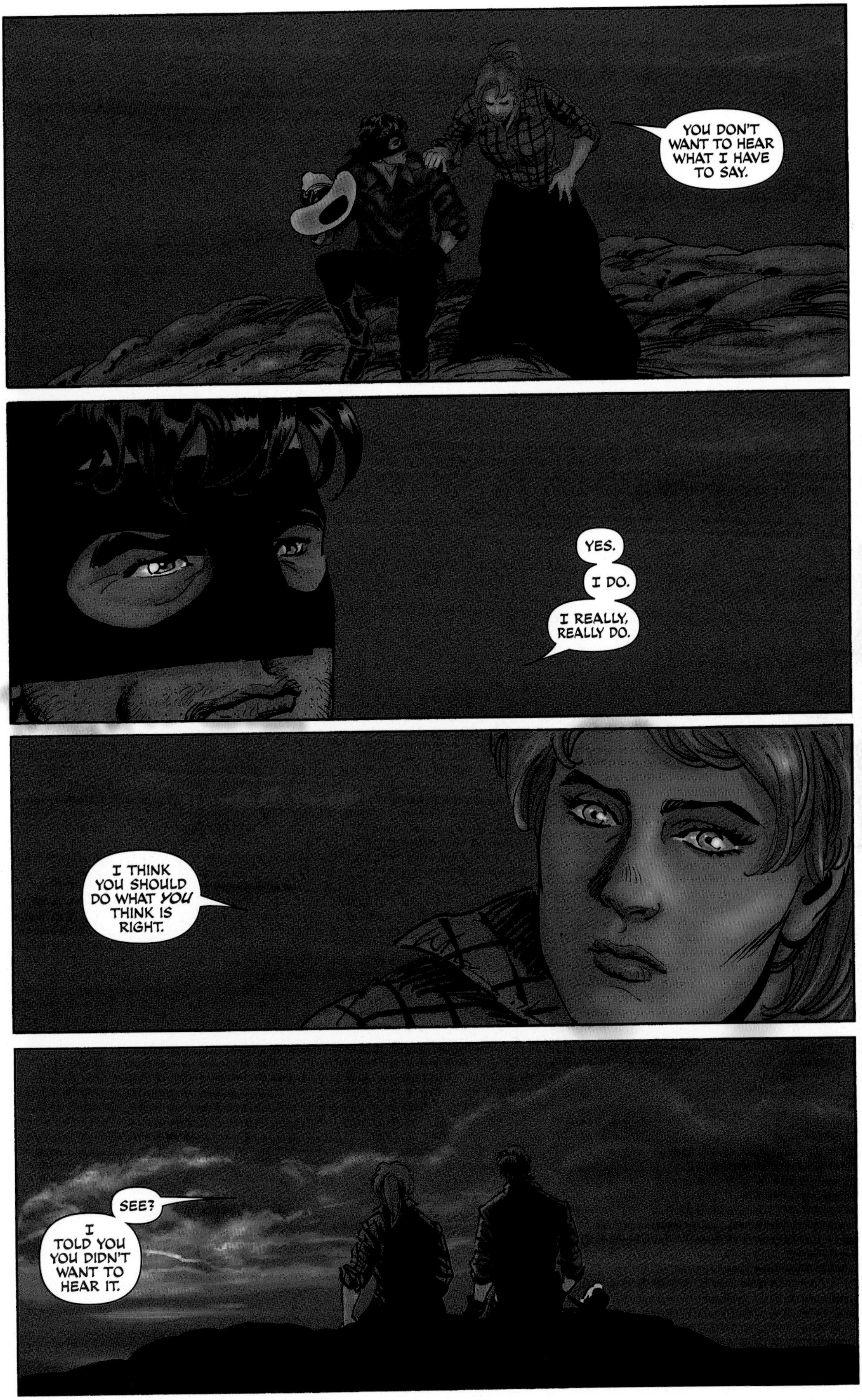
YOU DON'T WANT TO HEAR WHAT I HAVE TO SAY.
YES.
I DO.
I REALLY, REALLY DO.
I THINK YOU SHOULD DO WHAT *YOU* THINK IS RIGHT.
SEE?
I TOLD YOU YOU DIDN'T WANT TO HEAR IT.

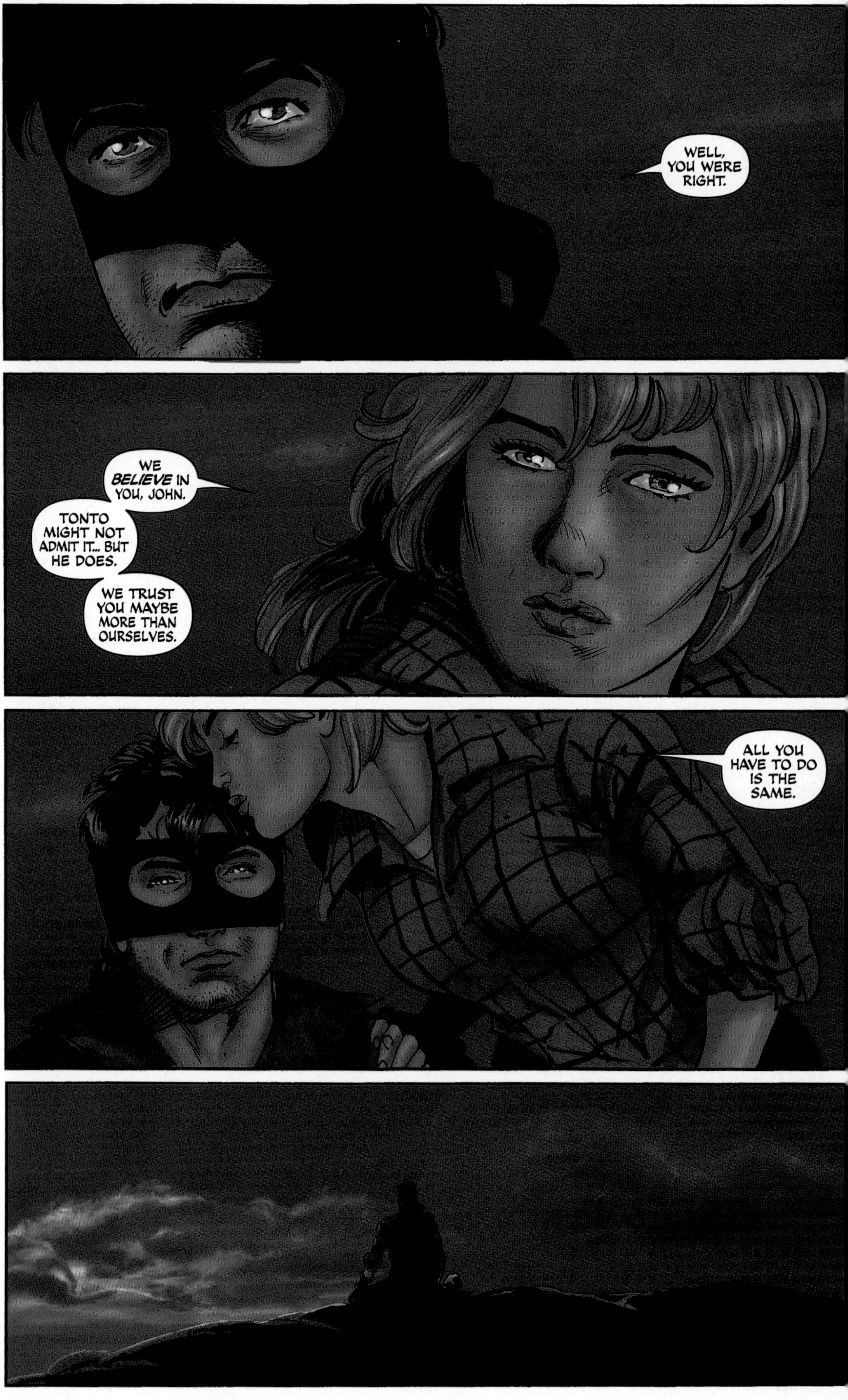
WELL, YOU WERE RIGHT.
WE *BELIEVE* IN YOU, JOHN.
TONTO MIGHT NOT ADMIT IT... BUT HE DOES.
WE TRUST YOU MAYBE MORE THAN OURSELVES.
ALL YOU HAVE TO DO IS THE SAME.

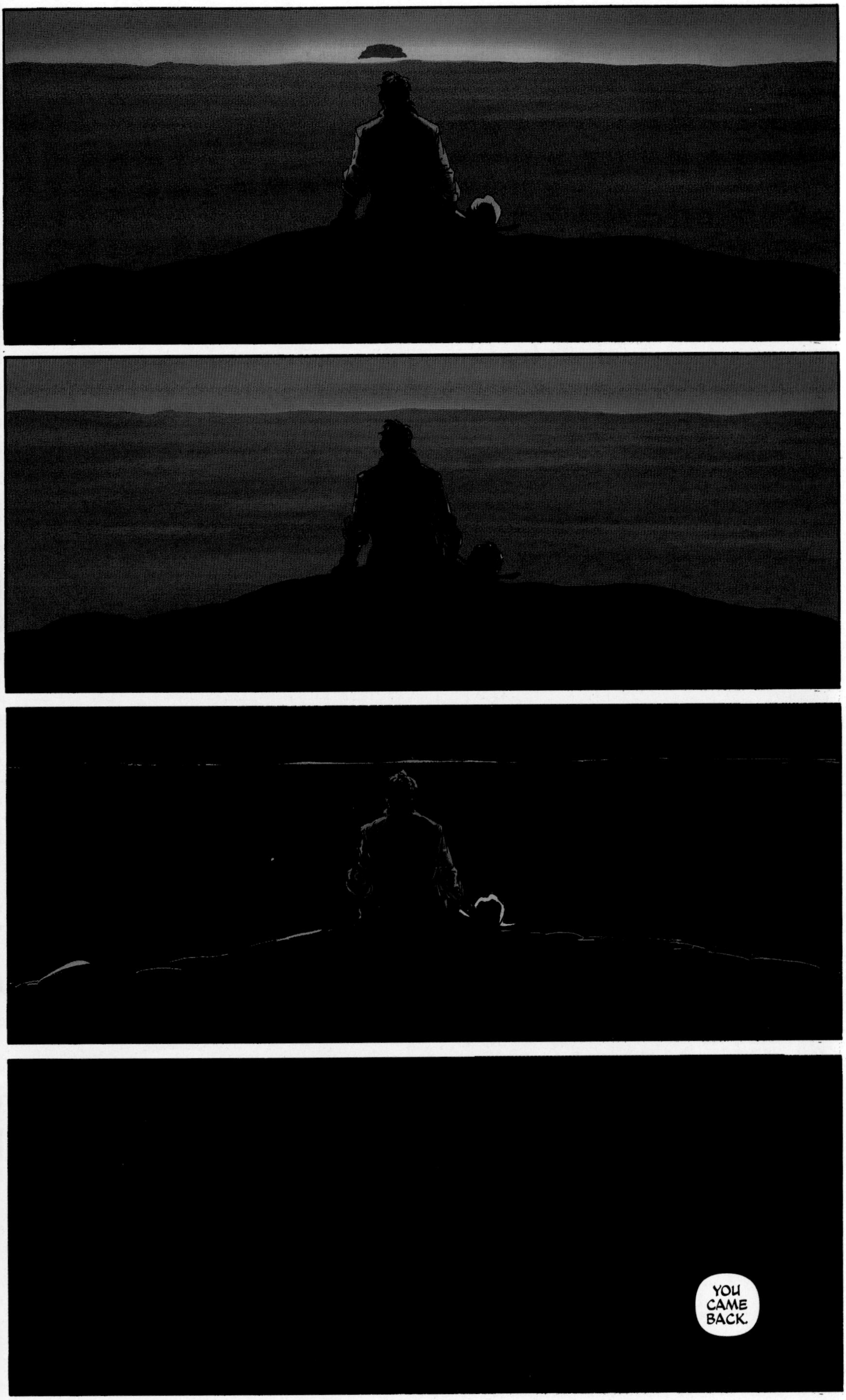
YOU CAME BACK.

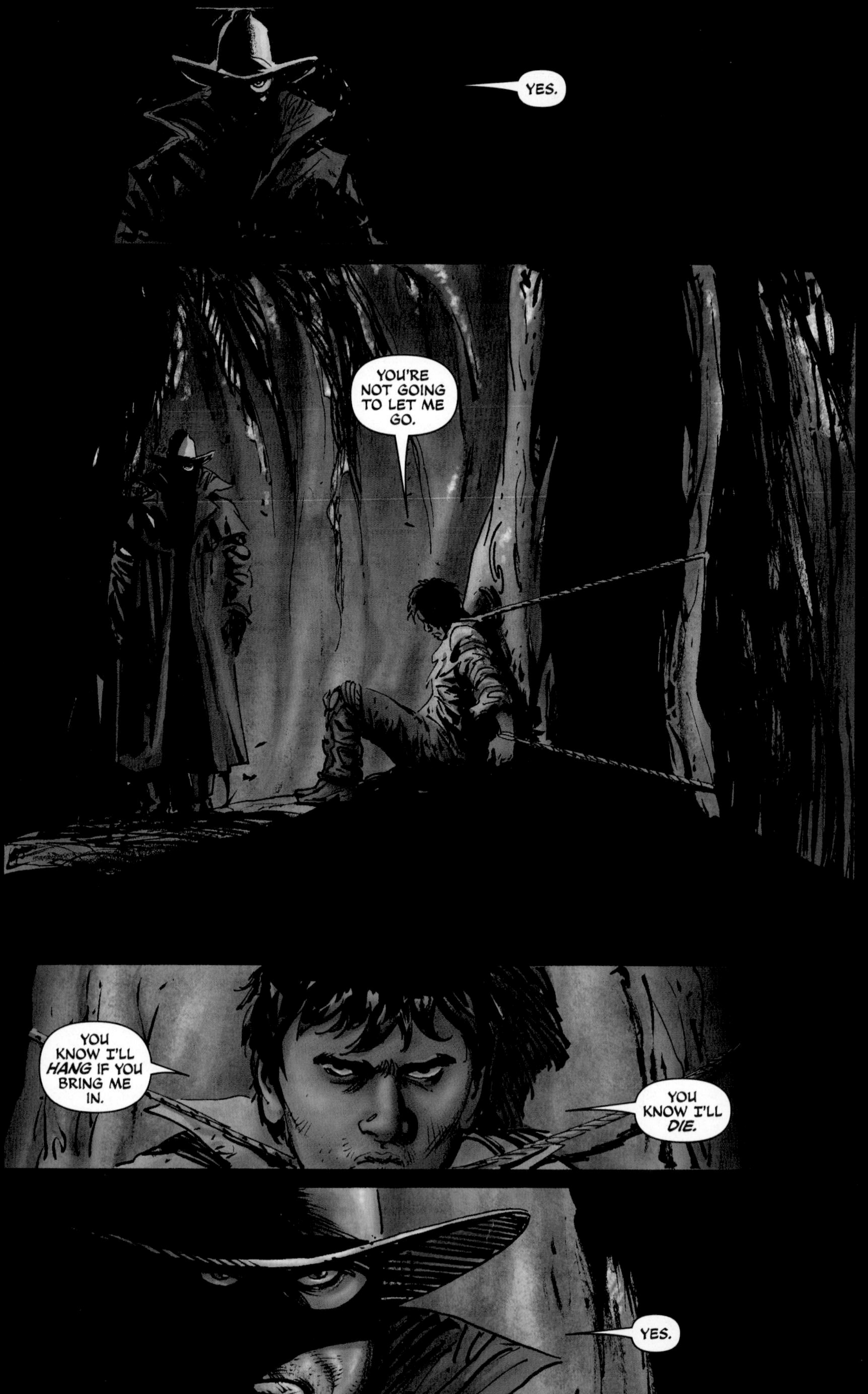
YES.
YOU'RE NOT GOING TO LET ME GO.
YOU KNOW I'LL *HANG* IF YOU BRING ME IN.
YOU KNOW I'LL *DIE*.
YES.

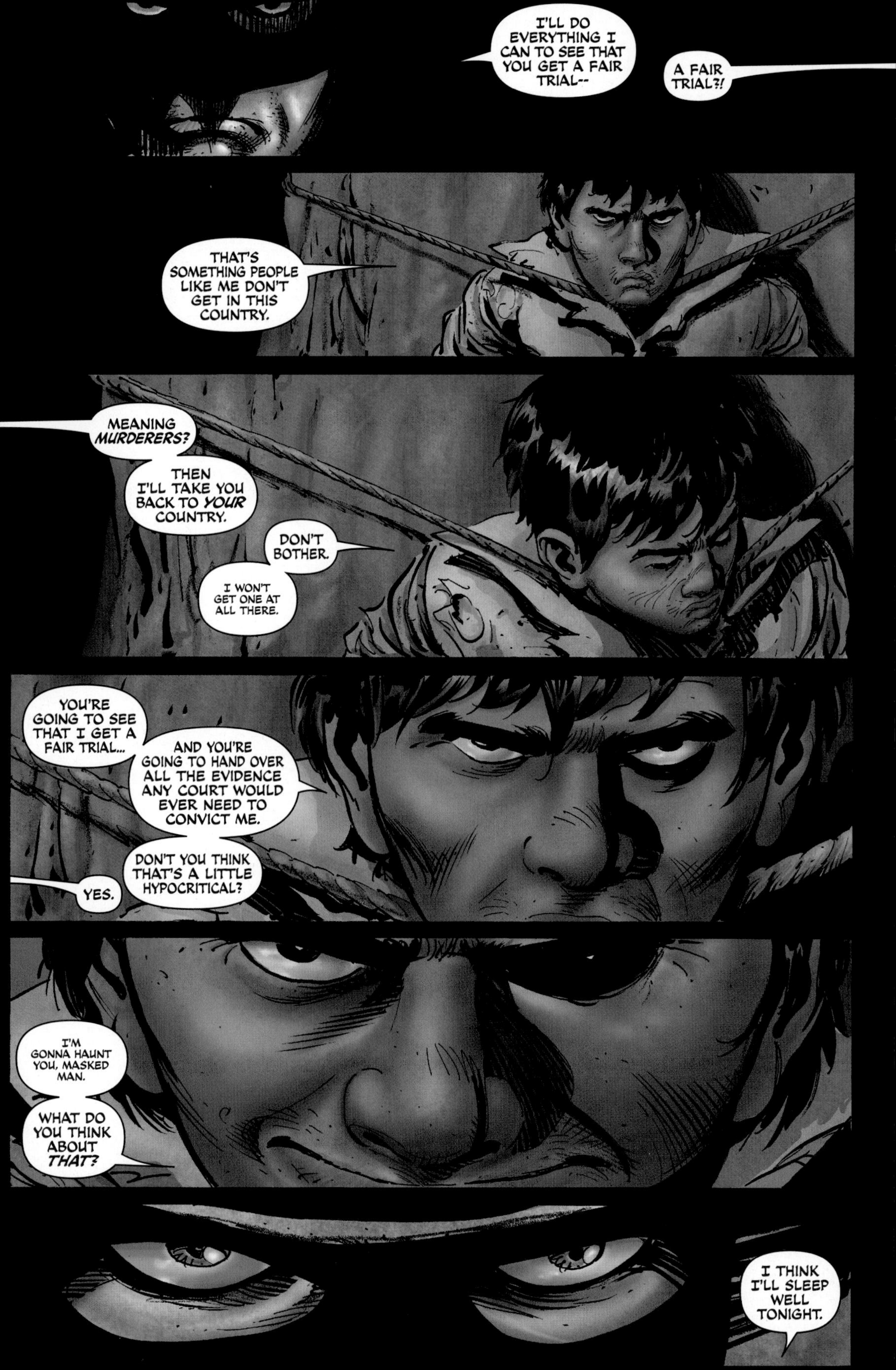

I'LL DO EVERYTHING I CAN TO SEE THAT YOU GET A FAIR TRIAL--
A FAIR TRIAL?!
THAT'S SOMETHING PEOPLE LIKE ME DON'T GET IN THIS COUNTRY.
MEANING *MURDERERS?*
THEN I'LL TAKE YOU BACK TO *YOUR* COUNTRY.
DON'T BOTHER.
I WON'T GET ONE AT ALL THERE.
YOU'RE GOING TO SEE THAT I GET A FAIR TRIAL...
AND YOU'RE GOING TO HAND OVER ALL THE EVIDENCE ANY COURT WOULD EVER NEED TO CONVICT ME.
DON'T YOU THINK THAT'S A LITTLE HYPOCRITICAL?
YES.
I'M GONNA HAUNT YOU, MASKED MAN.
WHAT DO YOU THINK ABOUT *THAT?*
I THINK I'LL SLEEP WELL TONIGHT.

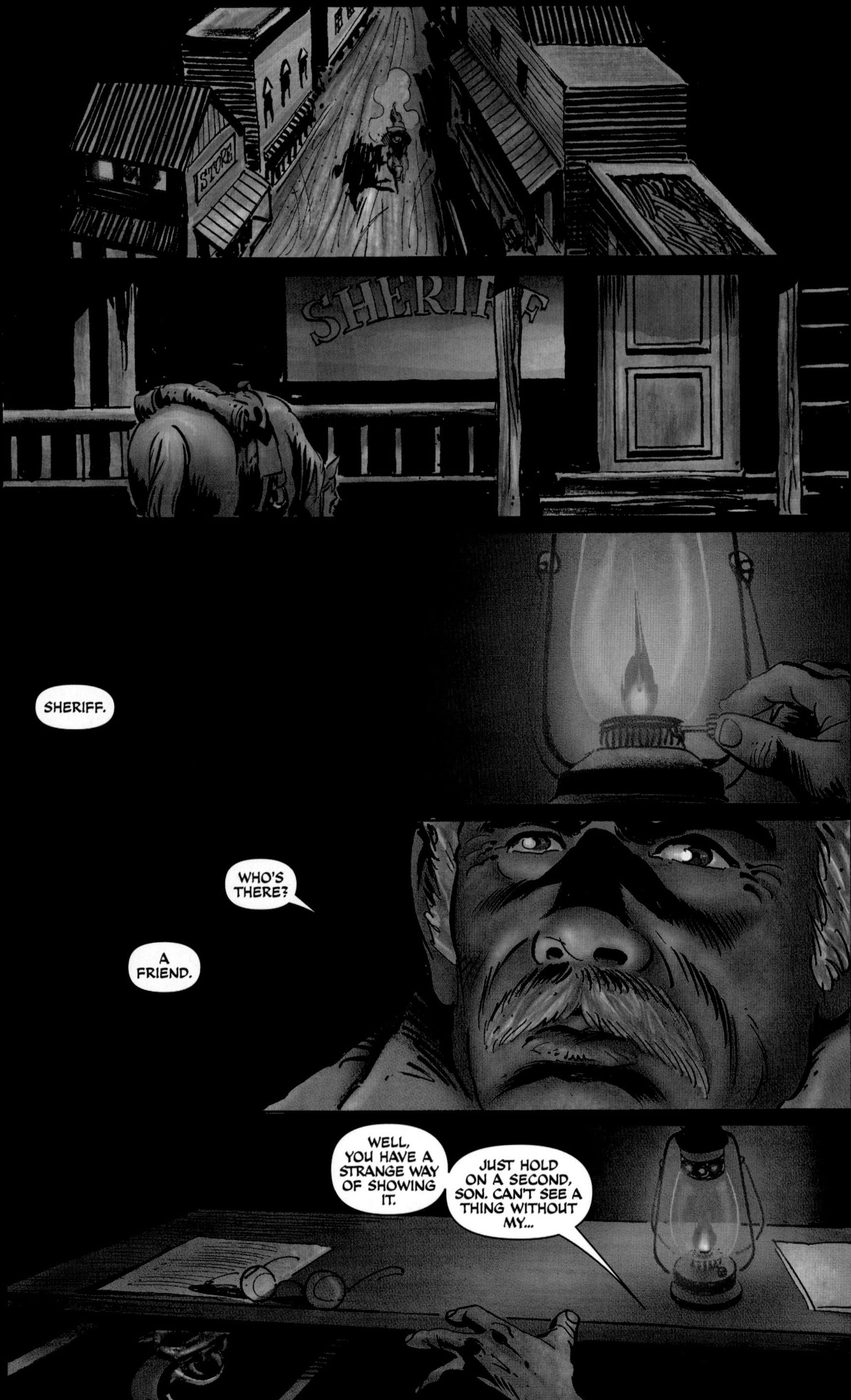
SHERIFF.
WHO'S THERE?
A FRIEND.
WELL, YOU HAVE A STRANGE WAY OF SHOWING IT.
JUST HOLD ON A SECOND, SON. CAN'T SEE A THING WITHOUT MY...

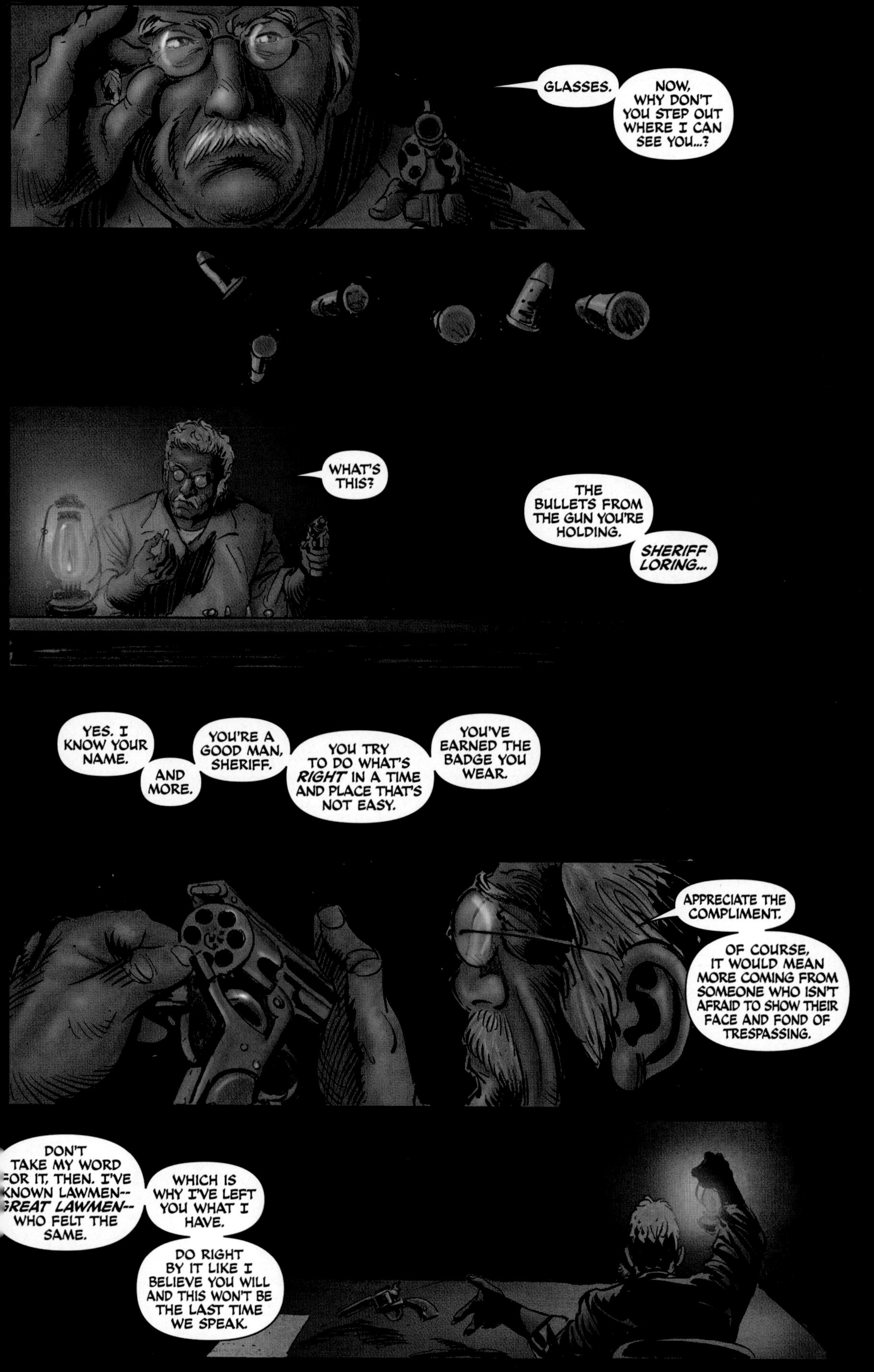
GLASSES.
NOW, WHY DON'T YOU STEP OUT WHERE I CAN SEE YOU...?
WHAT'S THIS?
THE BULLETS FROM THE GUN YOU'RE HOLDING.
SHERIFF LORING...
YES. I KNOW YOUR NAME.
AND MORE.
YOU'RE A GOOD MAN, SHERIFF.
YOU TRY TO DO WHAT'S *RIGHT* IN A TIME AND PLACE THAT'S NOT EASY.
YOU'VE EARNED THE BADGE YOU WEAR.
APPRECIATE THE COMPLIMENT.
OF COURSE, IT WOULD MEAN MORE COMING FROM SOMEONE WHO ISN'T AFRAID TO SHOW THEIR FACE AND FOND OF TRESPASSING.
DON'T TAKE MY WORD FOR IT, THEN. I'VE KNOWN LAWMEN-- *GREAT LAWMEN--* WHO FELT THE SAME.
WHICH IS WHY I'VE LEFT YOU WHAT I HAVE.
DO RIGHT BY IT LIKE I BELIEVE YOU WILL AND THIS WON'T BE THE LAST TIME WE SPEAK.

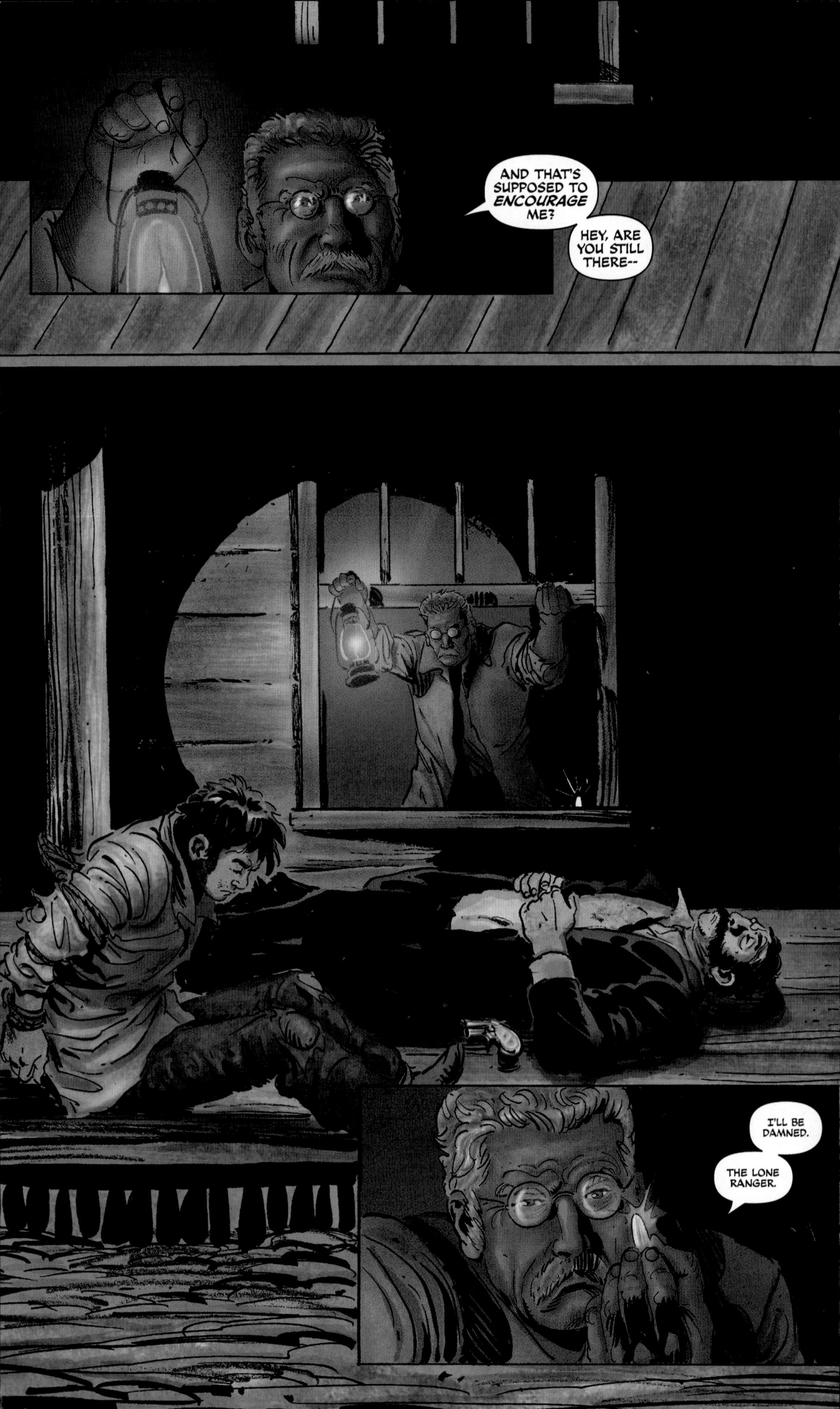

AND THAT'S SUPPOSED TO *ENCOURAGE* ME?
HEY, ARE YOU STILL THERE--
I'LL BE DAMNED.
THE LONE RANGER.

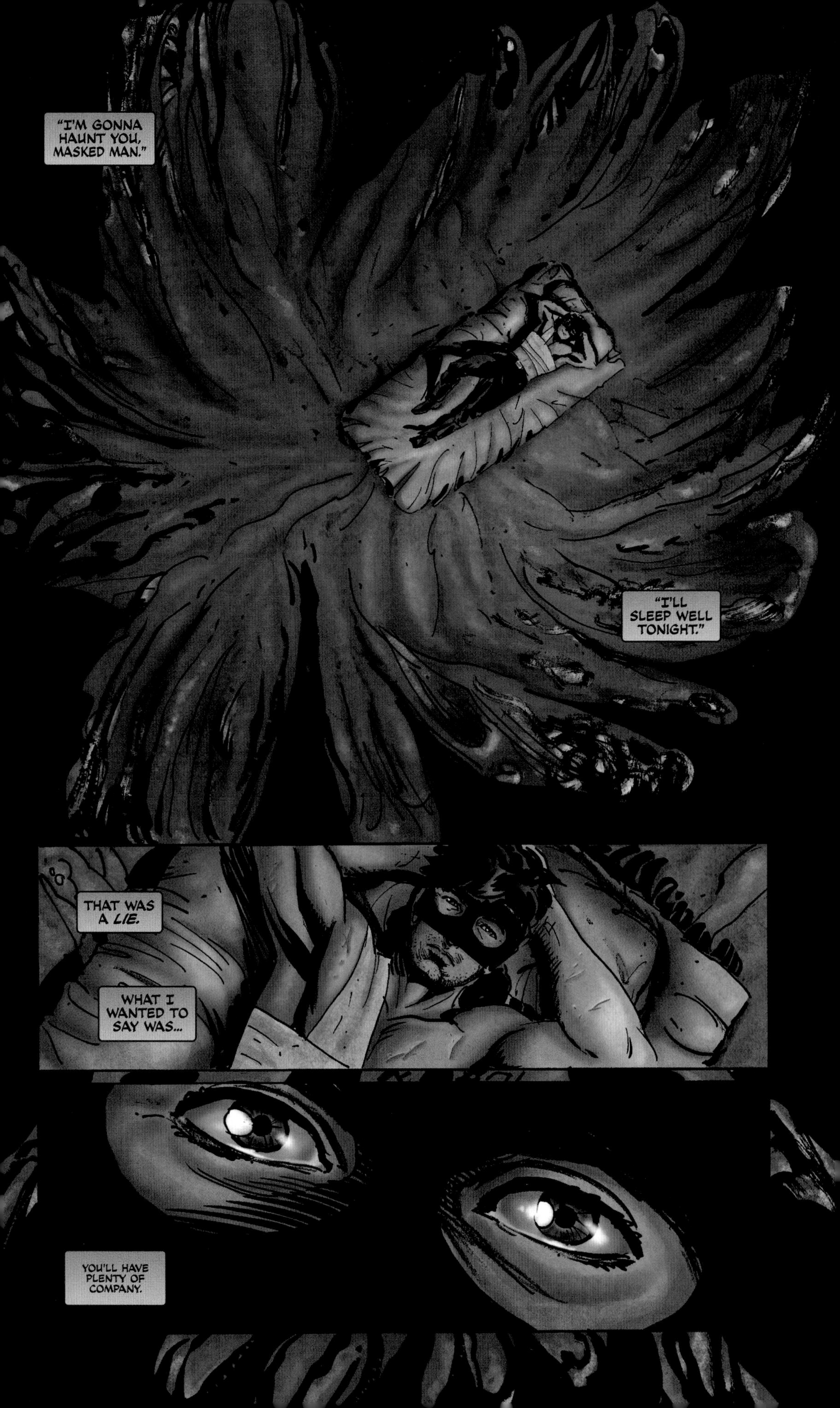
"I'M GONNA HAUNT YOU, MASKED MAN."
"I'LL SLEEP WELL TONIGHT."
THAT WAS A *LIE.*
WHAT I WANTED TO SAY WAS...
YOU'LL HAVE PLENTY OF COMPANY.

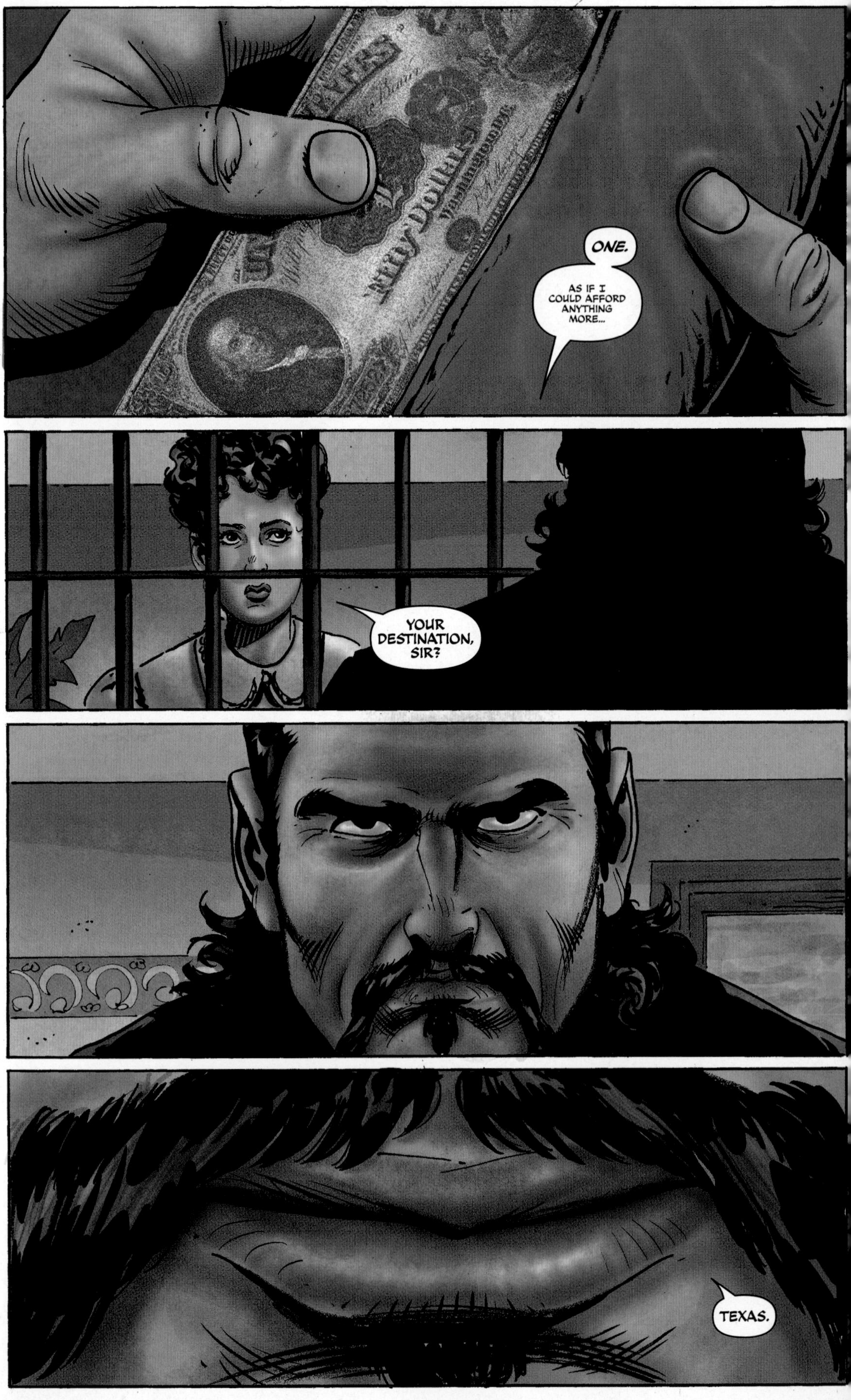
ONE.
AS IF I COULD AFFORD ANYTHING MORE...
YOUR DESTINATION, SIR?
TEXAS.

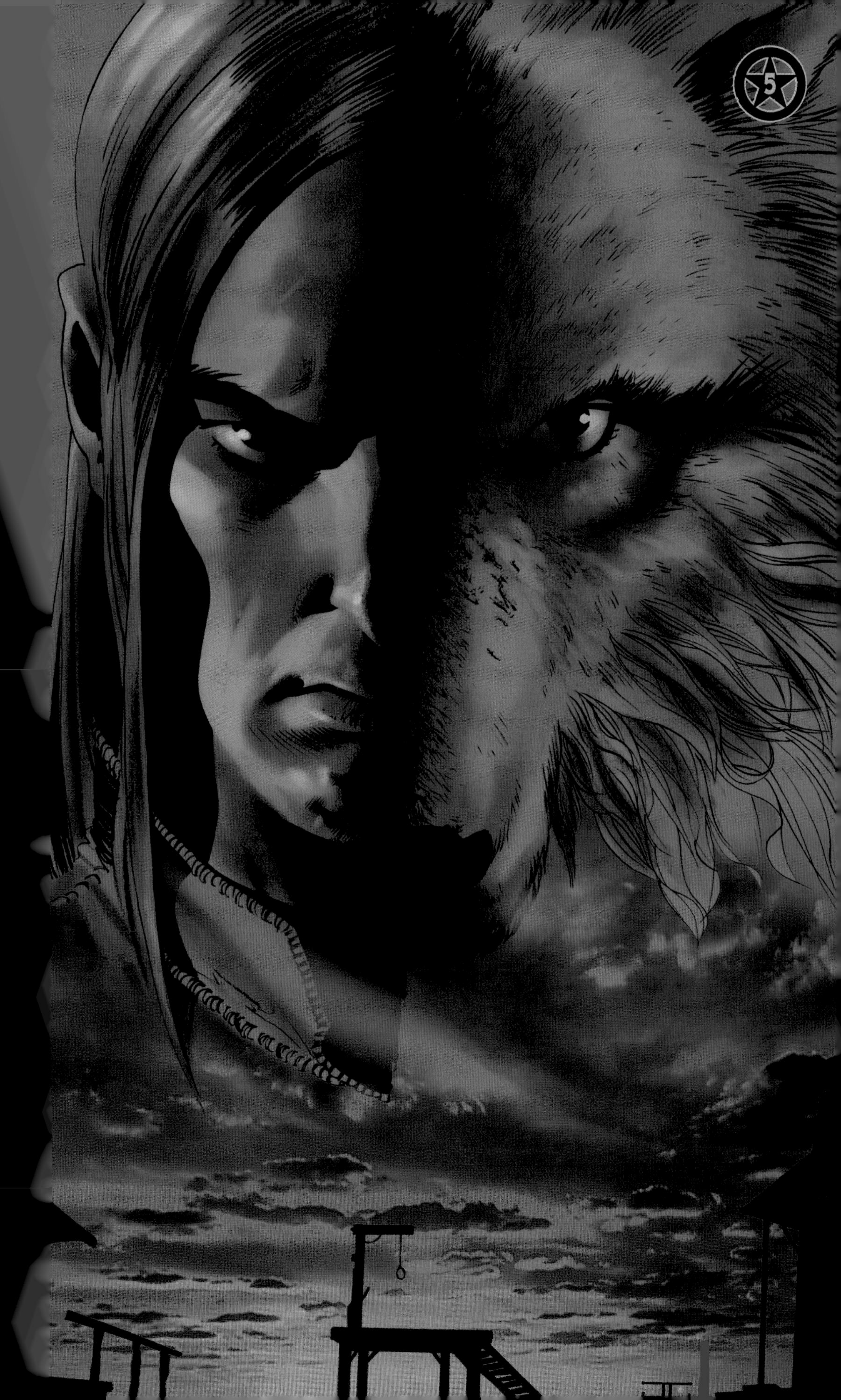

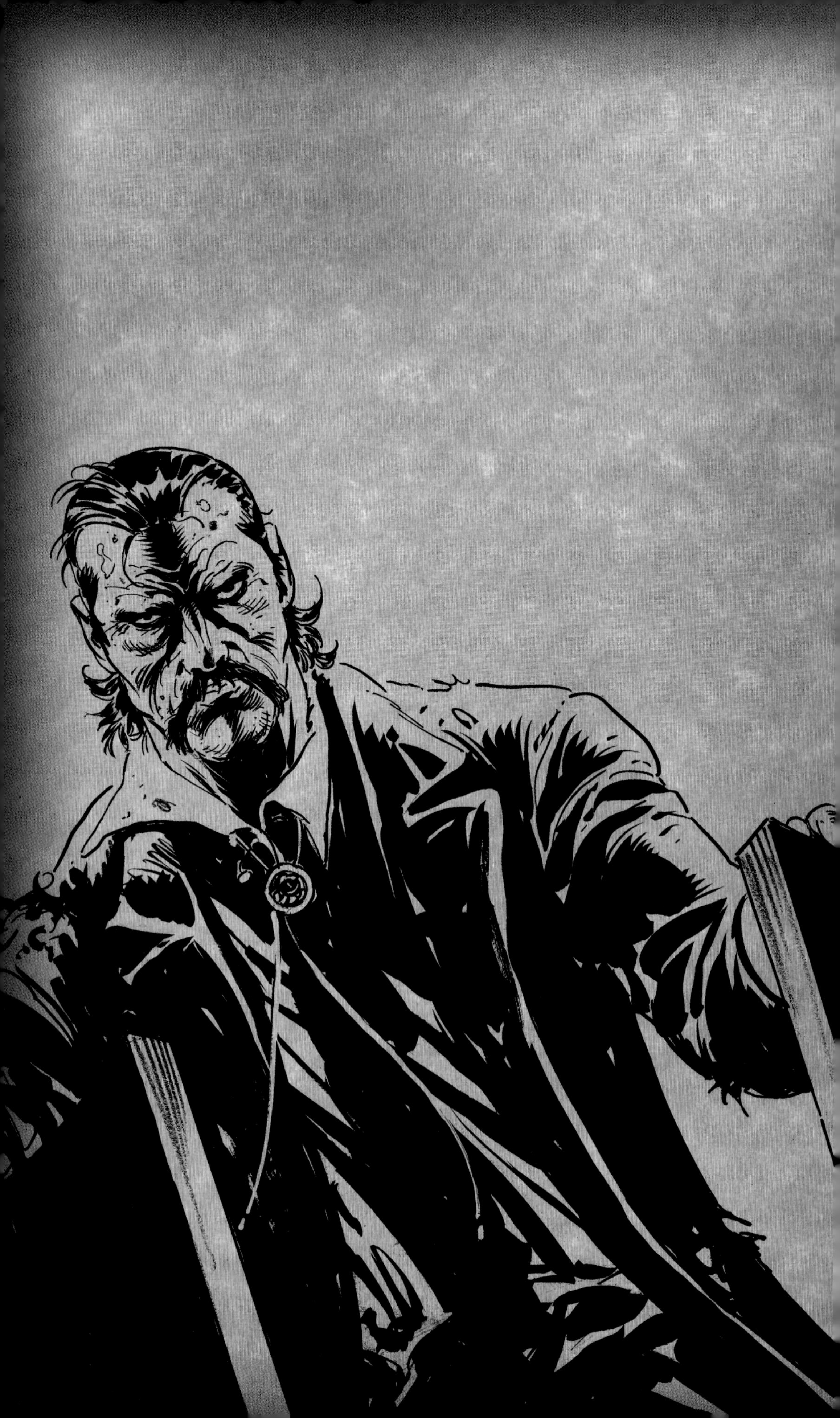

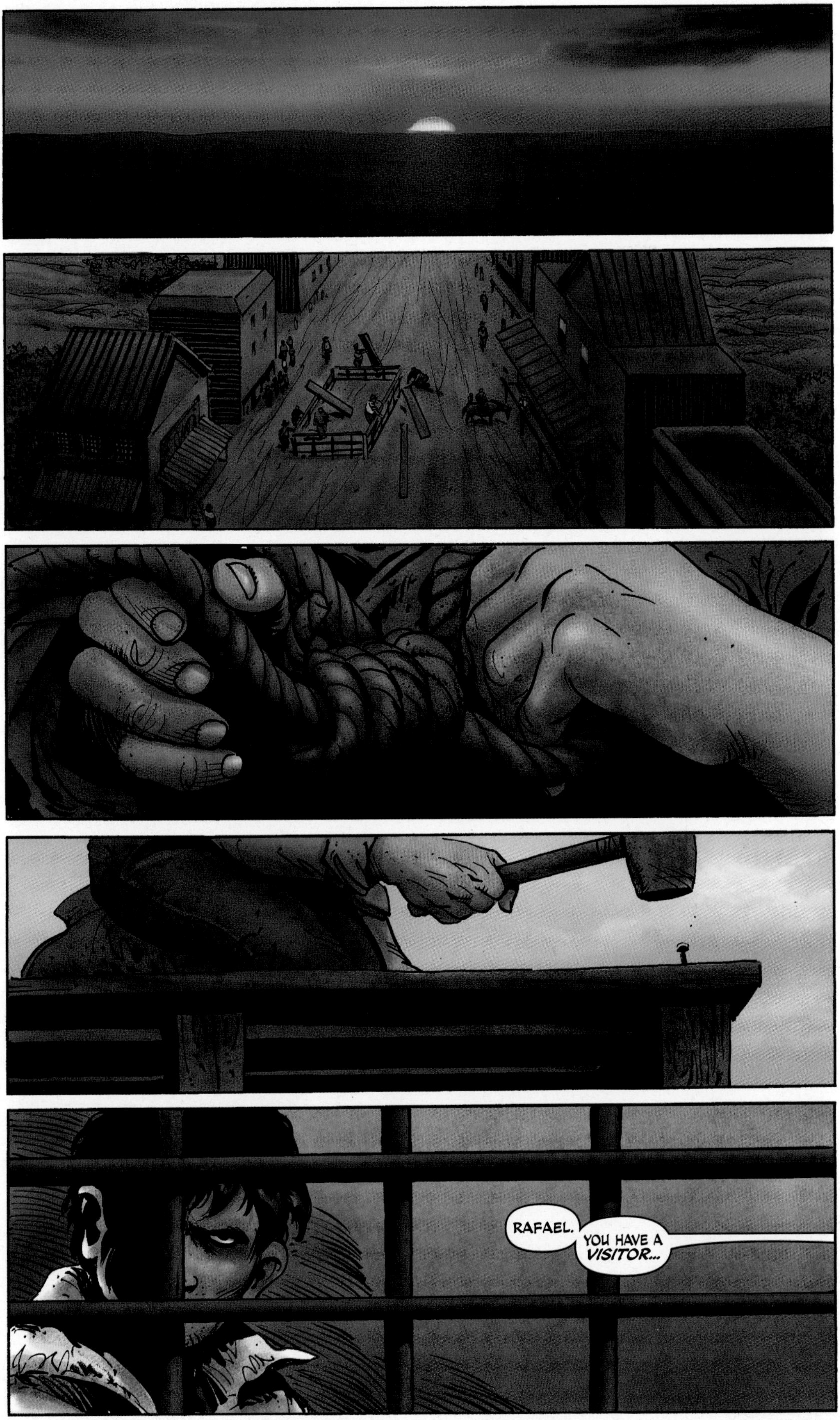
RAFAEL.
YOU HAVE A VISITOR...

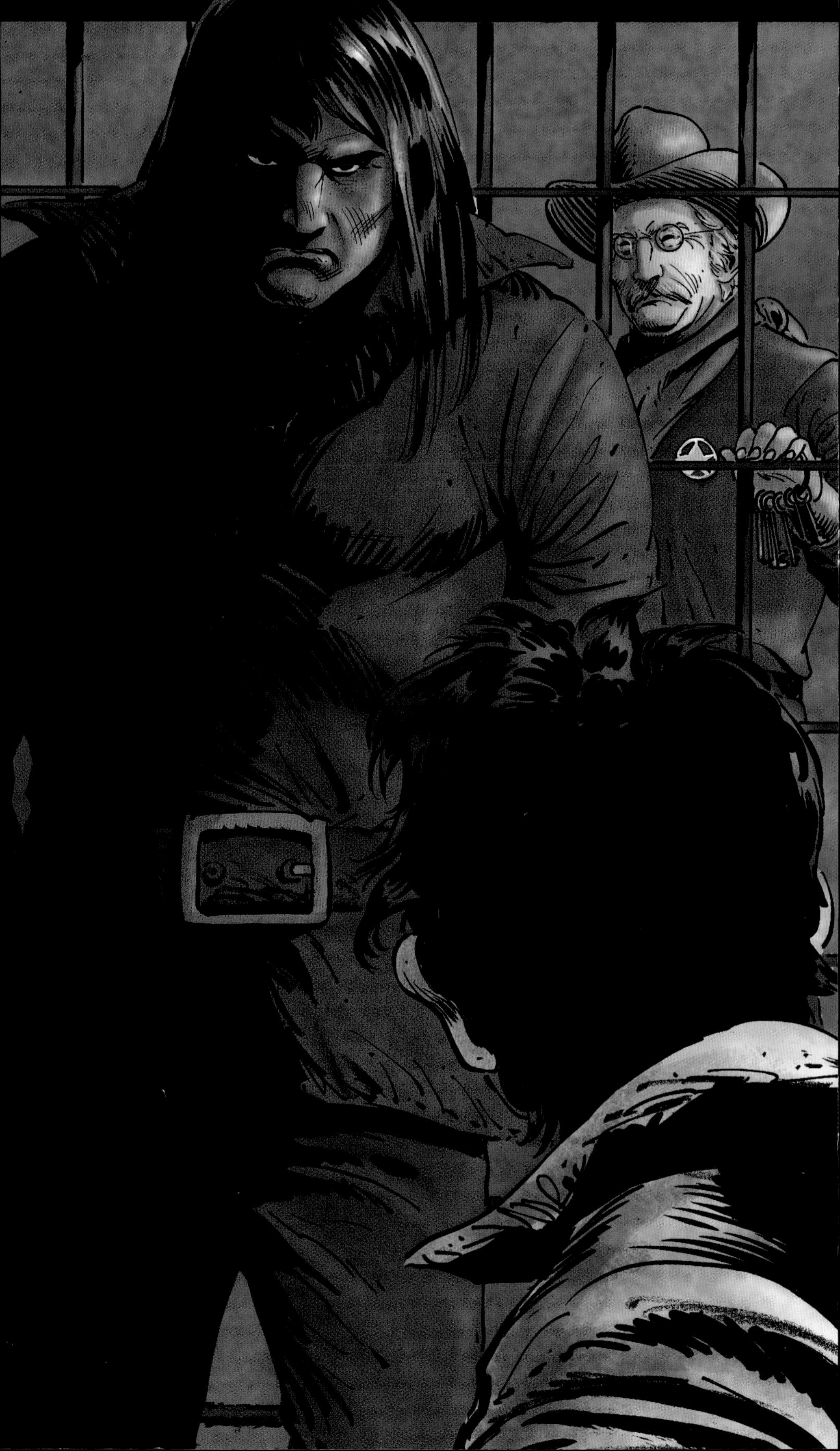

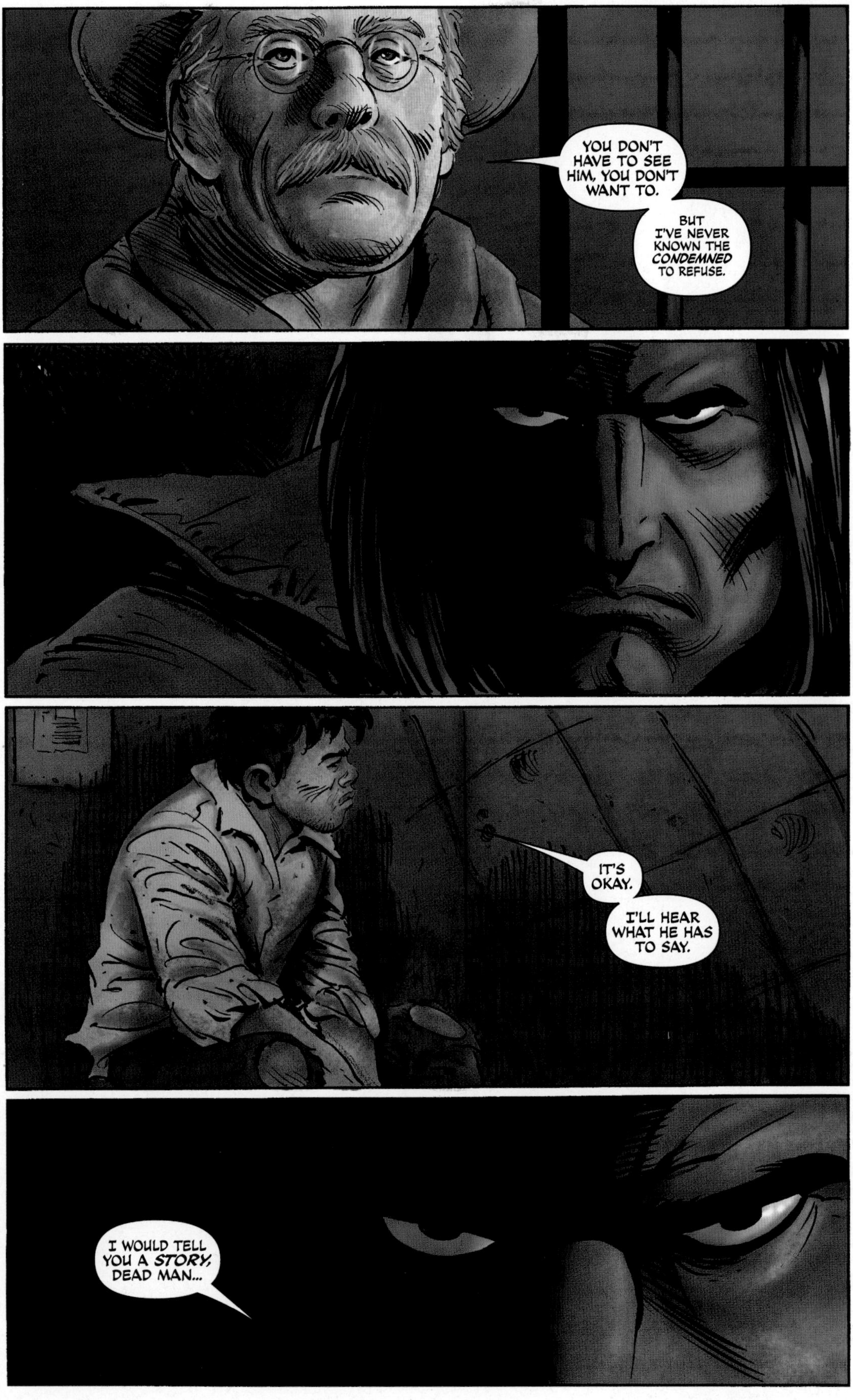
YOU DON'T HAVE TO SEE HIM, YOU DON'T WANT TO.
BUT I'VE NEVER KNOWN THE *CONDEMNED* TO REFUSE.
IT'S OKAY.
I'LL HEAR WHAT HE HAS TO SAY.
I WOULD TELL YOU A *STORY*, DEAD MAN...

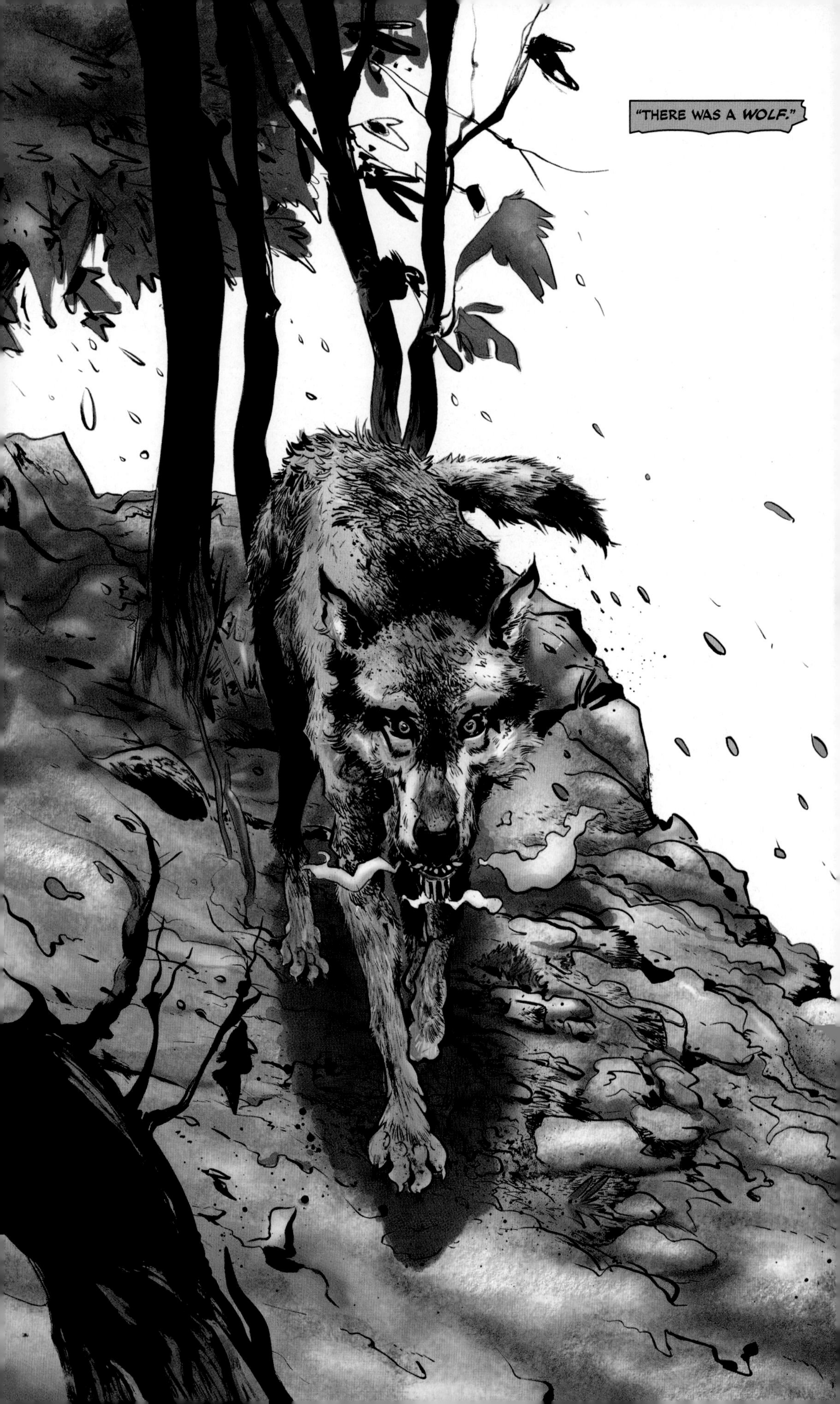
"THERE WAS A *WOLF.*"

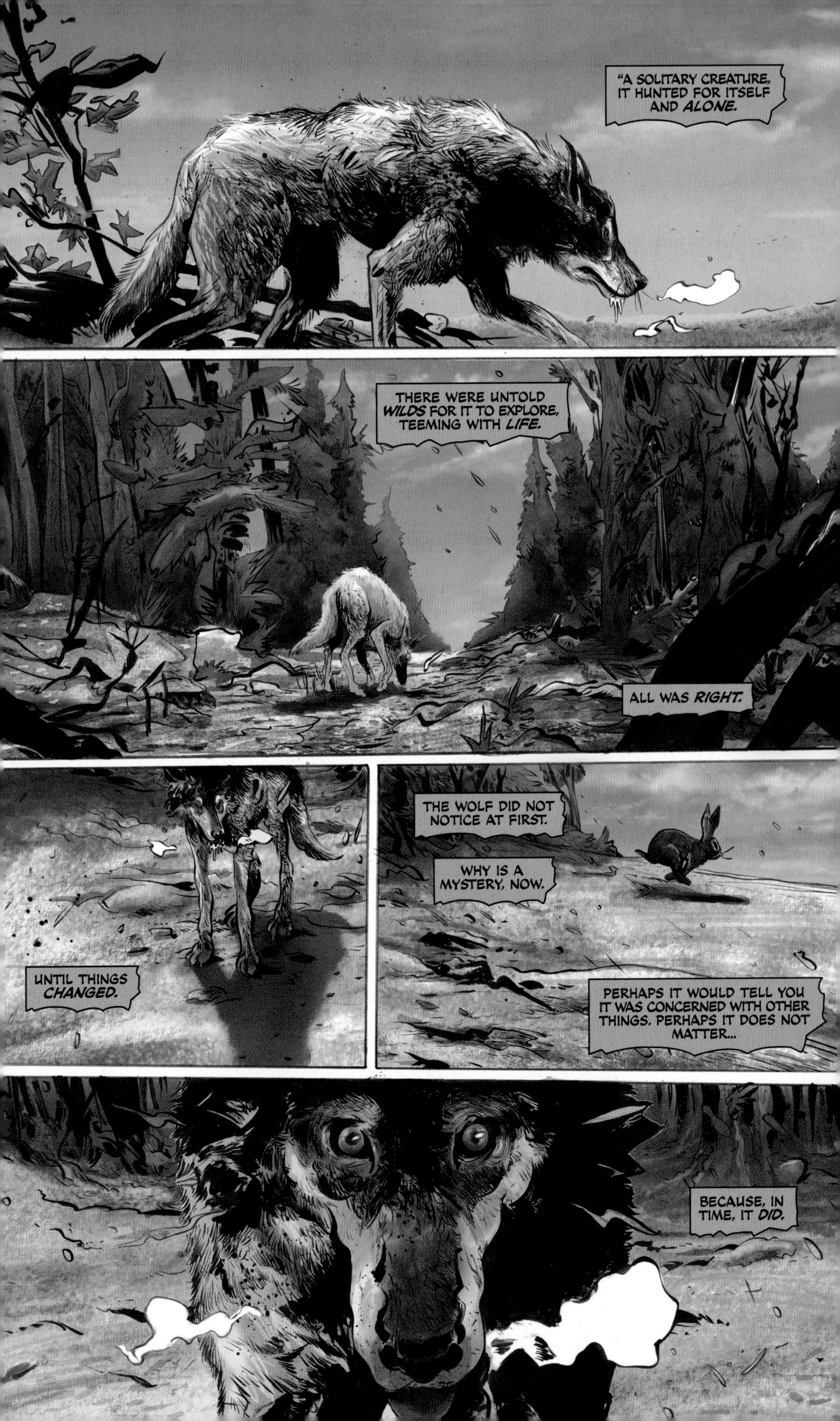
"A SOLITARY CREATURE, IT HUNTED FOR ITSELF AND *ALONE.*
THERE WERE UNTOLD *WILDS* FOR IT TO EXPLORE, TEEMING WITH *LIFE.*
ALL WAS *RIGHT.*
UNTIL THINGS *CHANGED.*
THE WOLF DID NOT NOTICE AT FIRST.
WHY IS A MYSTERY, NOW.
PERHAPS IT WOULD TELL YOU IT WAS CONCERNED WITH OTHER THINGS. PERHAPS IT DOES NOT MATTER...
BECAUSE, IN TIME, IT *DID.*

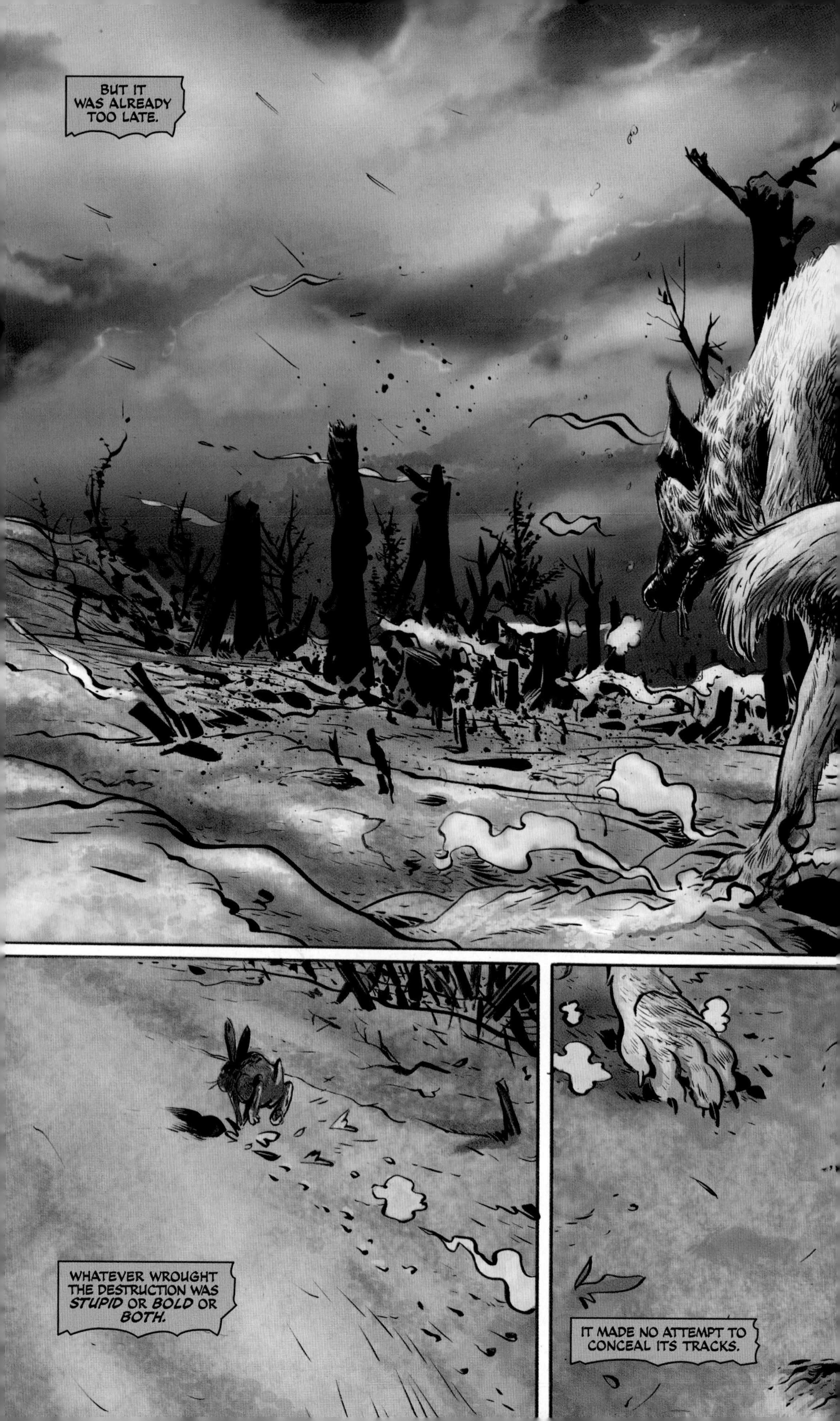
BUT IT WAS ALREADY TOO LATE.
WHATEVER WROUGHT THE DESTRUCTION WAS *STUPID* OR *BOLD* OR *BOTH*.
IT MADE NO ATTEMPT TO CONCEAL ITS TRACKS.

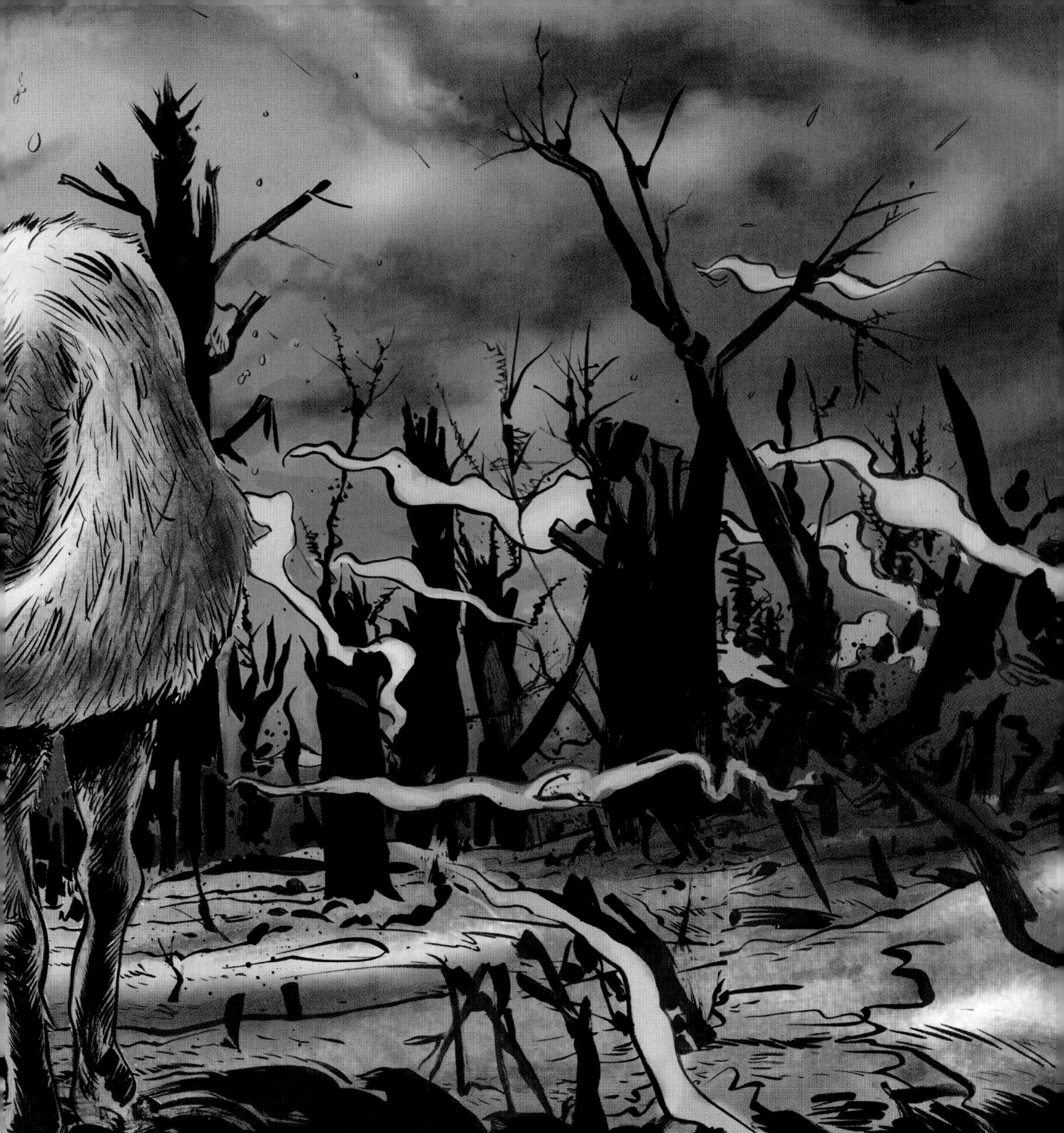

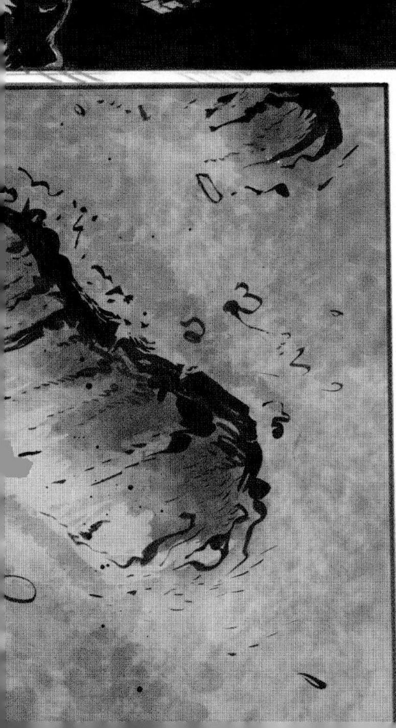

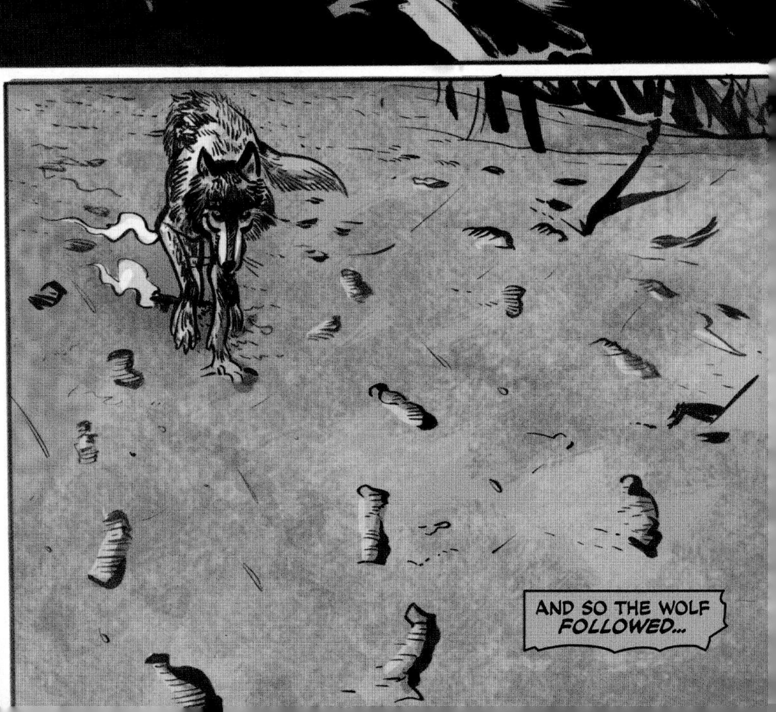
AND SO THE WOLF *FOLLOWED*...

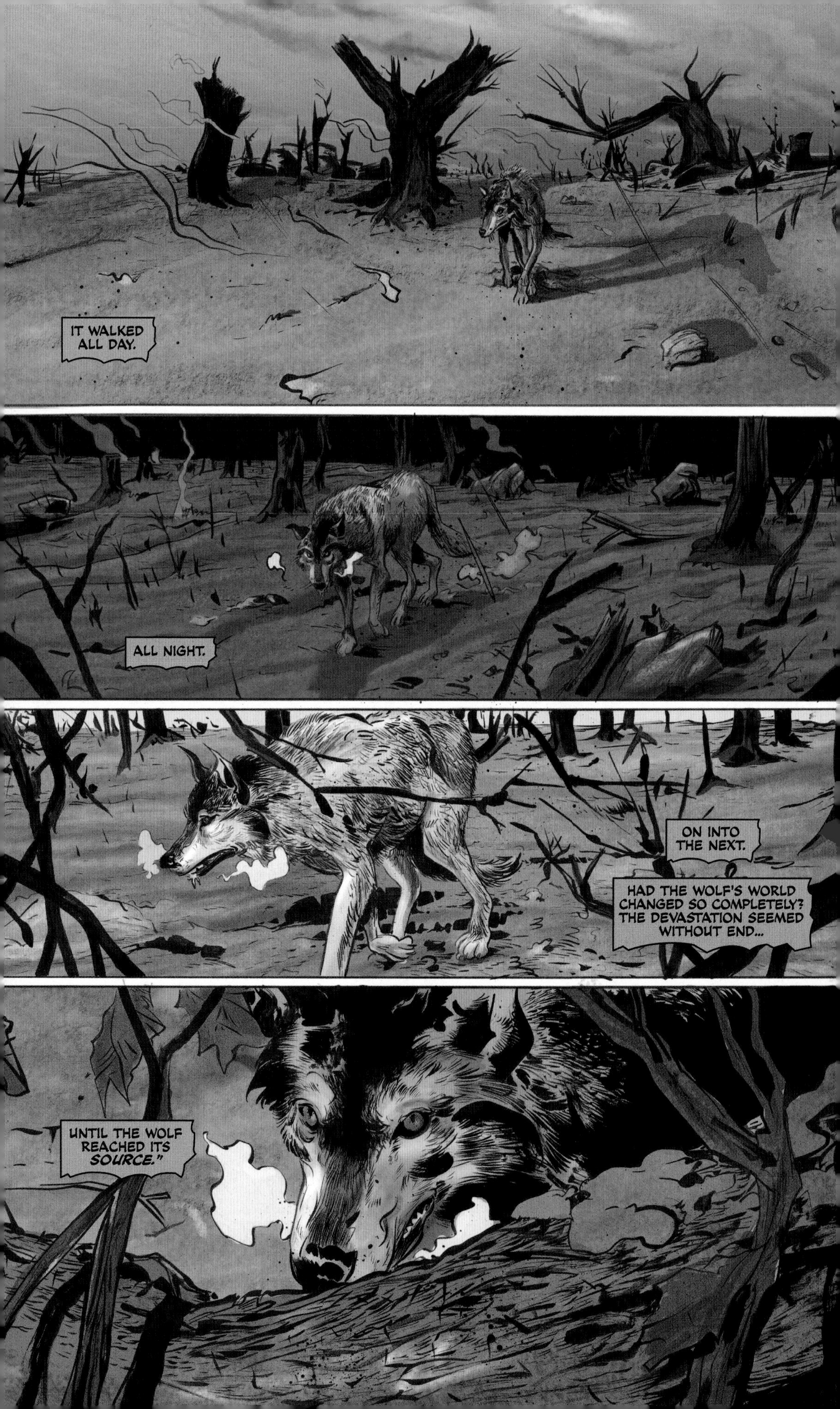
IT WALKED ALL DAY.
ALL NIGHT.
ON INTO THE NEXT.
HAD THE WOLF'S WORLD CHANGED SO COMPLETELY? THE DEVASTATION SEEMED WITHOUT END...
UNTIL THE WOLF REACHED ITS *SOURCE.*"

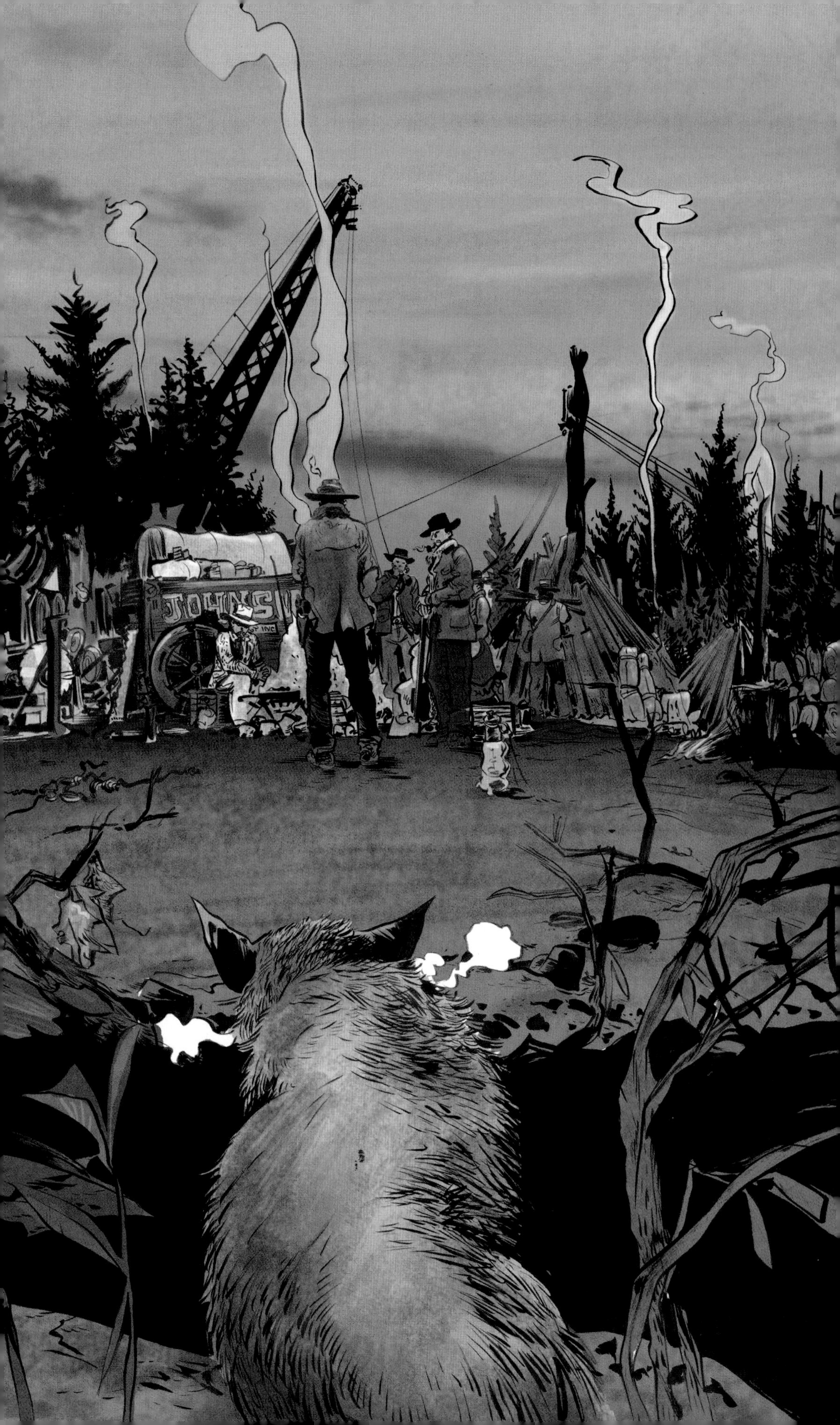
JOHNS

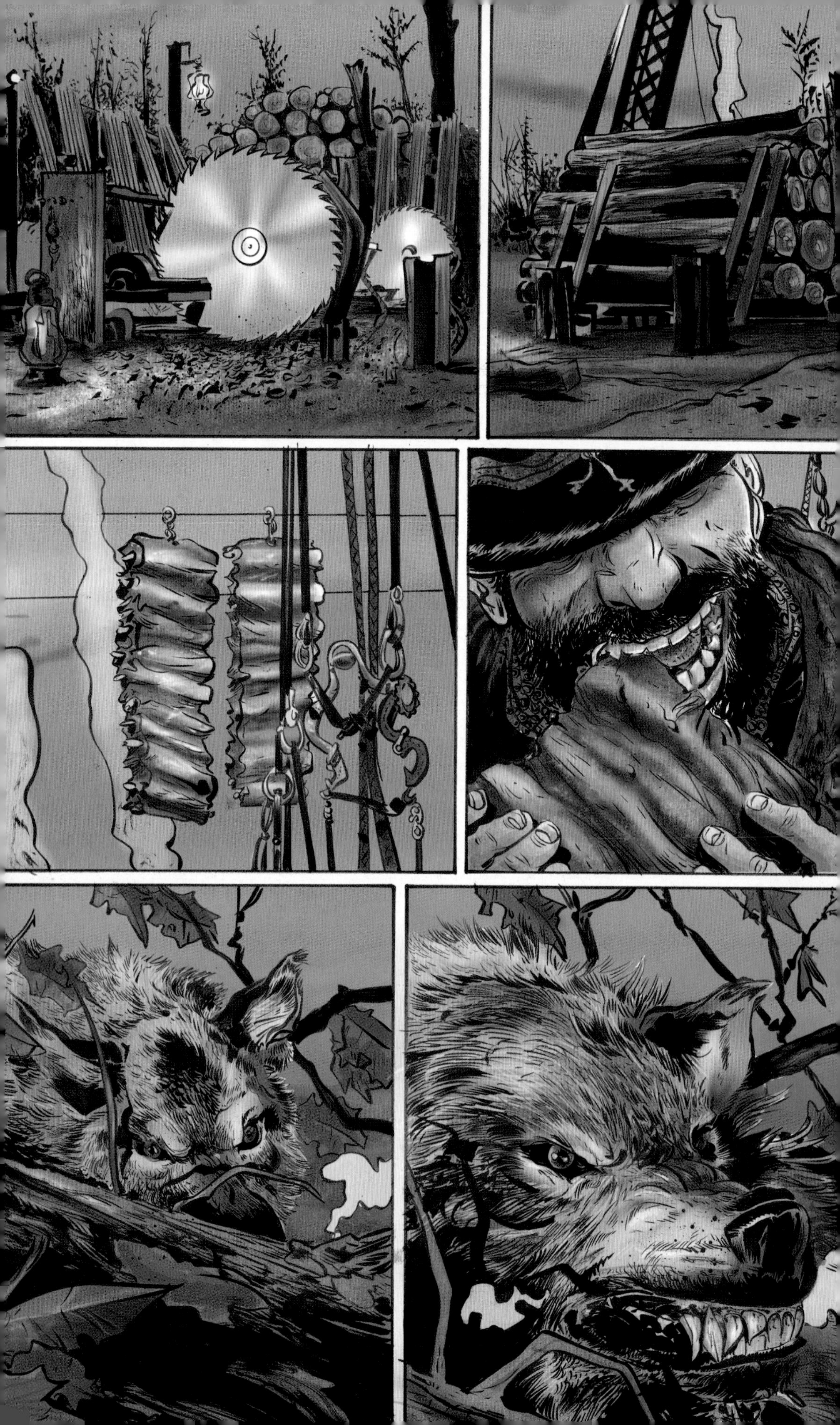

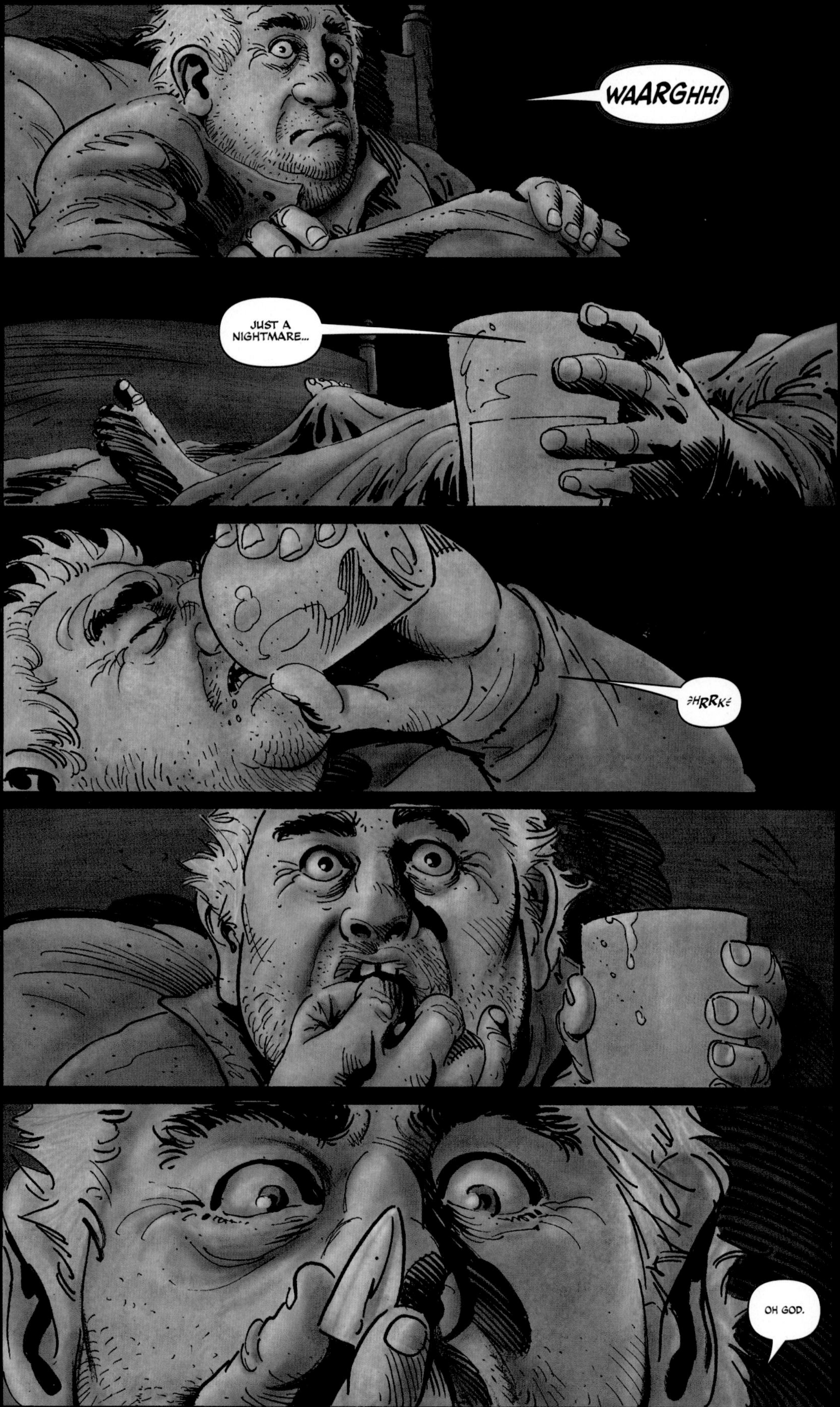
WAARGHH!
JUST A NIGHTMARE...
HRRK
OH GOD.

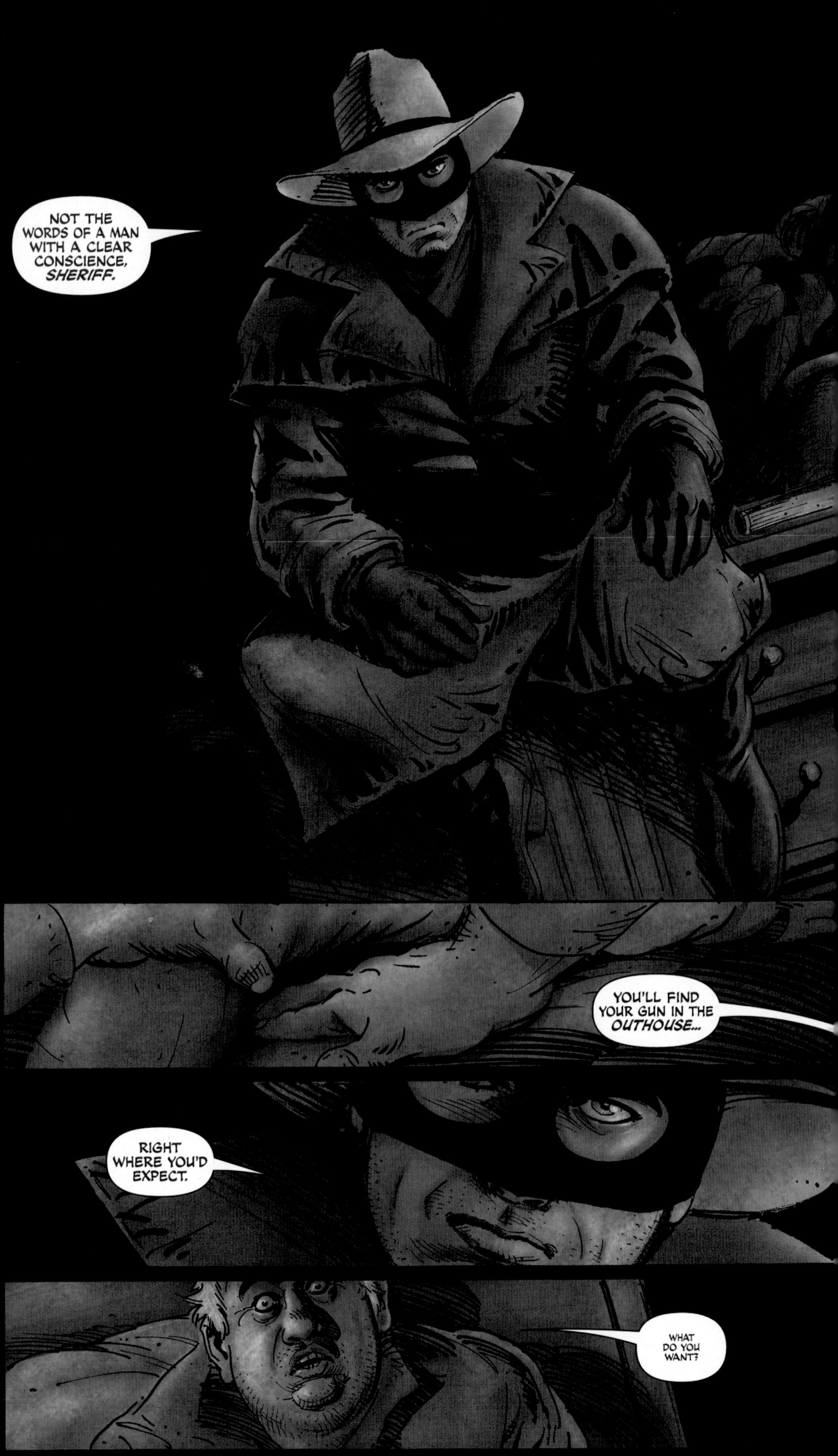
NOT THE WORDS OF A MAN WITH A CLEAR CONSCIENCE, *SHERIFF.*
YOU'LL FIND YOUR GUN IN THE *OUTHOUSE...*
RIGHT WHERE YOU'D EXPECT.
WHAT DO YOU WANT?

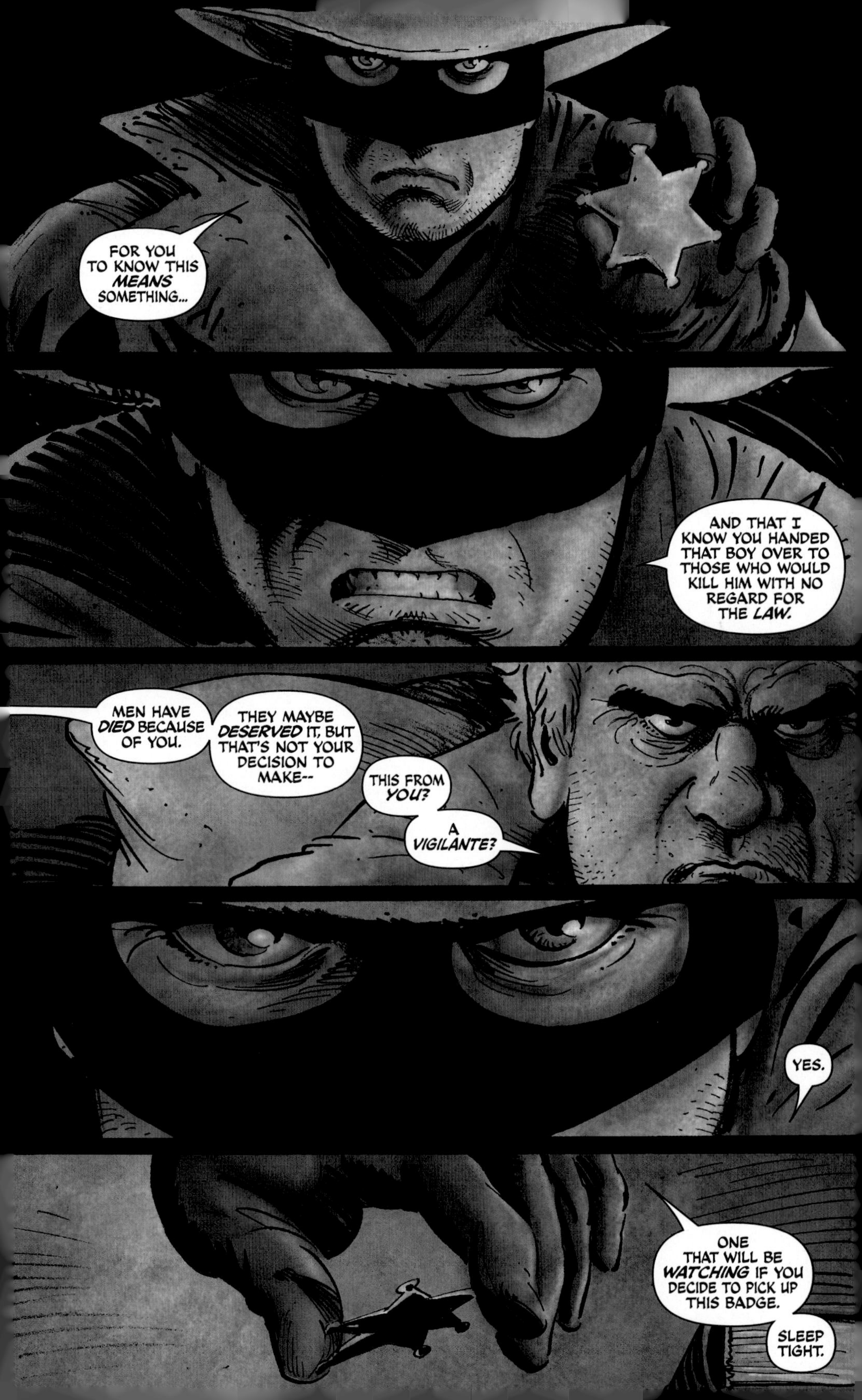
FOR YOU TO KNOW THIS MEANS SOMETHING...
AND THAT I KNOW YOU HANDED THAT BOY OVER TO THOSE WHO WOULD KILL HIM WITH NO REGARD FOR THE LAW.
MEN HAVE DIED BECAUSE OF YOU.
THEY MAYBE DESERVED IT, BUT THAT'S NOT YOUR DECISION TO MAKE--
THIS FROM YOU?
A VIGILANTE?
YES.
ONE THAT WILL BE WATCHING IF YOU DECIDE TO PICK UP THIS BADGE.
SLEEP TIGHT.

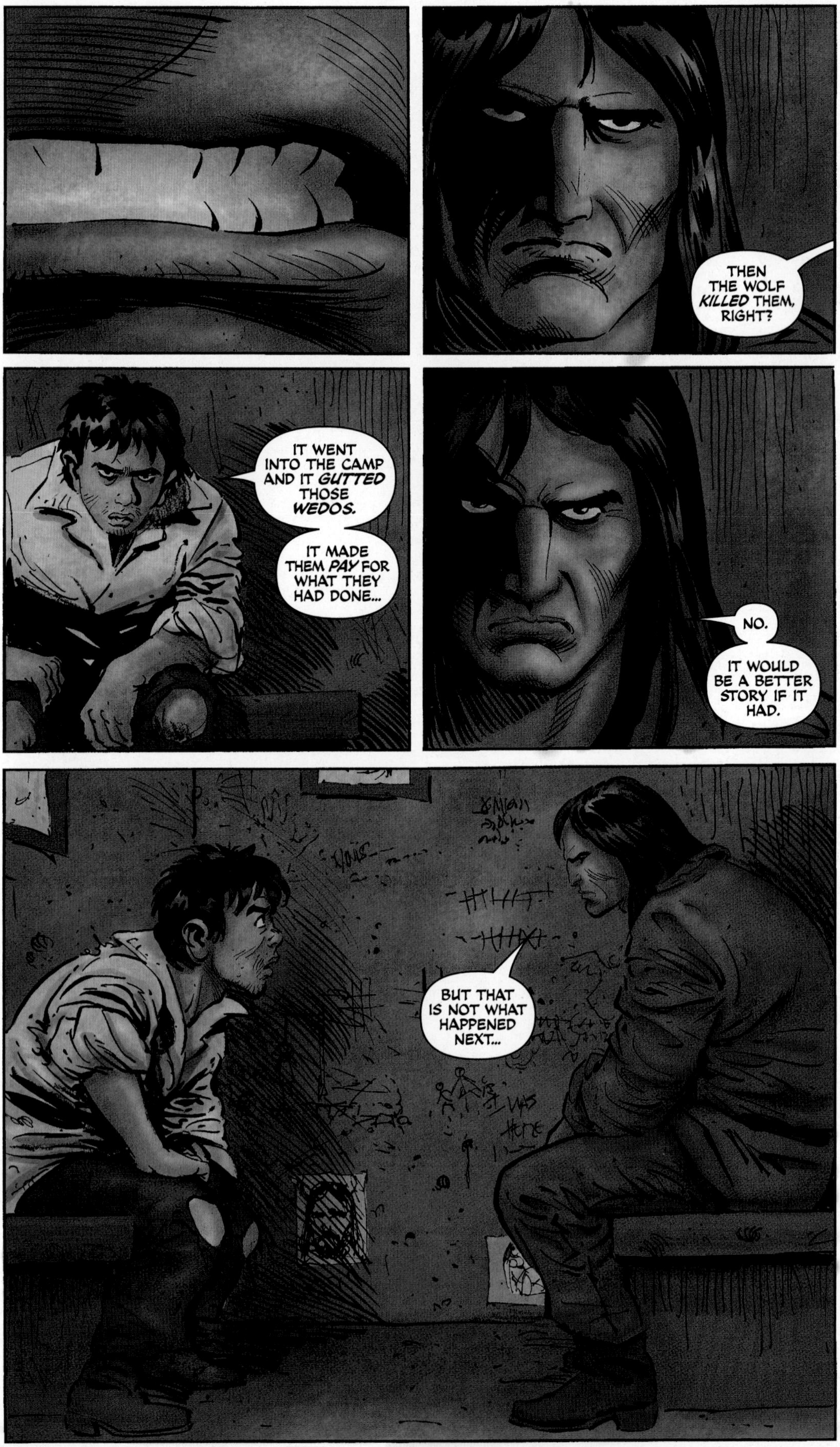
THEN THE WOLF *KILLED* THEM, RIGHT?
IT WENT INTO THE CAMP AND IT *GUTTED* THOSE *WEDOS.*
IT MADE THEM *PAY* FOR WHAT THEY HAD DONE...
NO.
IT WOULD BE A BETTER STORY IF IT HAD.
BUT THAT IS NOT WHAT HAPPENED NEXT...

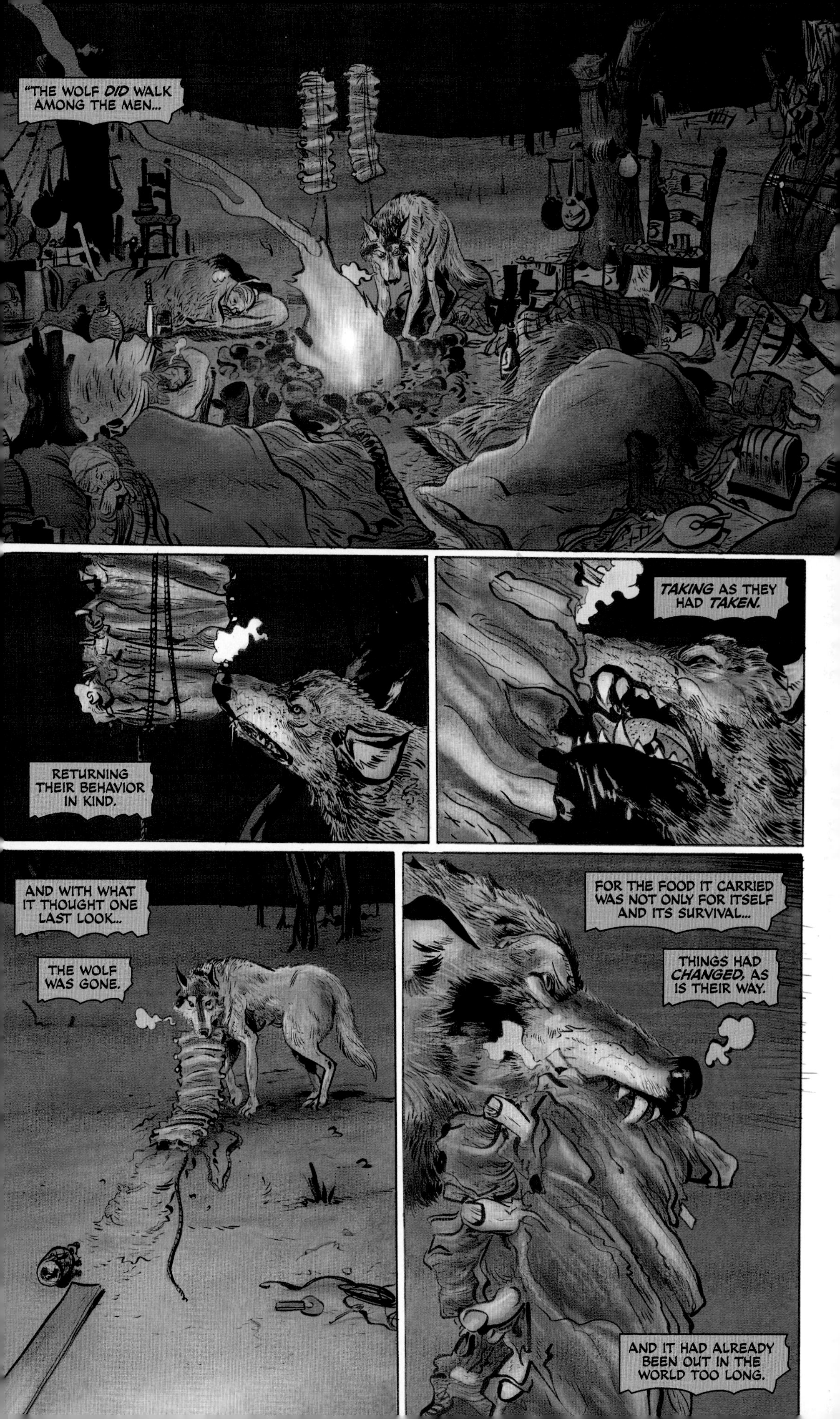
"THE WOLF *DID* WALK AMONG THE MEN...
RETURNING THEIR BEHAVIOR IN KIND.
TAKING AS THEY HAD *TAKEN.*
AND WITH WHAT IT THOUGHT ONE LAST LOOK...
THE WOLF WAS GONE.
FOR THE FOOD IT CARRIED WAS NOT ONLY FOR ITSELF AND ITS SURVIVAL...
THINGS HAD *CHANGED,* AS IS THEIR WAY.
AND IT HAD ALREADY BEEN OUT IN THE WORLD TOO LONG.

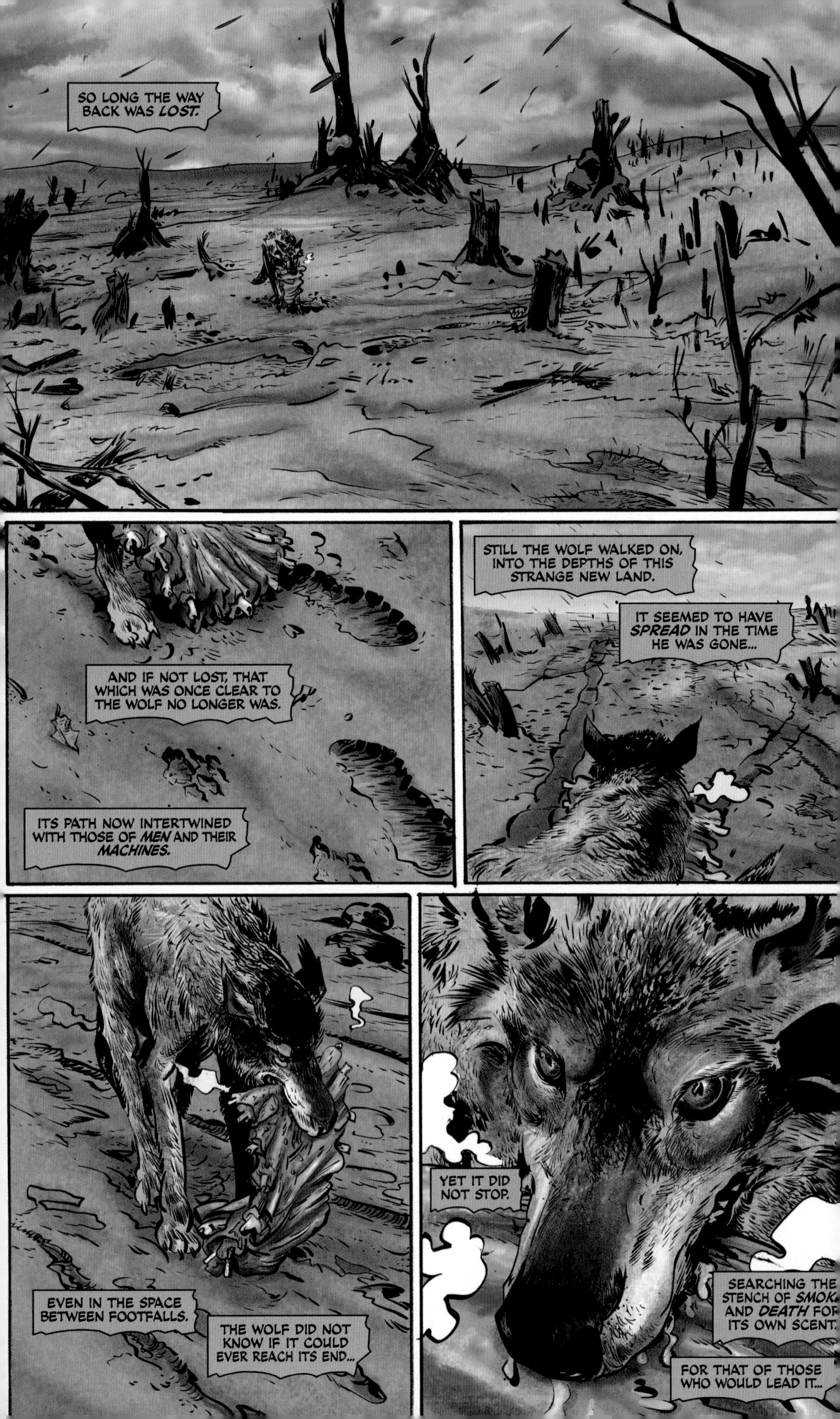
SO LONG THE WAY BACK WAS *LOST.*
AND IF NOT LOST, THAT WHICH WAS ONCE CLEAR TO THE WOLF NO LONGER WAS.
ITS PATH NOW INTERTWINED WITH THOSE OF *MEN* AND THEIR *MACHINES.*
STILL THE WOLF WALKED ON, INTO THE DEPTHS OF THIS STRANGE NEW LAND.
IT SEEMED TO HAVE *SPREAD* IN THE TIME HE WAS GONE...
EVEN IN THE SPACE BETWEEN FOOTFALLS.
THE WOLF DID NOT KNOW IF IT COULD EVER REACH ITS END...
YET IT DID NOT STOP.
SEARCHING THE STENCH OF *SMOK* AND *DEATH* FOR ITS OWN SCENT.
FOR THAT OF THOSE WHO WOULD LEAD IT...

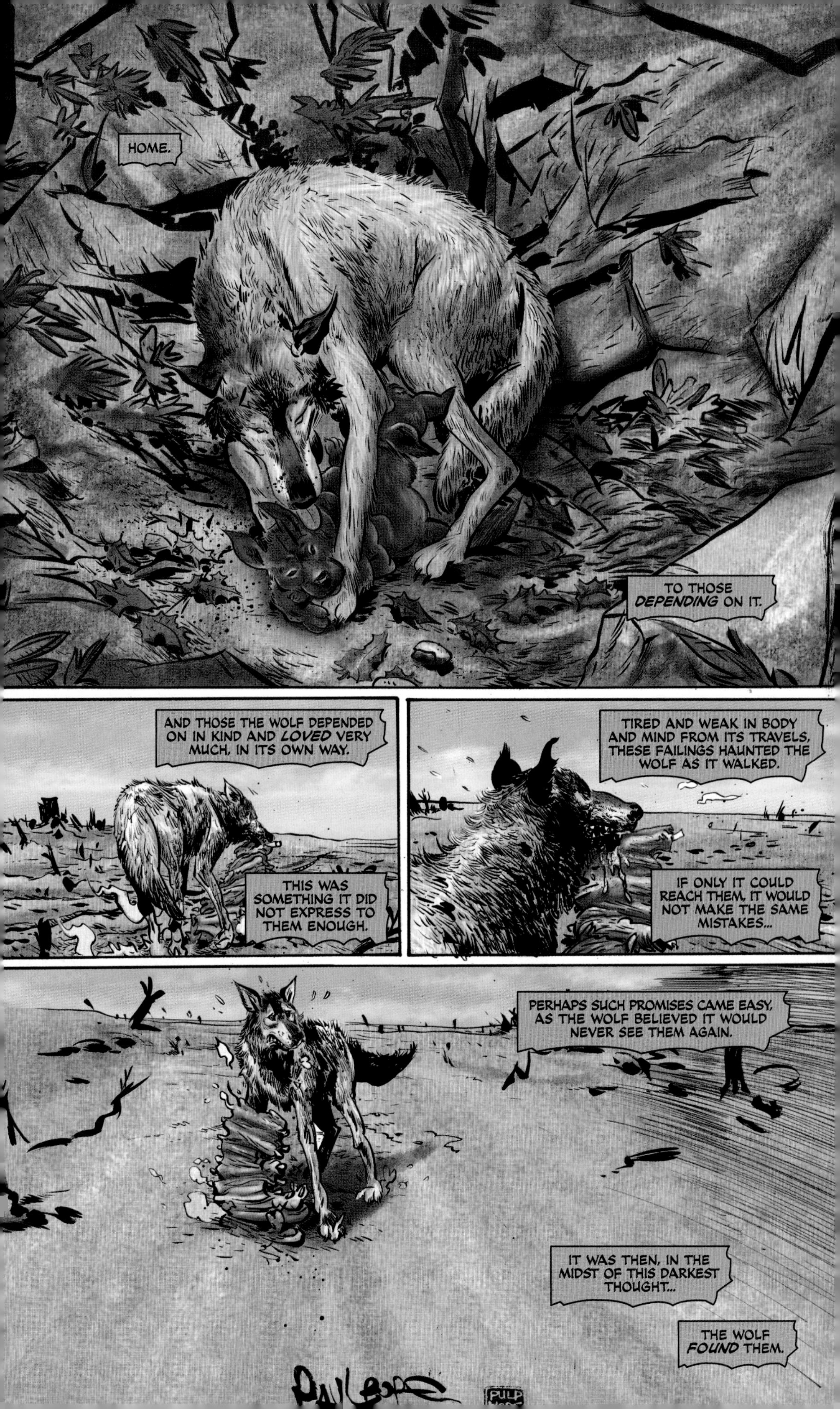
HOME.
TO THOSE DEPENDING ON IT.
AND THOSE THE WOLF DEPENDED ON IN KIND AND LOVED VERY MUCH, IN ITS OWN WAY.
THIS WAS SOMETHING IT DID NOT EXPRESS TO THEM ENOUGH.
TIRED AND WEAK IN BODY AND MIND FROM ITS TRAVELS, THESE FAILINGS HAUNTED THE WOLF AS IT WALKED.
IF ONLY IT COULD REACH THEM, IT WOULD NOT MAKE THE SAME MISTAKES...
PERHAPS SUCH PROMISES CAME EASY, AS THE WOLF BELIEVED IT WOULD NEVER SEE THEM AGAIN.
IT WAS THEN, IN THE MIDST OF THIS DARKEST THOUGHT...
THE WOLF FOUND THEM.
PULP

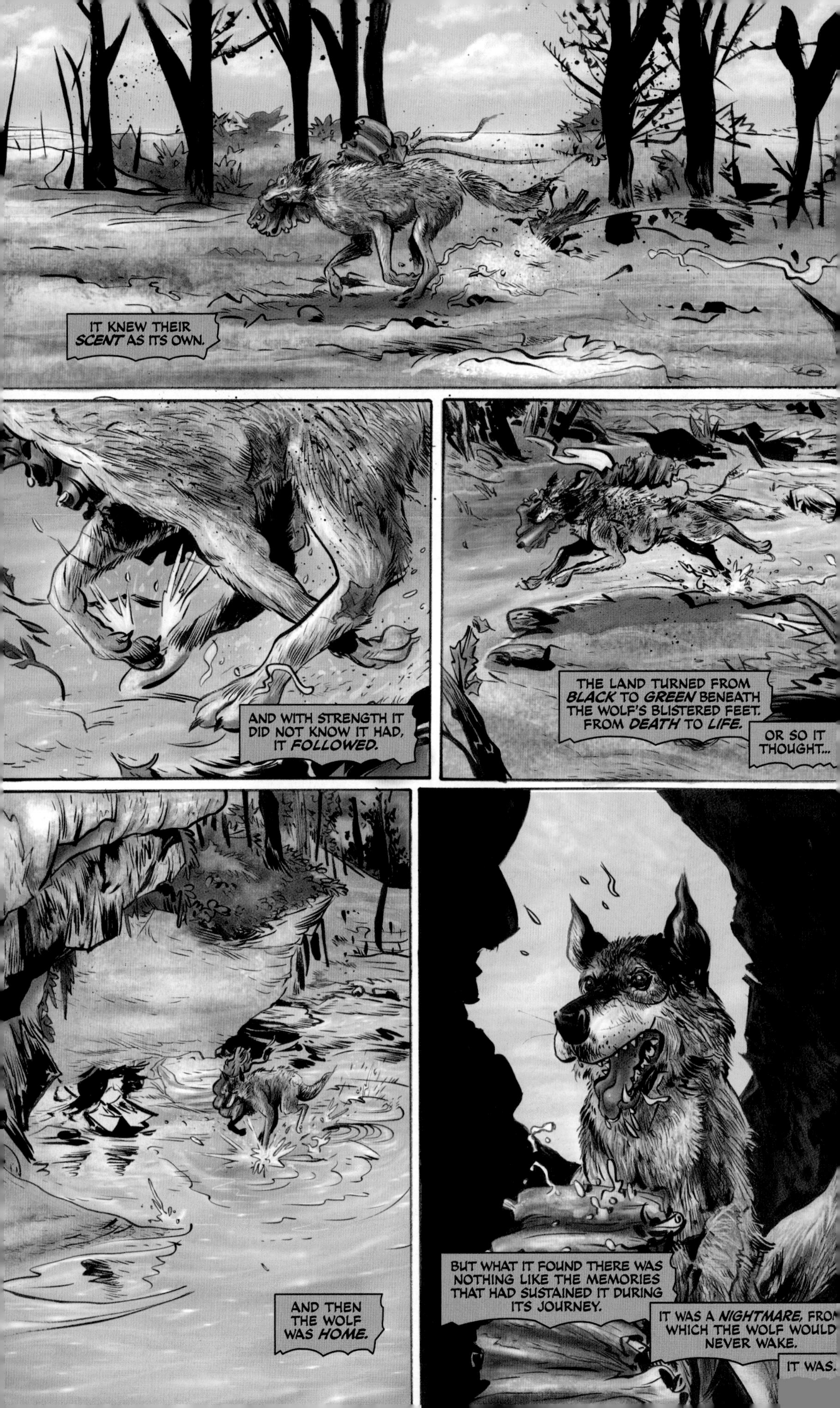
IT KNEW THEIR SCENT AS ITS OWN.
AND WITH STRENGTH IT DID NOT KNOW IT HAD, IT FOLLOWED.
THE LAND TURNED FROM BLACK TO GREEN BENEATH THE WOLF'S BLISTERED FEET. FROM DEATH TO LIFE.
OR SO IT THOUGHT...
AND THEN THE WOLF WAS HOME.
BUT WHAT IT FOUND THERE WAS NOTHING LIKE THE MEMORIES THAT HAD SUSTAINED IT DURING ITS JOURNEY.
IT WAS A NIGHTMARE, FRO WHICH THE WOLF WOULD NEVER WAKE.
IT WAS

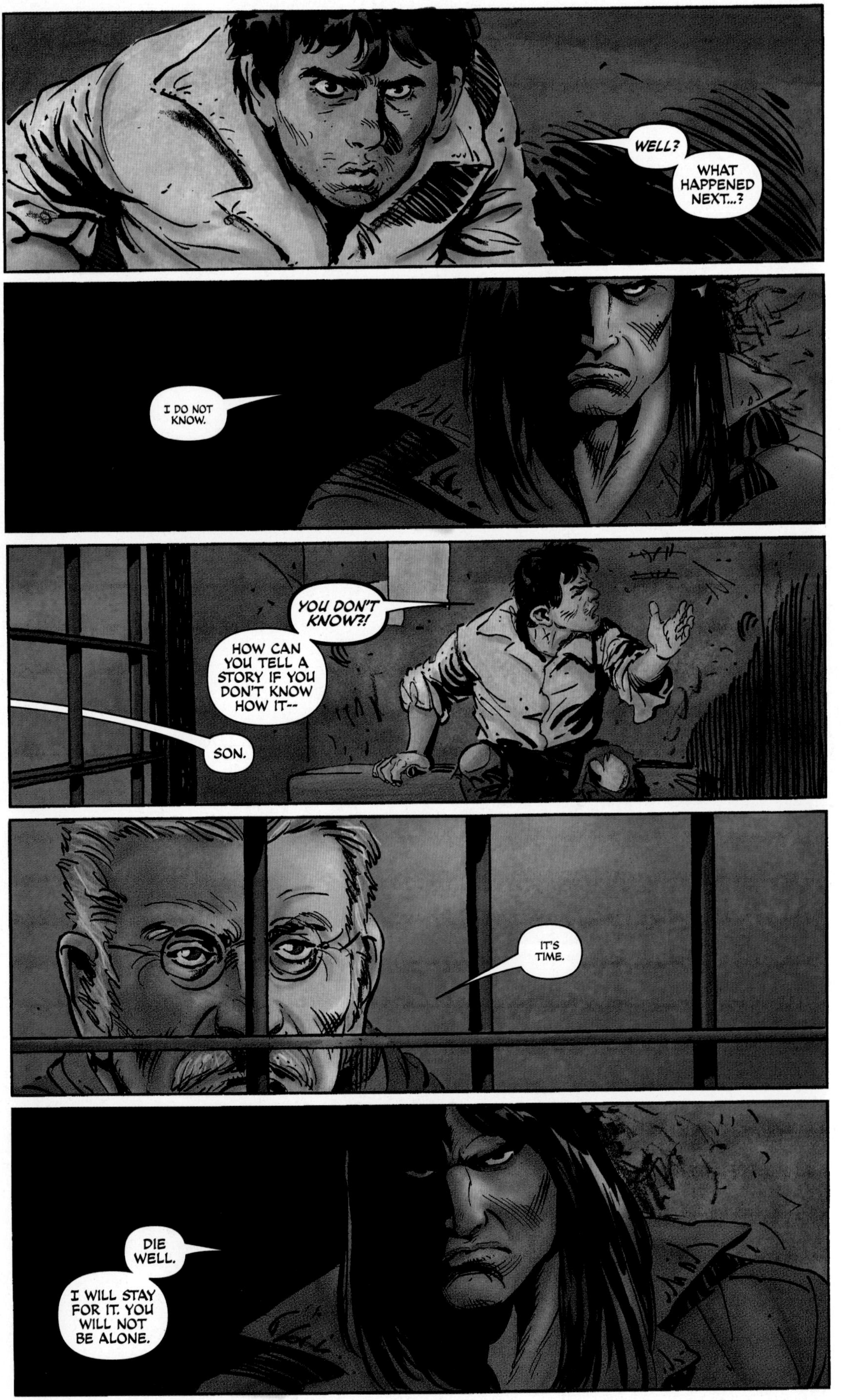
WELL?
WHAT HAPPENED NEXT...?
I DO NOT KNOW.
YOU DON'T KNOW?!
HOW CAN YOU TELL A STORY IF YOU DON'T KNOW HOW IT--
SON.
IT'S TIME.
DIE WELL.
I WILL STAY FOR IT. YOU WILL NOT BE ALONE.

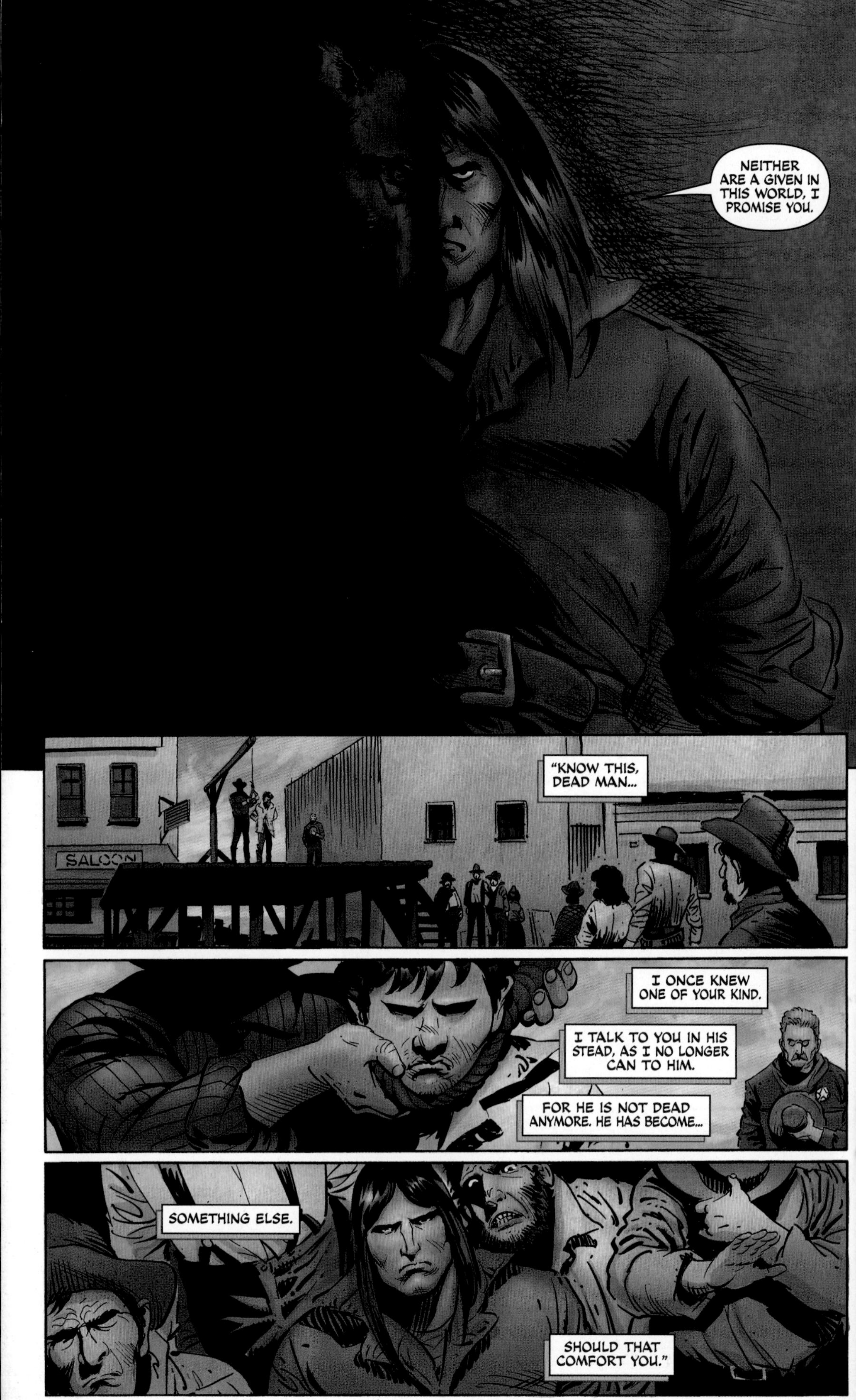
NEITHER ARE A GIVEN IN THIS WORLD, I PROMISE YOU.
SALOON
"KNOW THIS, DEAD MAN...
I ONCE KNEW ONE OF YOUR KIND.
I TALK TO YOU IN HIS STEAD, AS I NO LONGER CAN TO HIM.
FOR HE IS NOT DEAD ANYMORE. HE HAS BECOME...
SOMETHING ELSE.
SHOULD THAT COMFORT YOU."

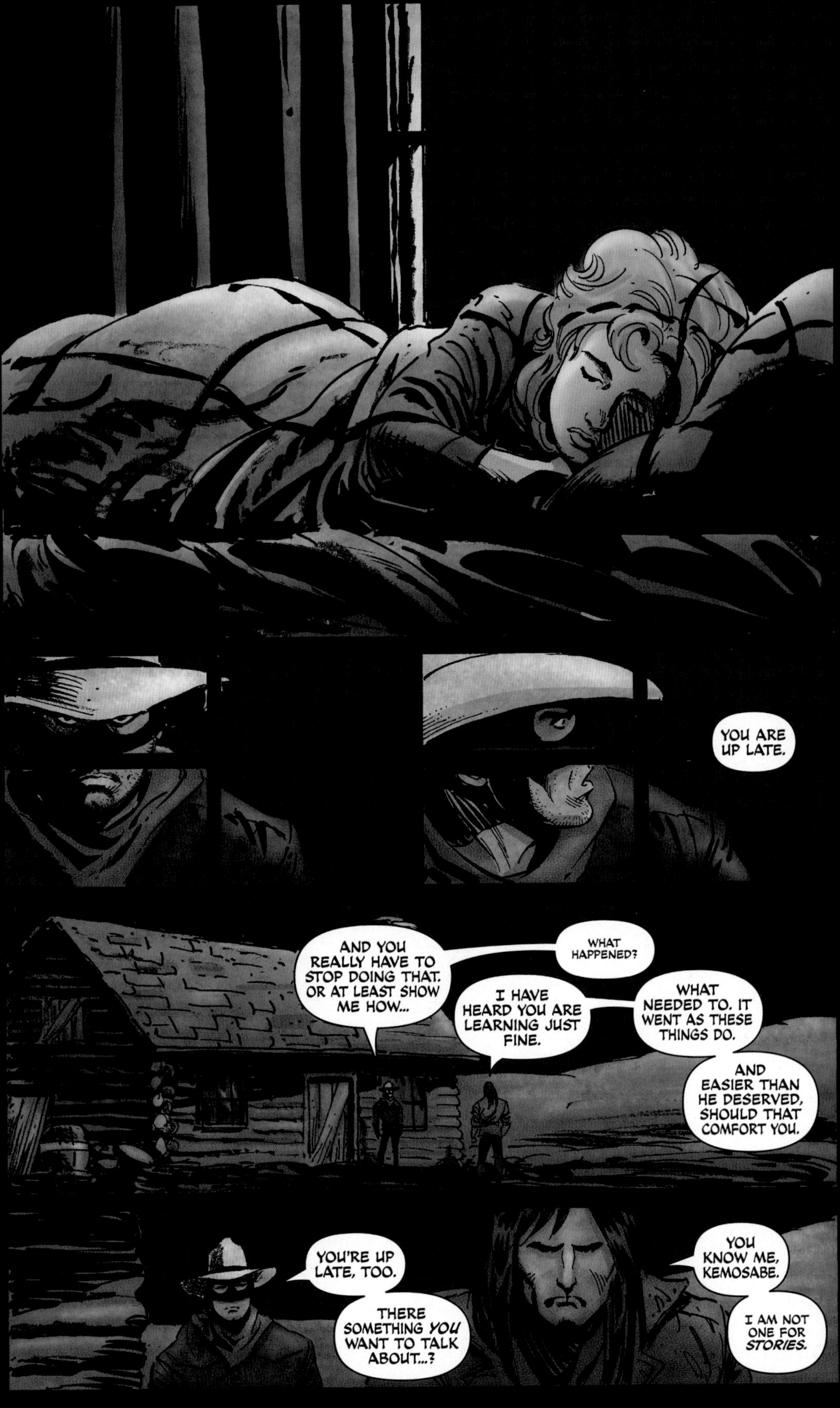
YOU ARE UP LATE.
AND YOU REALLY HAVE TO STOP DOING THAT. OR AT LEAST SHOW ME HOW...
I HAVE HEARD YOU ARE LEARNING JUST FINE.
WHAT HAPPENED?
WHAT NEEDED TO. IT WENT AS THESE THINGS DO.
AND EASIER THAN HE DESERVED, SHOULD THAT COMFORT YOU.
YOU'RE UP LATE, TOO.
THERE SOMETHING *YOU* WANT TO TALK ABOUT...?
YOU KNOW ME, KEMOSABE.
I AM NOT ONE FOR *STORIES.*

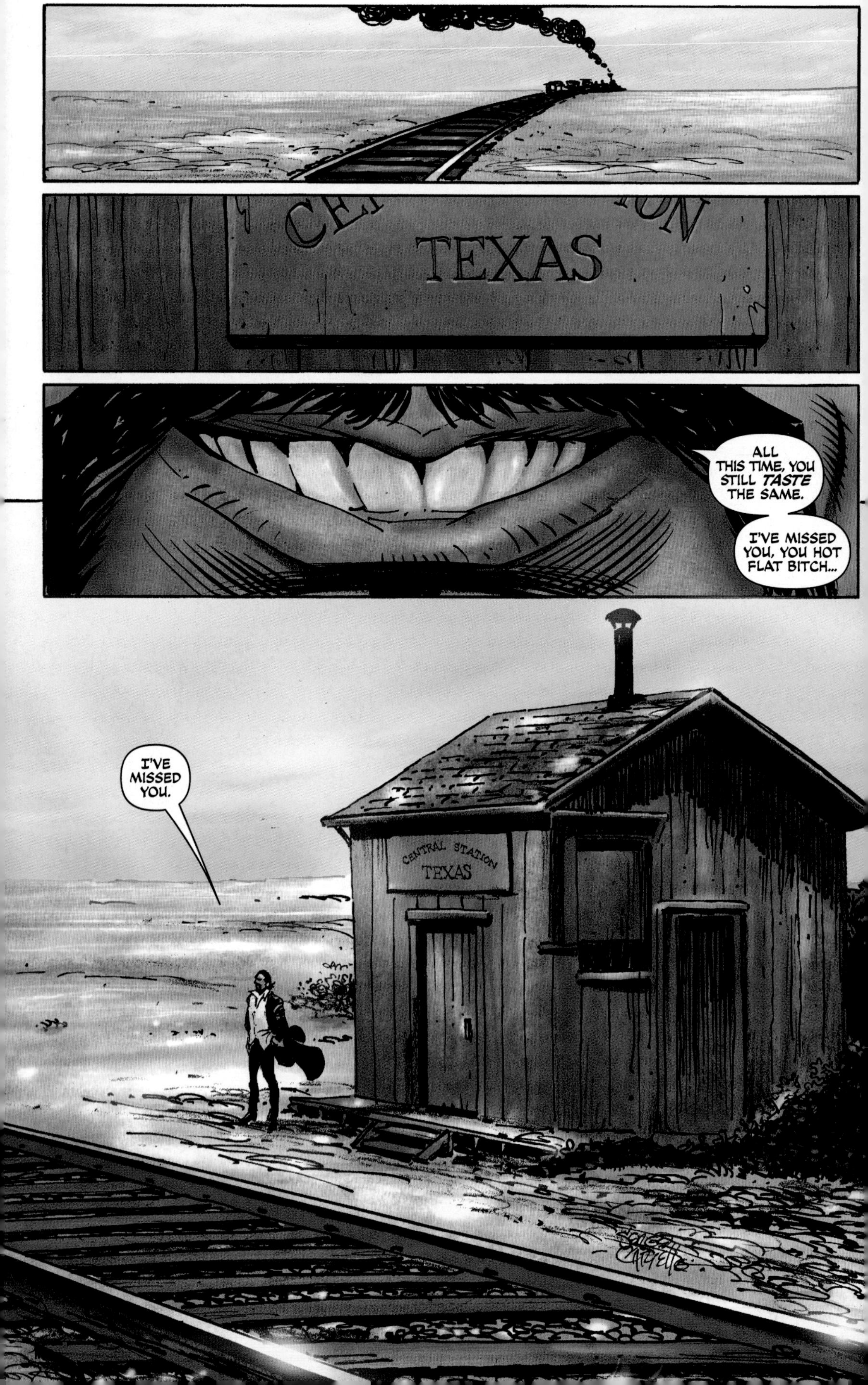
TEXAS
ALL THIS TIME, YOU STILL *TASTE* THE SAME.
I'VE MISSED YOU, YOU HOT FLAT BITCH...
CENTRAL STATION TEXAS
I'VE MISSED YOU.

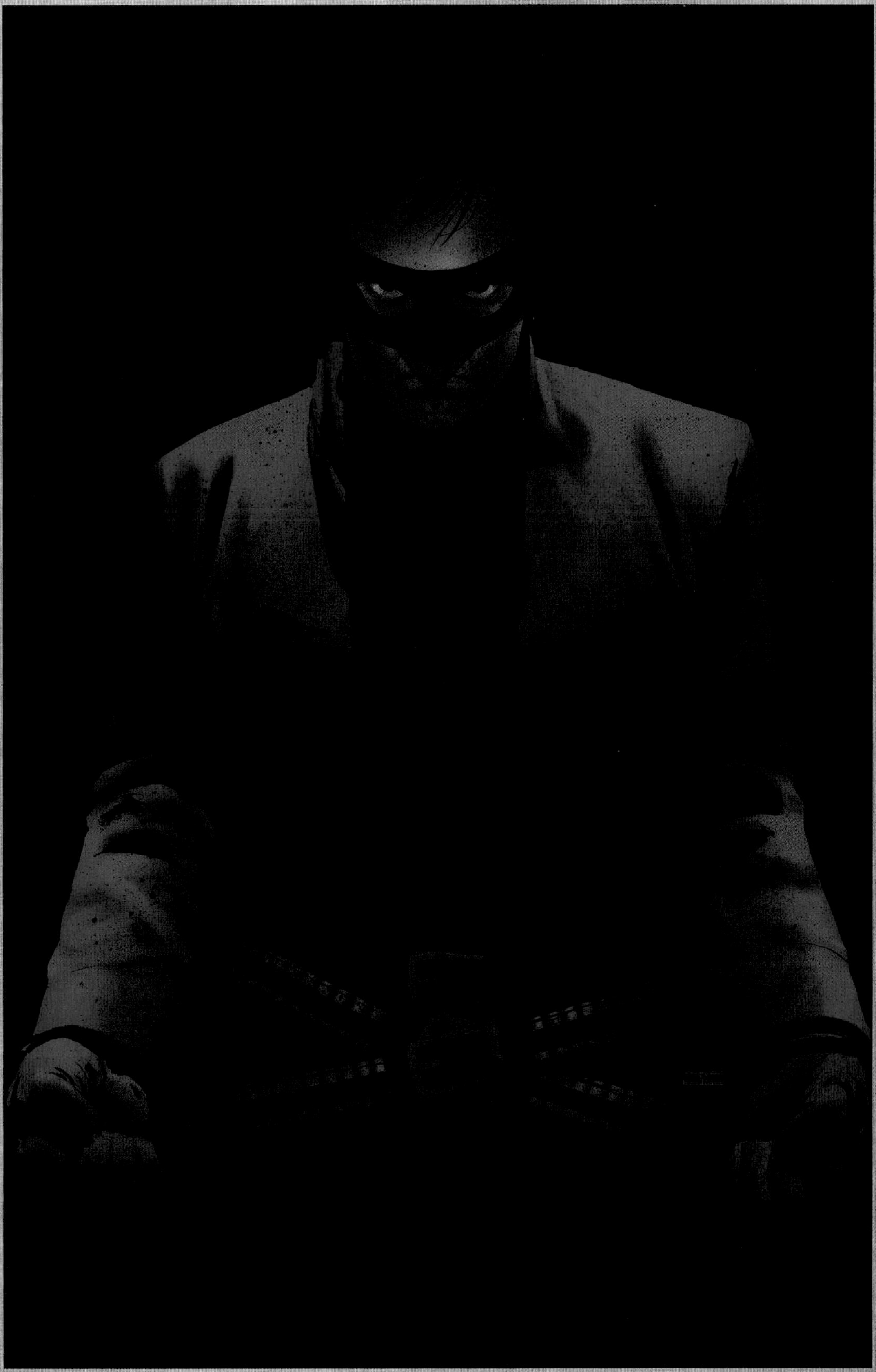

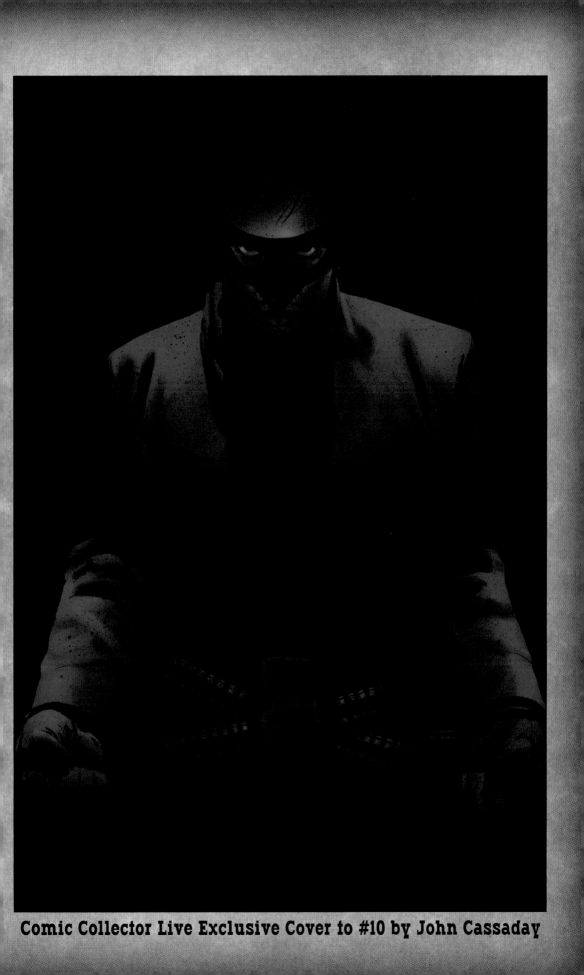

Comic Collector Live Exclusive Cover to #10 by John Cassaday

THE LONE RANGER®

★ MATTHEWS ★ CARIELLO ★ WHITE ★ CASSADAY ★

DIRECT MARKET COVER

MASS MARKET COVER

THE LONE RANGER: NOW & FOREVER HARDCOVER VOLUME 1
$24.99 • Full Color • Direct and Mass Market Edition Covers by Cassaday

WRITER:	COVERS:	ART:	COLORS:
BRETT MATTHEWS	JOHN CASSADAY	SERGIO CARIELLO	DEAN WHITE

"AN UNRELENTING TALE OF THE WEST. A YOUNG MAN SEARCHES FOR REVENGE, ONLY TO FIND JUSTICE...
AND THAT HE'S SOMETHING GREATER THAN HE EVER THOUGHT HE COULD BE."

THIS EDITION FEATURES:
- DYNAMITE'S SMASH HIT THE LONE RANGER #1-6
- A COMPLETE COVER GALLERY FEATURING ALL OF JOHN CASSADAY'S COVERS FOR THE SERIES
- A LOOK INSIDE THE SKETCHBOOKS OF BOTH SERGIO CARIELLO AND JOHN CASSADAY!

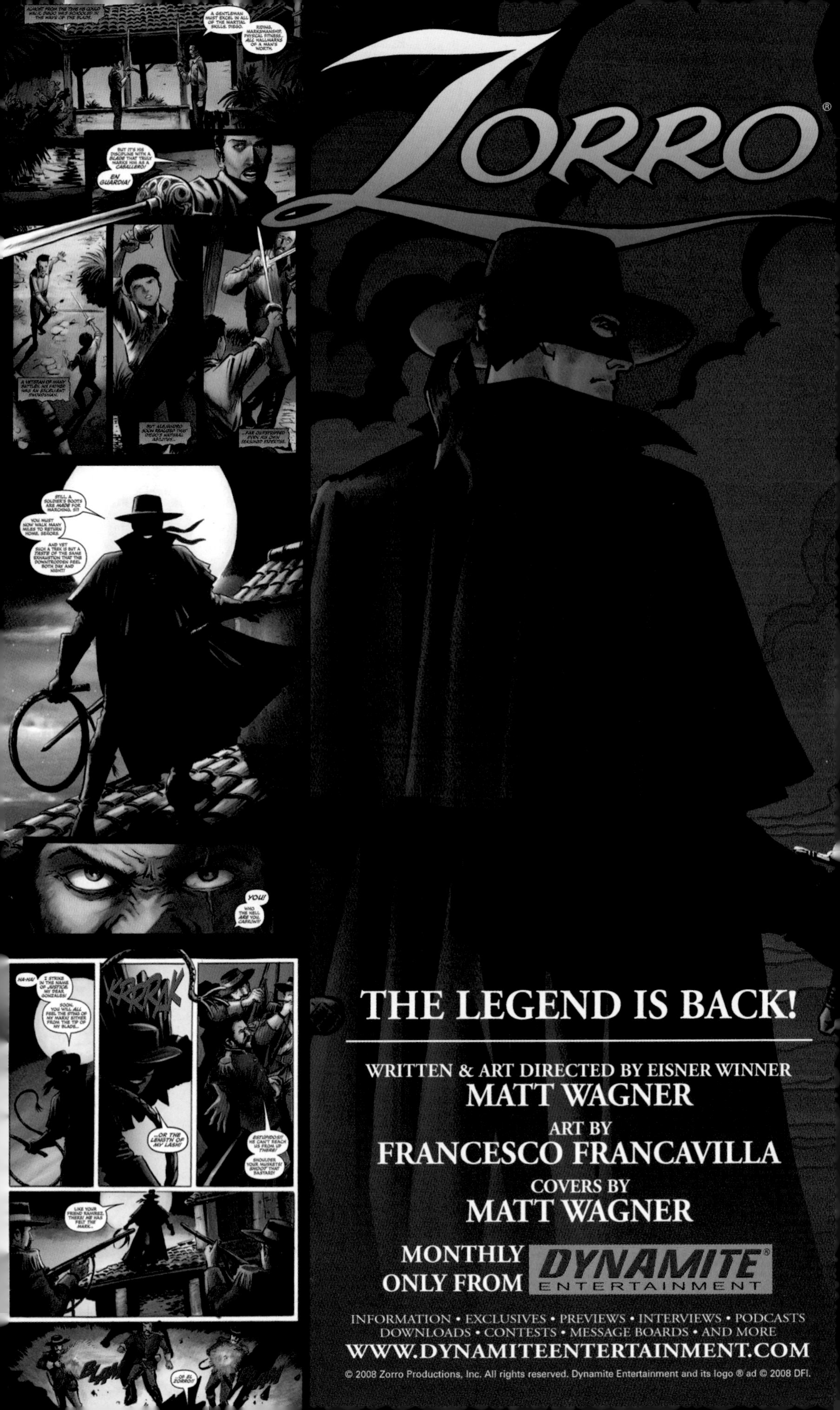
ALMOST FROM THE TIME HE COULD WALK, DIEGO WAS SCHOOLED IN THE WAYS OF THE BLADE.
A GENTLEMAN MUST EXCEL IN ALL OF THE MARTIAL SKILLS, DIEGO.
RIDING, MARKSMANSHIP, PHYSICAL FITNESS... ALL HALLMARKS OF A MAN'S WORTH.
BUT IT'S HIS DISCIPLINE WITH A BLADE THAT TRULY MARKS HIM AS A CABALLERO!
EN GUARDIA!
A VETERAN OF MANY BATTLES, HIS FATHER WAS AN EXCELLENT SWORDSMAN.
BUT ALEJANDRO SOON REALIZED THAT DIEGO'S NATURAL ABILITIES...
...FAR OUTSTRIPPED EVEN HIS OWN SEASONED EXPERTISE.
STILL, A SOLDIER'S BOOTS ARE MADE FOR MARCHING, SI?
YOU MUST NOW WALK MANY MILES TO RETURN HOME, SEÑORS.
AND YET SUCH A TREK IS BUT A TASTE OF THE SAME EXHAUSTION THAT THE DOWNTRODDEN FEEL BOTH DAY AND NIGHT!
YOU!
WHO THE HELL ARE YOU, CABRON?!
HA-HA!
I STRIKE IN THE NAME OF JUSTICE, MY DEAR GONZALES!
SOON, YOU WILL ALL FEEL THE STING OF MY MARK! EITHER FROM THE TIP OF MY BLADE...
KRRAK
...OR THE LENGTH OF MY LASH!
ESTÚPIDOS!! HE CAN'T REACH US FROM UP THERE!
SHOULDER YOUR MUSKETS! SHOOT THAT BASTARD!
LIKE YOUR FRIEND RAMIREZ, THERE! HE HAS FELT THE MARK...
...OF EL ZORRO!!
ZORRO®
THE LEGEND IS BACK!
WRITTEN & ART DIRECTED BY EISNER WINNER
MATT WAGNER
ART BY
FRANCESCO FRANCAVILLA
COVERS BY
MATT WAGNER
MONTHLY
ONLY FROM
DYNAMITE® ENTERTAINMENT
INFORMATION • EXCLUSIVES • PREVIEWS • INTERVIEWS • PODCASTS
DOWNLOADS • CONTESTS • MESSAGE BOARDS • AND MORE
WWW.DYNAMITEENTERTAINMENT.COM
© 2008 Zorro Productions, Inc. All rights reserved. Dynamite Entertainment and its logo ® ad © 2008 DFI.

THE DYNAMITE ENTERTAINMENT COLLECTION

CURRENTLY AVAILABLE AND UPCOMING COLLECTIONS FROM DYNAMITE ENTERTAINMENT

Adventures of Red Sonja Vol. 1
Roy Thomas, Frank Thorne, More
SC ISBN: 1-933305-07-X

Adventures of Red Sonja Vol. 2
Roy Thomas, Frank Thorne, More
SC ISBN: 1-933305-12-6

Adventures of Red Sonja Vol. 3
Roy Thomas, Frank Thorne, More
SC ISBN: 1-933305-98-3

Army of Darkness: Movie Adaptation
Sam Raimi, Ivan Raimi, John Bolton
SC ISBN: 1-933305-17-7

Army of Darkness: Ashes to Ashes
Andy Hartnell, Nick Bradshaw
SC ISBN: 0-9749638-9-5

Army of Darkness: Shop 'Till You Drop Dead
James Kuhoric, Nick Bradshaw,
Sanford Greene
SC ISBN: 1-933305-26-6

Army of Darkness vs. Re-Animator
James Kuhoric, Nick Bradshaw,
Sanford Greene
SC ISBN: 1-933305-13-4

Army of Darkness: Old School & More
James Kuhoric, Kevin Sharpe
SC ISBN: 1-933305-18-5

Army of Darkness: Ash vs. The Classic Monsters
James Kuhoric, Kevin Sharpe,
Fernando Blanco
SC ISBN: 1-933305-41-X

Army f Darkness: From The Ashes
James Kuhoric, Fernando Blanco
SC ISBN: 1-933305-77-0

Bad Boy 10th Anniversary Edition
Frank Miller, Simon Bisley
HC ISBN: 1-933305-54-1

Borderline Vol. 1
Eduardo Risso, Carlos Trillo
SC ISBN: 1-933305-05-3

Borderline Vol. 2
Eduardo Risso, Carlos Trillo
SC ISBN: 1-933305-99-1

The Boys Vol. 1: The Name of the Game
Garth Ennis, Darick Robertson
SC ISBN: 1-933305-73-8

The Boys Vol. 2: Get Some
Garth Ennis, Darick Robertson,
Peter Snejbjerg
SC ISBN: 1-933305-68-1

Classic Battlestar Galactica Vol. 1
Rick Remender, Carlos Rafael
SC ISBN: 1-933305-45-2

Classic Battlestar Galactica Vol. 2: Cylon Apocalypse
Javier Grillo-Marxuach, Carlos Rafael
SC ISBN: 1-933305-55-X

Darkman vs. Army of Darkness
Kurt Busiek, Roger Stern, James Fry
SC ISBN: 1-933305-48-7

Dreadstar The Definitive Collection
Jim Starlin
HC ISBN: 0-9749638-0-1
SC part 1 ISBN: 0-9749638-1-X
SC part 2 ISBN: 0-9749638-2-8

Dreadstar: The Beginning
Jim Starlin
HC ISBN: 1-933305-10-X

Eduardo Risso's Tales of Terror
Eduardo Risso, Carlos Trillo
SC ISBN: 1-933305-23-1

Highlander Vol. 1: The Coldest War
Michael Avon Oeming, Brandon Jerwa,
Lee Moder, Kevin Sharpe
HC ISBN: 1-933305-31-2
SC ISBN: 1-933305-34-7

Highlander Vol. 2: Dark Quickening
Brandon Jerwa, Fabio Laguna
SC ISBN: 1-933305-59-2

Highlander Vol. 3: Armageddon
Brandon Jerwa, Carlos Rafael
SC ISBN: 1-933305-67-3

Jungle Girl Vol. 1
Frank Cho, Doug Murray, Adriano Batista
HC ISBN: 1-933305-78-9

Kid Kosmos: Cosmic Guard
Jim Starlin
SC ISBN: 1-933305-02-9

Kid Kosmos: Kidnapped
Jim Starlin
SC ISBN: 1-933305-29-0

The Lone Ranger Vol. 1: Now & Forever
Brett Matthews, Sergio Cariello,
John Cassaday
HC ISBN: 1-933305-39-8
SC ISBN: 1-933305-40-1

The Lone Ranger Vol. 2: Lines Not Crossed
Brett Matthews, Sergio Cariello,
John Cassaday, Paul Pope
HC ISBN: 1-933305-66-5
SC ISBN: 1-933305-70-3

Mercenaries Vol. 1
Brian Reed, Edgar Salazar
SC ISBN: 1-933305-71-1

Monster War
Christopher Golden, Joyce Chin, more
SC ISBN: 1-933305-30-4

New Battlestar Galactica Vol. 1
Greg Pak, Nigel Raynor
HC ISBN: 1-933305-33-9
SC ISBN: 1-933305-34-7

New Battlestar Galactica Vol. 2
Greg Pak, Nigel Raynor
HC ISBN: 1-933305-53-3
SC ISBN: 1-933305-49-5

New Battlestar Galactica Vol. 3
Greg Pak, Nigel Raynor, Jonathan Lau
HC ISBN: 1-933305-58-4
SC ISBN: 1-933305-57-6

New Battlestar Galactica: Zarek
Brandon Jerwa, Adriano Batista
SC ISBN: 1-933305-50-9

New Battlestar Galactica: Season Zero Vol. 1
Brandon Jerwa, Jackson Herbert
SC ISBN: 1-933305-81-9

Essential Painkiller Jane Vol. 1
Joe Quesada, Jimmy Palmiotti,
Rick Leonardi, Amanda Conner
SC ISBN: 1-933305-97-5

Painkiller Jane Vol. 1: The Return
Joe Quesada, Jimmy Palmiotti, Lee Moder
SC ISBN: 1-933305-42-8

Painkiller Jane Vol. 2: Everything Explodes
Joe Quesada, Jimmy Palmiotti, Lee Moder
SC ISBN: 1-933305-65-7

Raise The Dead
Leah Moore, John Reppion, Hugo Petrus
HC ISBN: 1-933305-56-8

Red Sonja She-Devil With a Sword Vol. 1
Michael Avon Oeming, Mike Carey, Mel Ru
HC ISBN: 1-933305-36-3
SC ISBN: 1-933305-11-8

Red Sonja She-Devil With a Sword Vol. 2: Arrowsmiths
Michael Avon Oeming, Mel Rubi, more
HC ISBN: 1-933305-44-4
SC ISBN: 1-933305-43-6

Red Sonja She-Devil With a Sword Vol. 3: The Rise of Kulan Gath
Michael Avon Oeming, Mel Rubi, more
HC ISBN: 1-933305-51-7
SC ISBN: 1-933305-52-5

Red Sonja She-Devil With a Sword Vol. 4: Animals & More
Michael Avon Oeming, Homs, more
HC ISBN: 1-933305-64-9
SC ISBN: 1-933305-63-0

Red Sonja vs. Thulsa Doom Vol. 1
Peter David, Luke Lieberman, Will Conrad
SC ISBN: 1-933305-96-7

Savage Red Sonja: Queen of the Frozen Wastes
Frank Cho, Doug Murray, Homs
HC ISBN: 1-933305-37-1
SC ISBN: 1-933305-38-X

Red Sonja: Travels
Ron Marz, Josh Ortega, Roy Thomas, more
SC ISBN: 1-933305-20-7

Sword of Red Sonja: Doom of the Go
Red Sonja vs. Thulsa Doom 2
Luke Lieberman, Lui Antonio
SC ISBN: 1-933305-76-2

Scout Vol. 1
Timothy Truman
SC ISBN: 1-933305-95-9

Scout Vol. 2
Timothy Truman
SC ISBN: 1-933305-60-6

Six From Sirius
Doug Moench, Paul Gulacy
SC ISBN: 1-933305-03-7

Street Magik
Luke Lieberman, Kevin McCarthy,
Rodney Buchemi
SC ISBN: 1-933305-47-9

Terminator: Infinity
Simon Furman, Nigel Raynor
SC ISBN: 1-933305-74-6

Witchblade: Shades of Gray
Leah Moore, John Reppion, Stephen Sego
Walter Geovani
SC ISBN: 1-933305-72-X

Xena Vol. 1: Contest of Pantheons
John Layman, Fabiano Neves
SC ISBN: 1-933305-35-5

Xena Vol. 2: Dark Xena
John Layman, Keith Champagne,
Noah Salonga
SC ISBN: 1-933305-61-4

To find more collected editions and monthly comic books from Dynamite Entertainment,
visit your local comic book store or call 1-888-COMIC-BOOK to locate the nearest comic store to you.

For more information visit
WWW.DYNAMITEENTERTAINMENT.COM